THE JESUS WHO WAS
THE JESUS WHO IS

For
Marilyn Morgan
whose love
makes these pages and other pages possible

Joseph O'Hanlon

The Jesus who was
The Jesus who is

the columba press

First published in 2005 by
the columba press
55A Spruce Avenue, Stillorgan Industrial Park,
Blackrock, Co Dublin

Cover by Bill Bolger
Origination by The Columba Press
Printed in Ireland by ColourBooks Ltd, Dublin

ISBN 1 85607 479 X

Acknowledgements

Most of the New Testament quotations and not a few of the Old Testament are my own. I have, however, made use of two modern translations which are, in my view, the best of the many available in English. I hereby acknowledge my debt:

Some scripture quotations contained herein are from the New Revised Standard Version of the Bible, Anglicised Edition, copyright © 1989, 1995 by the Division of Christian Education of the National Council of the Churches of Christ in the United States of America, and are used by permission. All rights reserved.

Some scripture quotations contained herein are from the Revised Standard Version of the Bible, copyright © 1946, 1952, and 1971 by the Division of Christian Education of the National Council of Churches of Christ in the United States of America, and are used by permission. All rights reserved.

Table of Contents

WE SHALL NOT CEASE FROM EXPLORATION
AND THE END OF ALL OUR EXPLORING
WILL BE TO ARRIVE WHERE WE STARTED
AND KNOW THE PLACE FOR THE FIRST TIME

T. S. Eliot, *Little Gidding*

Preface

Psalm 136 is a psalm for slow learners. It is a song which sings of God from the dawning of creation to the giving of our daily bread. It is long, as any catalogue of God's goodness must be long. The song leaps from one gift of God's open hand to the next, in a cascade of giving that calls for a chorus. And the chorus is repeated with all the affrontery of an old come-all-ye. It is repeated twenty-six times. Twenty-six times we are invited to join in the song: *God's steadfast love endures forever!* Psalm 136 is a psalm for slow learners.

What this book tries to do is to sing the song again. These are dark days, days when many we know and love walk away from Christian churches because they have not found there the God whose steadfast love endures for them forever and amen. Those of us who remain are battered and storm-tossed and, like St Paul, are daily made aware that we carry faith in vessels of clay. Fragile faith, faith like mine, which at the next shattering storm, may crack, needs to shout with the men in the boat, 'Teacher, don't you care that we are perishing?' And hope there's an answer from the man asleep.

Where is God's steadfast love? What I wish to do is to ask where the gift of God's heart is to be found in our time and in our place. Nobody has a bad word to say about the man from Nazareth who went about doing good. Few have a good word to say about the churches which seek to perpetuate his name on this earth. How can we rehabilitate who we are, who we claim to be, so that the Jesus who was may live again in our time and in our place? Not an ambitious book, then.

I take some thirty-six sentences of one chapter of the Gospel of St Luke and ask my readers to journey with me to learn what they meant and what they mean. It is a voyage of discovery. I believe that the God whose steadfast love endures each day for each and all of us is to be found in the man from Galilee. I believe, as he himself did, that the words of God tell all we need to know. If we learn to read what was said in ancient times and how to translate what we learn to our time and our place, we will have something to sing about. But we must first learn to read. The Bible, the Gospels, were not written for us. They are not our library; we are but borrowers there. Our lending card is imagination, study, prayer.

I have tried to keep everything as simple as I can. To make Jesus live in our time and our place requires work but it does not have to be back-breaking. Like an old come-all-ye, I repeat some things again and again, if only because God does the same and our holy books, as Psalm 136 maintains, could be slimmed down to a line of a song: *God's steadfast love endures forever*. I want readers to learn to read with imagination. I start from conviction, borne in upon me by years of teaching, that you can't begin too far back. Most people know very little about the Bible and, consequently, most people know little of who Jesus was. It is hardly surprising, therefore, that most people don't know who he is. Or where to find him in our time and in our place.

I have tried, too, to make reading as congenial as possible. I have quoted sentences from the Bible rather than refer to them. I have repeated key texts, not because I distrust your memory but because I share your indolence. I have puts lots of material in italics and capital letters because I want you to pause in surprise, in reflection, even in prayer. I have tried to anticipate your bad habits when reading by confronting my own. When matters of complexity come up, and they often do, I have explained without simplifying into banality. Hard work cannot be forever avoided. So we will travel with all the signposts clearly visible, the navigational instructions endlessly repeated, the destination constantly before our eyes. A few sentences of one Gospel cannot be expected to yield all that may be revealed and needs to be grasped about Jesus of Nazareth. There is much more in our Bible, our traditions, our creeds and our worship than may be said in a few paragraphs of one Gospel. But if attention to a few lines lifts up our hearts and minds to God, and if, in the process, we learn how to read the holy words of God, we will have started the journey well. The reward, I hope and pray, will be to discover that the Jesus who was can once again be resurrected to our time and to our place.

Feast of the Transfiguration,
6 August, 2004.

A Prologue

The birth of a baby is a joy. Even if the circumstances surrounding the coming of a child into the world are fraught with misgivings and anguish, even if the pain of its delivery must be bravely borne, in the moment of its coming, all disquiet is set aside:

> When a woman is in labour she has sorrow because her hour has come but when she is delivered of the child, she no longer remembers the pain, for joy that a child is born into the world. *Gospel of John 16:21*

And when the parents are past hope and have begun to look to a childless old age, rejoicing is beyond measure:

> Abraham was a hundred years old when his son Isaac was born to him. And Sarah said, 'God has made laughter for me; everyone who hears will laugh with me. Who would have said to Abraham that Sarah would suckle children? Yet I have borne him a son in his old age.' *Book of Genesis 21:5-7*

She called the child Isaac, which mean 'He laughs'.

Childless Hannah, the pitied wife (how cruel pity can be!) in a household overrun with children, turned to desperate prayer:

> O Lord of hosts, if only you will look on the misery of your servant, and not forget your servant, but will give to your servant a son, then I will give him back to the Lord to serve him all his days ... *First Book of Samuel 1:11*

She named the child after God, for Samuel means 'The name of God'.

The child of Elizabeth and Zachariah, too, was, an answer to prayer. An angel of the Lord, Gabriel by name, said to the old priest in the Temple,

> 'Do not be afraid, Zechariah, for your prayer has been heard. Your wife Elizabeth will bear you a son ... you will have

great joy and gladness, and many will rejoice at his birth.'
Gospel of Luke 1:13

The child danced for joy in Elizabeth's womb and the old couple
called the lad John, which means 'God is gracious'.

Joseph and Mary had a child. He was not old. She was not
old. There would be other children about the house. We know
their names: James, Joseph, Judah, Simeon, and the girls, too,
perhaps named Salome and Mary *(Gospel of Mark 6:3)*. But the
circumstances surrounding the conception and birth of the son
called Jesus were so extraordinary, so beyond human hope and
expectation, that his name is above the names of Isaac, Samuel,
John, above the names of other little ones in the Nazareth home.
For these children were named in thanksgiving to the God who
heard the prayers of the childless or in memory of great ones of
old. Jesus was named for the future. He will save people from
their sins:

'Joseph, son of David, do not be afraid to take Mary as your
wife, for that which is conceived in her is of the Holy Spirit.
She will bear a son, and you are to call him Jesus for he will
save the people from their sins.' *Gospel of Matthew 1:20-21*

Who was Jesus?

Who IS Jesus?

CHAPTER ONE

Conception and Birth: Fact and Fiction

Gospels are rare books. Thousands of plays have been written, hundreds of thousands of novels have been published, millions of poems penned. History and science, religion and philosophy, politics and economics, all have spawned googols of books. But there are only about thirty books which are called gospels. But only four are venerated by millions of people as holy. Only two of these four speak of the circumstances surrounding the conception and birth of Jesus. We do not have much to go on.

Of the four Gospels venerated by Christian people, the Gospels according to Matthew, Mark, Luke, and John, only Matthew's and Luke's contain accounts of the events surrounding the coming into the world of Jesus of Nazareth. When compared, one with the other, these Gospels, at first sight, create so much confusion that we are hard put to answer the simplest of questions. We cannot name with any certainty the year in which Jesus was born; we cannot say with unassailable certitude that Jesus was born in Bethlehem; we cannot say without fear of contradiction that Joseph and Mary were forced into Egyptian exile by Herod the Great. We may be reluctant to accuse King Herod of killing babies, if proof positive is demanded of us. We have no absolute assurance that magi ever journeyed to the little town of Bethlehem; we cannot be confident of a guiding star; we must be careful what we say about shepherds and mangers and our ears must be especially sensitive to pick up the strains of heavenly choirs.

The contradictions and contrasts between the accounts of Matthew and Luke of the infancy of Jesus are easily listed. The more obvious are:

Gospel of Matthew	*Gospel of Luke*
1. Joseph and Mary are natives of the village of Bethlehem.	Joseph and Mary are natives of the village of Nazareth.
2. Joseph is married to Mary.	Mary has no husband.
3. An unnamed angel tells Joseph of the child to be born.	Gabriel tells Mary of the child she will conceive.
4. Joseph is told to name the child.	Mary is told to name the child.
5. The child is born in a house.	The child is placed in a manger.
6. Magi visit the home of the child.	Shepherds visit the manger.
7. The family are forced to flee to Egypt by Herod's evil plans.	The family make a peaceful pilgrimage to Jerusalem's Temple.
8. Children are slain in Bethlehem.	Jesus is presented in the Temple.
9. The family are forced to resettle in the obscure village of Nazareth.	The family return 'to their own town of Nazareth' safely.
10. Matthew has many quotations.	Luke has beautiful hymns.

What are we to make of these contradictions, inconsistencies, and confusions? We could try to reconcile them, to perform some plastic surgery to eradicate the wrinkles and tuck in the awkward protuberances. This, in fact, is what Christians do. They call it Christmas.

Our Christmas Crib, invented by St Francis of Assisi, has much to answer for. Francis saw the power of a visual aid, an aid to understanding, to appreciation, to prayer. To see the infant in a manger, to look on the mother, to stand guard with Joseph, to join with shepherds and wise men, to sing with the angels, is to open hearts to the wonder of God and the simplicity of love. That is what happened when, on Christmas Eve in 1223 in Greccio, Francis staged the Nativity in a cave. In his biography, the *Vita Prima*, Thomas of Celano records that, as he prayed, Francis took up the infant Jesus who seemed to come alive in his arms. It has been happening in every Christian heart and home ever since. But at a price.

The price to be paid for filleting the Gospel of Matthew and the Gospel of Luke to the dimensions of our crib is to rob each of its individual voice. It is to create our story by destroying the integrity of their stories. It is to turn their poetry into our prose. In short, it is to corrupt the very word of God, for it creates a Christmas exclusively for children, a Christmas devoid of the cross, reeking of sentimentality and pious illusion. The price paid corrupts the purposes for which Matthew and Luke composed their stories. They were not writing a history of the infant Jesus. Each in his own way was constructing a prologue, an overture, to the Jesus who would emerge in their pages. In their sure and certain faith in the resurrection of Jesus, they sought to sustain in faith men and women who, like them, saw in the person of Jesus the human face of God. They were not writing a history story; rather, they travelled beyond history into realms of faith, and contemplation, and prayer. To travel with them, we must ask, not only who Jesus was, but, more demandingly, who Jesus is.

To clarify what our four gospels are, and how we ought to read them, we will make two excursions. First, we will make our way through the infancy presentation of Saint Matthew, trying to listen to what he has to say, and trying to appreciate the way he says it. We will allow him to have his say, leaving aside, painfully perhaps, our cherished opinions and unsuspected prejudices. Secondly, we will journey through Saint Luke's infancy presentation, in the knowledge of what we have learned from Saint Matthew, and keenly aware that Luke is telling a very different and contradictory story. Out of our confusion will grow an understanding of what gospels are. If we learn to read Gospels aright, we will be well on the way to learning who Jesus was and who he is.

Saint Matthew's Infancy Presentation

Gospel of Matthew, chapters 1-2

Matthew opens his majestic overture boldly: *The book of the origin of Jesus Messiah, son of David, son of Abraham*. Not only is Jesus God's representative, anointed by God to shoulder God's designs in the world (that us what Messiah implies), but he is a royal personage, descended from the royal family of David. And descended, too, from Abraham, to whom God had spoken words of universal significance:

> I will make you a great nation, and I will bless you, and make your name great, so that you will be a blessing. I will bless those who bless you, and those who curse you, I will curse; and in you all the families of the earth shall be blessed.
> *Book of Genesis 12:2-3*

The origins of Jesus lie in the promises made to Abraham and David. His responsibility is to bring into being great expectations, to fulfil hopes long cherished and often dashed. Matthew's genealogy, an apparently boring list of begetters and begettings, will reveal all.

A Genealogy (1:2-16)

Genealogies have a purpose. If you were a priest in ancient Israel, you had to remember your lineage back six generations in order to show that your family was not tainted with non-priestly blood. The higher up the priestly tree you were, the longer the genealogical credentials had to be. Genealogies are, of course, of importance to kings (and queens), for obvious reasons. But, in the Bible, while genealogies serve priestly and royal concerns, for the most part they witness to continuity. That is why we must wade through all the names from Adam down to Noah *(Book of Genesis 5:1-32)*, and from Noah down to Abraham *(Book of Genesis 11:10-30)*, and from Adam, through the twelve sons of Jacob, down to the exile in Babylon which happened in 587 BC *(First Book of Chronicles, chapters 1-9)*. All this is not about human

roots or historical research. It is a declaration of faith: genealogies show that there is continuity in God's concern for humanity.
The past is linked to the present in order to show that the human
story is God's story. Genealogies join up huge swathes of history
about which nobody knows anything and declares that what is
hidden from us is not hidden from God. Men and women may
come, men and women may go, but God goes on forever.

Matthew's genealogy of Jesus is an act of faith. It is a declaration that, from Abraham to Jesus, God had been preparing,
from one generation to the next, to bring about the blessing
promised to humanity on the dusty roads of Iraq (*Book of Genesis
12:1-3*). We will not be surprised, therefore, to learn that Jesus is
Emmanuel, God-with-us (*Gospel of Matthew 1:23*), nor that his
presence will endure in our midst (*Gospel of Matthew 28:20*). The
first words of Matthew's Gospel are his last words.

Matthew does, however, have a surprise up his genealogical
sleeve. The genealogy in the Gospel of Luke (3: 23-38) traces
Jesus back through Abraham to Adam but he does not include a
single woman, not even Mary. Matthew has five women. Of
these four women, Tamar, Rahab, and Ruth are non-Jews, and
the wife of Uriah the Hittite, whom Matthew does not name, by
marrying a pagan renounces her Jewishness and loses her status
as one of God's people. To each of these great women belongs a
story (please, honour them by reading their stories). It was not
customary (but not unheard of) to include women in genealogies. And, we might ask, if women must be included, why not
Sarah, and Rebecca, and Leah and Rachel, and Miriam and
Abigail, for their stories may be deemed more 'holy' than those
of the quartet of street-wise ladies assembled by Matthew. And
why associate Mary with such worldly-wise women? Then,
again, why not?

The answer may be twofold. First, Matthew is concerned that
both Jewish and pagan people who had come to believe in Jesus
and who formed the Christian community for which he wrote
should live in harmony together. If the gospel is to be preached
to all nations, as the risen Lord Jesus commands (28:11-20), then
people of all races and cultures must live together in one community of praise. What better way of underlining his point than
to include in the family tree of Jesus himself mothers from all

over the place. If it is good enough for Jesus' family, it is good enough for Jesus' church.

Could it be that the rather colourful behaviour of these wonderful women (again, read for yourself, and ask, for instance, why the prostitute Rahab is twice praised in the New Testament for her faith) is seen by Matthew as instances of what we all know to be true: God works in mysterious ways. Not least in the case of Mary who was found to be with child by the Holy Spirit and not by her husband Joseph.

The name mentioned most frequently in Matthew's genealogy in not that of Jesus. It is that of David the King whose name and role are emphasised to warn careful readers that Jesus, a descendant of King David of old, will die with these words skirling around the cross in the mocking but ironic words of chief priests, scribes and elders:

> He saved others; he cannot save himself. He is the king of Israel; let him come down now from the cross, and we will believe in him. He trusts in God; let God deliver him now, if he desires him; for he said, 'I am the Son of God'.
> *Gospel of Matthew 27:41-43*

Matthew emphatically confirms the synthetic nature of his genealogy by his instructive nudge at its conclusion:

> Therefore, all the generations from Abraham to David are fourteen, and from David to the deportation to Babylon fourteen generations, and from the deportation to Babylon to the Messiah, fourteen generations. *Gospel of Matthew 1:17*

Readers who have the patience to check, particularly by painstakingly cross-referencing with the opening nine chapters of the First Book of Chronicles, will notice that Matthew has omitted some names and mentioned others more than once in order to arrive at his three groups of fourteen (and think about the number seven here). Indeed, he is one generation short in the last group of fourteen. In other words, he is not trying to narrate an historically accurate genealogical account of the family tree of Jesus (actually, he makes mistakes). His concern is to open the eyes of faith to the will of God coursing through history, even in the most unlikely of backwaters, and to alert his readers to the hand which firmly grasps the tiller of the little ship of humanity as it makes its way in a seemingly Godless world.

Joseph the Dreamer (1: 18-25)

In Luke's genealogy, the father of Joseph is a man called Eli. Matthew calls him Jacob. Again, we will be wide of the mark if we entangle ourselves in historical conundrums. Matthew is not concerned to identify who Joseph's biological parents were. His concern is to identify what kind of man has been chosen by God for what lies ahead. Matthew imagines Joseph to be the son of a Jacob because that famous Joseph, the one with the technicolour dream-coat, was the son of the great patriarch Jacob, the man who wrestled with God and whose name was changed to Israel, giving his name to a people. The new Joseph is modelled on ancient Joseph the dreamer. To understand Matthew's Joseph, you must read the story of Joseph of old. It is to be found in the Book of Genesis, chapters 37-50. Is what you find there an old man who is content to remain in the background?

The picture of St Joseph which many Christians unthinkingly accept is of an old man caring for a young mother and child. There is nothing in Matthew's gospel to support this caricature. For that, we are, in the main, indebted to a document now called *The Protevangelium of James*, a late second-century (?) apocryphal gospel which was popular for hundreds of years in very many Christian communities. Scholars know of editions in many languages: Greek, Latin, Coptic, Georgian, Armenian, Arabic, Ethiopic and Slavonic. The book purports to have been written by James, the brother of the Lord, allegedly a son of Joseph by a former marriage. We know of a James, called the brother of the Lord, from our Gospels and other New Testament writings, and, indeed, he may very well have written the Letter of James. It is extremely unlikely that this James was the author of the *Protevangelium* (a title which intends to convey the content of the work which concerns itself with matters which 'happened' before our Gospels pick up the story of Joseph, Mary, and Jesus).

The *Protevangelium* tells of an elderly couple, Joachim and Anna, whose prayer for a child was answered with a daughter, Mary. Like Samuel of old, the girl was lodged in the Temple where she was fed by an angel. When she was twelve years old and approaching puberty, the high priest assembled all the widowers in the land to select a husband. A dove alighted on the head of Joseph, and, objecting that he has sons already and was an old man, he was coerced into marrying the girl. An angel of the Lord appeared to Mary to tell her that she was to have a child. In her sixth month, Joseph discovered what he regarded as a deception and was unsure what to do. Luckily, an angel of the Lord assured him in a dream. The high priest tested the truthfulness of both Joseph and Mary and the child is born in a cave outside Bethlehem. With much cribbing from our Gospel of Matthew (and a little from the Gospel of Luke), and a great deal of an imaginative retelling of ancient bits and pieces, we have stars, visiting magi, angry Herod, slaughtered babies, and an intriguing escape for baby John the Baptist.

It is from such works of fiction that the popular picture of Joseph is cobbled together. Matthew has an altogether surer guide. He models his Joseph on the great son of Jacob. To know Matthew's Joseph, we must look to Joseph the dreamer whose talents took him from slave-boy to estate manager, prison governor, and prime-minister of Egypt. The ancient Joseph was a man of courage, insight, intelligence, a man with a great heart, a forgiving nature, and, above all, a profound trust in God. He saved the whole world when Pharaoh could not. He believed in his dreams.

Matthew's Joseph is made of the same stuff. Young, energetic, thoughtful, magnanimous, with a profound trust in God, he does not lightly dismiss his pregnant wife nor does he lightly take responsibility for what God proposes: only the foolhardy give in lightly to God. The angel in his dreams has to deal with a man who has a passion for doing what is right and a reverence for God which counsels caution. Responsibility for one whose destiny it will be to save his people from their sins, who will be God-with-us, is not to be undertaken without hesitation, reflection, and prayer. He takes the child and names it as his own.

Magi, the Star, and the Gifts (2:1-8)
There were no three kings. They were not called Balthasar, Melchior, and Caspar, one white, one black, one brown. Because the visitors conversed with King Herod, it was assumed that they, too, were kings. Because there were three gifts, it was assumed there were three givers. And it was an Englishman who decided that one came from Asia, one from Africa, and one from Europe.

Because human beings like to name the nameless, the names of the magi were given as Balthasar, Melchior, and Caspar in a sixth century text known as *Excerpta Latina Barbari*. The English monk, Venerable Bede, in his commentary *Exposition of Matthew*, recorded that each of the wise men came from one of the three known continents, Asia, Africa, and Europe, and coloured accordingly. Bede also claimed that the three were descended from Shem, Ham, and Japheth, the sons of Noah. More wondrous, out of Africa, an Ethiopian text, the *Book of Adam and Eve*, named the three as Hor, King of the Persians, Basanater, King of Sab, and Karsudan, King of the East. And in the East, according to Syrian and Armenian traditions, twelve magi journeyed to the court of King Herod in Jerusalem, and their names, as well as the names of their fathers, are recorded. All agree that the magi were from the pagan world.

Matthew is at once more, and less, exciting. The word *magus* (plural: *magi*) is an Old Persian word which refers to a priest. The priest practised *mageia*, not magic, but work befitting a priest, such as the pursuit of knowledge and wisdom, and astronomy/astrology and any arcane arts likely to reveal the divine mind. When the word found its way into Greek, it took a downturn. Sophocles, in his play, *Oedipus, King of Thebes*, describes a soothsayer as a *magos*, meaning 'a fraudulent quack'. Then there is the story of one Simon Magus in the Acts of the Apostles (chapter 8). Matthew's magi are, however, the real thing.

In the Book of Daniel, which has a very oriental feel about it, we find Nebuchadnezzar of Babylon threatening to put all his magi to death because they fail to interpret a royal dream. Daniel, a Jew, one of the King's wise men, who had proved himself to be ten times better than the court magi in learning, skill in all matters, and wisdom in understanding all visions and dreams, interpreted Nebuchadnezzar's dream and saved all the Chaldean magi from a sorry end *(Book of Daniel, chapters 1-2)*. Wise Daniel and his wise companions are the prototypes of Matthew's men from the East.

The star, the magi and their expensive presents, must not be placed under the historical microscope. They will be seen more clearly when looked at through the eyes of imagination and from the perspective of prayerful reflection on Old Testament hopes and expectations.

The star

This is no ordinary star. Not only does it travel from north to south, it drops from the heaven to stand still over a house. To attempt to identify Matthew's star with a comet, a planetary conjunction, or a supernova, is to chase moonbeams. Matthew, a man steeped in his Jewish Bible, will have known of the ancient words of that strange man from the East, a pagan called Balaam, who, inspired by God, turned a curse to a blessing, and sung of a star to be born. Balaam's star is David the King:

> The oracle of Balaam the son of Peor,
> the oracle of one whose eye is perfect,
> the oracle of one who hears the words of God,
> and knows the knowledge within the Most High,
> the man who sees the vision of the Almighty,
> a man who falls down but whose eyes are uncovered.

> I see him, but not yet;
> I behold him, but not near:
> a star shall come forth out of Jacob,
> a sceptre shall rise out of Israel.
> *Book of Numbers 24:15-17*

As Balaam points to the 'star' who will be David the King, so Matthew's star, in his genealogy, points to another 'star' to be born in Bethlehem, the son of David, King of Israel. *The Protevangelium of James*, St Ephrem of Syria, in his commentary on a work called the *Diatessaron*, and St John Chrysostom, in his commentary on the Gospel of Matthew, all point out that the so-called star does not remain in the high heavens but moves as a guide and comes to rest over the house where the child was, leading faithful pilgrims to worship on bended knees. And moreover, God reminded Job of a day,

> when the morning stars sang together,
> and all the sons of God shouted for joy. *Book of Job 38:7*

In the quotation 'morning stars' and 'sons of God' refer to angels, and it is no great leap of imagination to see a star as a symbol of a guiding angel. Indeed, a work entitled *The Arabic Gospel*

of the Infancy [of Jesus], which may have be known to the
prophet Mohammed (Peace be upon his name) for some of its
legends are to be found in the Koran, identifies the magi's star
with an angel. Notice, too, that God promised Moses that a guiding angel would see the wandering people safely to the land of
promise *(Book of the Exodus 23:20; 32:34)* and the divine guidance
is seen as a cloud by day and fire by night *(Book of the Exodus
13:21)*. The pillar of cloud is identified with God who speaks
with Moses *(Book of the Exodus 33:9-10)*. The star, the angel, the
cloud, the fire, all symbolise, in the poetry of prayer, divine presence guiding, protecting, and leading safely home.

Gold, Frankincense, Myrrh

What happened to the gold? Would not the (so-called) three
kings be as lavish as Henry VIII and Francis I at the Field of the
Cloth of Gold (1520)? Would not the Son of God merit more than
the King of France? Did the Holy Family live prosperously ever
after? To ask such questions is to expose the silliness of taking
Matthew's text as if he had set out to write unvarnished history.
It is to approach Matthew with feet of clay, and not with eagle's
wings.

Gold, it comes as no surprise, is the most frequently mentioned precious metal in the Old Testament. King Solomon's
gold mines are the stuff of fiction. But Matthew is not concerned
with a fortuitous increase in the financial resources of the Holy
Family. His eye is surely elsewhere.

Frankincense and myrrh, both botanical products of the
Burseraceae family, were expensive perfumes, and, accordingly,
the preserve, like gold, of the royal and the wealthy.

Matthew's magi seek the one who is born King of the Jews.
The gifts entirely endorse the royal status of the child. St Justin
Martyr was one of the first commentators to link the gifts with
lines from the Old Testament whose every word revealed to
Matthew the very mind of God. Consider a few lines from the
prophet Isaiah:

Arise, and shine; for your light has come,
and the glory of the Lord has risen upon you ...
Nations shall come to your light,
and kings to the brightness of your rising ...

Your sons shall come from afar,
and your daughters shall be carried in arms.
Then you shall see and be radiant,
your heart shall thrill and rejoice ...

... the wealth of the nations shall come to you.
A multitude of camels of Midian and Ephah ...

They will bring gold and frankincense,
and shall proclaim the praise of the Lord;
the children of your oppressors
shall come bending low to you ...

Violence no more shall be heard in your land ...
your city walls shall be called *Salvation*,
your city gates named *Praise*.
Book of Isaiah, chapter 60 passim

And a few lines from the Book of Psalms come to mind, especially
lines which invoke God's blessing on royal descendants of
David. Psalm 72 was regarded in some Jewish circles as a prayer
for God's Messiah King, and, be it noted, the psalm was the special psalm sung on the Feast of the Epiphany from a very early
date, the very feast day which remembers the importance of
Matthew's magi:

May the kings of Tarshish
and of the isles
render him tribute,
may the kings of Saba and Seba bring gifts!
May the kings fall down before him,
all the nations serve him!

For he delivers the needy who call upon him,
the poor who have no helper.
He has pity on the weak and the needy,
and saves the needy from death.
From oppression and violence he redeems their life;
and precious is their blood in his sight.
Psalm 72:10-14

Again, a poet declares, 'I address my verses to the *king*', and
pens,

Your godly throne endures forever and ever.
Your royal sceptre is a sceptre of justice;
you love righteousness and hate wickedness.

Therefore God your God, has *anointed* you
with the oil of gladness above your companions;
your robes are all fragrant with *myrrh* and aloes and cassia.
Psalm 45:6-7

A royal procession, in full regalia, catches the imagination of another poet:

What is that coming up from the desert,
like a column of smoke,
perfumed with myrrh and frankincense,
with the fragrant perfumes of the merchant?
Behold, it is the litter of Solomon!
Song of Songs, 3:6-7

The gifts of the magi, gold, frankincense, and myrrh, are fittingly brought to the new son of David, the King of the Jews. With a mind and an imagination steeped in the scriptures, Matthew draws his readers into contemplation of the new king, and invites them to worship with wise visitors from the great pagan world beyond the little town of Bethlehem. And beyond the little down of Bethlehem, just five miles away, is the city of Jerusalem and a place called Golgotha, where the King of Israel, the Son God, will save his people from their sins (*Gospel of Matthew 27:32-50*).

King Herod
Herod the Great, king of Palestine from 37 to 4 BC, was a genius, a benefactor and a paranoid villain. But we are hardly justified in adding to his many murderous crimes the death of children in Bethlehem. The Jewish historian, Flavius Josephus, born in 37 AD, provides a minute history of Herod, and, for political reasons, emphasises the crimes of a man he had little inducement to admire. He does not mention massacre of babies in Bethlehem. And is it not strange that whenever we meet members of Herod's family in the pages of the New Testament, none seems to know Jesus or to recall what terrors the old king inflicted at

his birth? Matthew makes no reference to the matter in the body of his gospel, and the other three gospels are silent on the matter, even when there is a dispute about whether Jesus was born in Bethlehem *(Gospel of John 7:40-42)*. The fact that there would have been few young children in a tiny village like Bethlehem does not add historical credibility when all other evidence casts a very thick pall of doubt.

Other paths to truth must be trod if we are to see what Matthew is about. Again, what determines his thought are the divine patterns he discerns in his Bible. He reworks old patterns so that his readers may come to see how it is that Peter can declare, *You are the Messiah, the Son of the living God (Gospel of Matthew 16:16)*, and themselves grow in the same faith.

We have seen Joseph modelled on Joseph the dreamer of old. The story of Moses' battle with Pharaoh provides Matthew with the strands to weave into his overture, strands of death and danger, of flight and return. When we move beyond the overture, we see the unfolding of themes laid down here. The ministry of Jesus will bring him from Galilee of the Gentiles to death in Jerusalem and back to Galilee of the Gentiles to meet with his disciples when he has been raised from the dead.

The Book of the Exodus 1-15 narrates the struggle between the Pharaoh and God. Moses is God's champion, the one appointed to wrest the people from the cruel tyranny of the king (as the Pharaoh is called). Moses is miraculously rescued from the programme of male infanticide and he grows in the wisdom of the Egyptians, thus enabled to lead the people out of slavery to meet with God on the holy mountain. For Pharaoh, read Herod. For the death of Hebrew boys, read the death of Bethlehem babies. For the flight of Moses to safety in the desert, read the flight of Joseph, Mary and child, into Egypt. For the death of first-born sons, read the death of Jesus. For the meeting with God on Mount Sinai, read the meeting of the Risen Lord on the mountain with worshipping disciples *(Gospel of Matthew 28:16-20)*.

Conclusions

1. We can easily discover how artificial Matthew's genealogy is, and, through its very artificiality, learn what he wants to say and

how he goes about his task, which is to identify who is to be born and die, the one who will be God-with-us.

2. We do not have access to the mind of Joseph or the mind of Mary. Yet Matthew, through his understanding of God's ways in lives of the great ones of old, fashions his material so that we may come to know what God was about in the calling of Joseph and Mary.

3. The weight of evidence indicates that we can have no historical certainty of any of the details surrounding the magi and their visit to Jerusalem and Bethlehem. But, by attending to Matthew's imaginative reflections on what he learned in his Bible, we may begin to grasp what God has given in the Jesus who saves the people from their sins and is God-with-us, Jews and Gentiles, till the end of the age.

4. There are many and serious reasons for concluding that the Flight into Egypt and the Massacre of the Holy Innocents did not happen. Yet prayerful meditation on these tales will reveal the finger of God writing our human story. We will be led to the cross, where political power in the person of Pilate, aligned with the Sanhedrin, as with Herod, the chief priests and the rest, combine to seek the life of the man Jesus. A son called out of Egypt will lead us to a Son called out of death.

5. Matthew guides us through his first two chapters by signposting our way with five explicit quotations from his Bible. The reader is invited to turn to them, in the light of all that has been said, and to wrestle with them and with the God of whom they speak. It is to that wrestling with the word of God to which Matthew invites his readers.

AND THE POINT IS …

The point is that the Gospels are not historical documents. They do not provide us with a biography of Jesus. They do not set out to satisfy our historical curiosity. They are that rare thing among all the books that ever were: good news, gospel.

EXCURSION II

Saint Luke's Infancy Presentation

Gospel of Luke, chapters 1-2

We are safe with our crib. Shepherds hobnob with three crowned kings, one black, one brown, one white. The ox and the ass are house-trained and the straw in the manger never smells. Elderly Joseph keeps well back. Mary wears a white frock.

Christians, for the most part, find Luke much more congenial than Matthew. Luke's presentation of the infancy story has no murderous king, no dead babies, and no flight into the desert. The keynote is joy and we feel that's the way it must have been. If we think about it at all, we are prepared to admit that, from the perspective of sober history and elementary astronomy, Matthew's star may be no more than an inner light, guiding the magi and nudging them whenever they stray. But we are loathe to concede much else to the historical junkyard. Certainly, we will not yield our manger, our shepherds, the swaddling clothes, the Angel Gabriel nor the heavenly choir. Yet, in our tenacity to hold in the grasp of history what we have always believed (but never examined), we may well miss what Luke strove to teach and be left with no more than a sentimental story, lovely for the children, of course, but hardly worth the cost of being a Christian.

If we outline the amazing design of Luke's drama, what he intended to convey will become clear. What we have are five tiny plays, all linked together, and all hinging on the central play which gives meaning to the other four. This, as I see it, was his plan:

PLAY I

THE ANNUNCIATION TO THE OLD PRIEST ZACHARIAH

PLAY II

THE ANNUNCIATION TO THE UNMARRIED MARY

PLAY III

THE MEETING OF THE MOTHERS

PLAY IV

WHAT HAPPENED WHEN JOHN WAS BORN

PLAY V

WHAT HAPPENED WHEN JESUS WAS BORN

Or, one might express it this way:

> Play 1: Gabriel makes an announcement to Zachariah (1:1-25)
> Play 2: Gabriel makes an announcement to Mary (1:26-38)
>
> **Play 3: Two Mothers Meet – Mary visits Elizabeth (1:39-56)**
>
> Play 4: The drama surrounding John's birth (1:57-80)
> Play 5: The drama surrounding Jesus' birth (2:1-40)

If my understanding is correct, the pivotal drama is the meeting of the two mothers. It is the Visitation which explains the other dramas. It supplies the key to the meaning of the whole. In order to understand what Luke is about in his infancy presentation, we will do well to begin with Mary's visit to her older relative.

The Visitation (1:39-56)
For the geographically minded, it is about seventy-two miles from Nazareth to Bethlehem and tradition places the home of Zachariah and Elizabeth in a village close by. It is difficult to imagine a pregnant thirteen or fourteen year old girl making her way alone through the dangerous Jordan Valley and the even more treacherous Judaean hills. Luke, like Matthew, forever interested in the ways of God, does not tarry over our concerns. Mary makes her way, as Jesus will make his way to Jerusalem and his death *(9:51; 13:22; 22:22)*, under divine impetus. This much we can gather by Abraham's *running, making haste,* and *making ready quickly*, which characterise his encounters with God *(Book of Genesis 18:1-8)*. When salvation comes to the house of Zacchaeus, he is advised to make haste in order to receive his guest *(Gospel of Luke 19:1-10)*. Simple words, such as 'arose', 'went', 'with haste', indicate Mary's obedience to God's will, for Luke is telling his story in the language used for great holy ones of the past.

The angel Gabriel did not greet old Zachariah but he did greet Mary: *Greetings, O favoured one, the Lord is with you! (1:28),* an early and cautionary indication that, great though he is, John is not Jesus. Mary, in her turn, greets Elizabeth, a greeting which causes the baby in her womb to leap about. So important is this leaping for joy that it is mentioned twice. Keep it in mind.

Elizabeth is filled with the Holy Spirit. God's Spirit has already been promised to Elizabeth's baby, whose birth will be a cause of joy and gladness to many who will come to listen and to be baptised. Gabriel's words had revealed as much to the father, the venerable Zachariah:

And you will have joy and gladness,
and many will rejoice at his birth;
for he will be great before the Lord,
and he shall drink no wine nor strong drink,
and he shall be filled with the Holy Spirit,
even from his mother's womb.
Gospel of Luke 1:14-15

The Holy Spirit, identified as *the power of the Most High*, had already overshadowed Mary with the mantle of God's creative power, and, consequently, *the child to be born will be called holy, Son of God* (1:35). It is the presence of this child in the young girl's womb and the identity of the child which are Luke's concerns in the meeting of the two mothers.

Twice we are told that Elizabeth's child jumped in her womb, a movement Elizabeth interprets as leaping for joy (just as true disciples will rejoice and jump for joy - see *Gospel of Luke 6:23*). With a loud cry (the sign of a prophet's voice), she proclaims that Mary is blessed by God, to a superlative (but not unique) degree. God's blessing, God's protective care, accomplishes and accompanies the call to motherhood given to Mary. The blessing, therefore, is centred on 'the fruit of your womb'; on account of her child, Mary is blessed as great women of old have been blessed. Elizabeth's next words to Mary repay careful scrutiny.

Elizabeth makes three statements:

How is it with me that the mother of my Lord should come to me?

For, behold, as the sound of your greeting came to my ears, the unborn child in my womb leapt for joy.

And blessed is the one who believed that the word uttered by the Lord would [come to] fulfilment.

To grasp what Luke is about here, we must go back in time to the days of David the King.

A Royal Procession
After the tempestuous reign of King Saul, David was anointed king at Hebron by all the elders of the tribes of Israel. For political, military, and economic reasons, David wanted to centralise his power and, accordingly, he needed a capital city to which all would give allegiance. For reasons entirely similar to the establishment of Washington DC and Canberra, Australia, he sought a city outside the tribal confederation. He captured the non-Israelite city of Jerusalem and made it his capital. It was his private city. That is why he called it *the city of David (Second Book of Samuel 5:1-10).*

David wanted to bind the religious aspirations of the tribes to Jerusalem. To this end, he wished to build a central temple in his city (his dalliance with Bathsheba thwarted this hope – *Second Book of Samuel 11:1-27*). His first move was to bring to Jerusalem the Ark of the Covenant, the chest of acacia wood which contained the stone slabs on which were inscribed the Ten Commandments. The Ark was the place where God's name dwelt, that is, it was the locus of God's presence among his people and functioned as a palladium or shield carried into battle *(Book of Numbers 10:35-36).*

The Ark of the Covenant was captured by enemies, re-captured, and lodged for safety in a place called Baalejudah (later, Keriath-Jearim), not far from Bethlehem. David decided that it should be brought to his city and organised a huge procession (think Corpus Christi here):

And David again assembled all the young men of Israel, seventy thousand strong. And David arose and went and all the people with him from among the leaders of Judah, going up to carry from that place the Ark of God, which is called by the name of the Lord of power who sits on the cherubim. And they carried the Ark of the Lord on a new cart, and they brought it out of the house of Abinadab which was on a hill. And Uzzah and his brothers, the sons of Abinadab, were leading the cart with the Ark, and his brothers went in front of the ark. And David and the sons of Israel were making

merry mightily before the Lord, with singers and with harps and with lutes, with timbrels, and with cymbals, and with trumpets.
Second Book of Samuel 6:1-5
(Translated from the Greek *Septuagint*)

Disaster struck the exuberant procession. When the oxen pulling the cart stumbled, Uzzah steadied the Ark with his hand, but God's anger struck him down. The story portrays the power and danger that ancient peoples associated with their holy objects and with the divine powers that inhabited them. The same Ark of God had brought plague and pestilence upon the Philistines when they captured it in battle *(First Book of Samuel, chapters 5 and 6)*. David, frightened because the Lord had burst forth against Uzzah, called off the procession. This is what the Bible says at this point:

And David was frightened of God that day, and he said, *How is it with me that the ark of the Lord should come to me?*
Second Book of Samuel 6:9

David lodged the Ark of God with a friend, where it remained for three months.

The God of the Ark showered blessings on his friend's household and David saw this as a sign to recommence the procession to Jerusalem with great rejoicing. The King was *leaping and dancing before the Lord*, so energetically that his wife Michal despised him in her heart for making a show of himself. Unlike Mary, unlike Elizabeth, *Michal had no child to the day of her death,* – perhaps the saddest sentence in the Bible.

Who is in the Ark?
Mary's hymn explains how it is that Elizabeth can call her the mother of my Lord. She looks beyond the immediate praise of Elizabeth to all generations who will bless what has been done in her, will rejoice in what God is about. Mary's whole being ('my soul' = 'I') marvels at and *rejoices in God who is my Saviour.* This Saviour God has done great things to her but the great things are not exclusively for her: great things have been done by mighty God to all generations, to the whole of humanity. The power of God is revealed to the world, not as destructive, aveng-

ing power, but as mercy: the God of Israel is the Saviour God
(*Book of Isaiah 45:15*). Limitless mercy is divine power: this is how
Mary sees God as Saviour. Remembering the blessings showered on Abraham in the past conjures up for Mary a future when
the blessing of mercy will be showered on all, wherever they
may be.

Of course, the surprising thing is that it is Jesus who is
Saviour; the baby swaddled in cloths is anointed/appointed
Saviour and Lord. All that Mary sings of in her song comes to
earth in the child in her womb. What must be said of God must
be said of the child. That is what the Visitation reveals and that is
why it is the play which explains all plays.

Where is God to be found?

Luke tells us that Jesus was born in Bethlehem, the city of David.
At first sight, this would appear to be nonsense. The city of
David was and is Jerusalem. True, David was the son of a farmer
of Bethlehem, but, as we have seen, Jerusalem was the personal
property of David because he captured it and made it his capital.
So why does Luke write this?:

> And Joseph also went up from Galilee, from the city of
> Nazareth, to Judaea, to the city of David, which is called
> Bethlehem, because he was of the house and family of David,
> to be enrolled with Mary, his betrothed, who was with child.
> *Gospel of Luke 2:4-5*

Another question. Why does Luke call attention to the fact that
Jesus is born in Bethlehem, in the city of David, during the reign
of Emperor Augustus? Notice, too, what the shepherds will find
there: for to you is born TODAY in the city of David a SAV-
IOUR, who is MESSIAH LORD, a cause of GLORY TO GOD and
PEACE on earth among its peoples with whom God is pleased:

> And the angel said [to the shepherds] 'Do not be afraid; for
> behold, I am gospelling you with great joy, which will be for
> all the people, because today is born for you in the city of
> David a saviour, who is Messiah Lord. And this will be a sign
> for you: you will find a baby swaddled in cloths and lying in
> a manger.'
>
> And suddenly there was with the angel a multitude of the

> heavenly army praising God and saying,
> 'Glory to God in the highest heaven,
> and peace on earth, goodwill to all people.'
> *Gospel of Luke 2:10-14*

A little history will help to clarify what Luke is about. Following the assassination of Julius Caesar in 44 BC, the Roman Empire descended into the chaos of civil war and it was not until 29 BC that the Augustus restored peace. Grateful citizens of the city of Rome erected an altar on which was inscribed the famous legend, *Ars Pacis Augustae*, the Altar of the Peace of Augustus. The Emperor's birthday was celebrated as the day of the birth of 'The Saviour of the World'. Indeed, a famous inscription commemorating the birth of Augustus reads, 'The birthday of the god [= Augustus] has marked the beginning of the gospel for the whole world' (Priene Inscription of Augustus).

Not Augustus! Not in Caesar's Rome! Not the Peace of Augustus! Not an imperial saviour! It is Jesus! It is in the city of David! It is the peace of Christ! Here you will find God's true Saviour, the true Messiah, the true Lord! This is the true good news, true gospel! Don't rely on here-today-gone-tomorrow peace! God's angels sing that the *Pax Christi*, the Peace of Christ, is God's peace to all peoples forever. God-in-Christ, our true Lord, is to be found, not on an altar in Rome, but in a manger in Bethlehem! Glory to God in the highest heaven!

What Luke has done is to move the imperial agenda and its propaganda from Rome to Bethlehem. Not only that, he has decided that the presence of God on earth is not now to be found in the temple in Jerusalem, but in the child in the manger, the child in the new city of David, to whom God has given 'the throne of his father David', and whose reign, unlike that of David or Augustus, will have no end *(Gospel of Luke 1:3-33)*.

Ten Lepers

There are many stories in Luke's Gospel which emphasise his point that, where Jesus is present, God is there too. In the story of the little man from Jericho *(Gospel of Luke 19:1-10)*, Jesus calls him out of the tree to tell him that *Today, salvation has come to this house*. Where Jesus is, there is God's salvation. The 'today' of

Jesus is the 'today' of God: a new time has arrived in the world, the time of Jesus, the time of God. The story of the ten people with leprosy who came to Jesus begging for mercy makes the point with crystal clarity *(Gospel of Luke 17:19)*.

Ten lepers cry to Jesus for help. They are commanded to go to their priests as to a public health officer. All are cured. One man, a Samaritan, making his way to his priest (not in Jerusalem but in the city of Samaria), on discovering that he has been cured, returns to Jesus, falls to the ground in worship before Jesus, and gives praise to God. The comments of Jesus explain the point:

Were not ten made clean? Where are the nine?

Was no one found to give praise to God, except this foreigner?

Gospel of Luke 17:17

One person came back to Jesus to give praise to God. But why, oh why, should anyone go to Jesus to give praise to God? Why not go to the Temple in the holy city of Jerusalem? And, why not pray to God for God's mercy in the first place? Because in the new 'Today' of St Luke, to seek for God's mercy, one must go to Jesus. In the new 'Today', to praise God, one must fall at the feet of Jesus of Nazareth. That is the kind of faith the Samaritan leper had. Therefore, to him is given what is beyond price. Ten people are cured; only one experiences that wholeness which comes from being where God is to be found: *Rise, go on your way; your faith has saved you.*

The Visitation Revisited

Let us retrace our steps. Mary came to the hill country of Judah, the very region where the Ark of the God was lodged in the house of David's friend. When Mary greeted her kinswoman, the child in her whom leapt and Elizabeth was filled with the Holy Spirit (David, too, was filled with God's Holy Spirit). Filled with the Spirit, she recognised the blessing showered on Mary, as God's presence in the Ark had showered blessing on David's friend and all his household. The words which David uttered long ago in fear and reverence before the very presence of God are echoed by Elizabeth as she proclaimed to the world in a loud cry:

Blessed are you among women,
and the fruit of your womb is blessed!
And how is this with me
that the mother of my Lord
should come to me?
For behold,
when the sound of your greeting
came to my ears,
the baby in my womb
leaped for joy.
Gospel of Luke 1:42-43

As David danced and made merry before the Lord, so the baby, a baby who was filled with the Holy Spirit, even from his mother's womb *(Gospel of Luke 1:15)*, leapt in joyous recognition of the presence of the Lord in his mother's house. According to the *First Book of Chronicles*, in its account of the procession of the Ark to the city of David, the celebrations were completed by a rousing psalm of thanksgiving composed for the occasion:

O give thanks to the Lord,
call on his name,
make known his deeds among the peoples ...

Deliver us,
O God of our salvation,
and gather and save us
from among the nations,
that we may give thanks
to your holy name,
and glory in your praise.
First Book of Chronicles 16:8-36

The Holy Spirit within Elizabeth pinpoints the root of Mary's blessedness: she believed the word spoken to her from the Lord. It comes as no surprise that Mary sings a rousing psalm of thanksgiving, as David commanded a rousing song from his choirmaster. One ought to bear in mind, too, that the blessing Elizabeth pronounced upon Mary *(Blessed are you among women ...)* is remarkably similar to that pronounced on Judith:

O daughter,
you are blessed by the Most High God,

above all women on earth ...
Book of Judith 13:18

Judith responded, as Mary does in the *Magnificat*, with a rousing song. And it comes as no surprise that the Ark of God was in the house of David's blessed friend for three months. Mary remained in Elizabeth's house for three months before returning to her home in Nazareth.

What is happening in Luke's story is plain enough. He has used an old story to tell a new story. In his first little play, Zachariah is told that his child will be a source of joy and gladness for he will, through the power of the Holy Spirit, be a prophet of God and prepare people for the coming of the Lord Jesus (*Gospel of Luke 1:14-17*). In the second play, the angel of the Lord discloses to Mary that her child will be greater still. For he will be, not prophet, but Son of the Most High; he will receive the throne of his ancestor David, he will reign over the house of Israel, and his kingdom will have no end (*Gospel of Luke 1:32-34*).

In the central play, the one which provides the key to the others, all is revealed. The presence of God has come into the world, showering blessings. This son of Mary is no less than, as Matthew puts it, God-with-us, as sure as the presence of God dwelt in the Ark which David brought to his city with much leaping and dancing in joy and gladness. The baby John, in the womb of Elizabeth, recognises and identifies where God is now to be found in our world. To be in the presence of the infant in Mary's womb is to be where the Lord is. Mary is the new Ark of the Covenant, the Gate of Heaven, the Morning Star. In Luke's story, John the Baptist never meets Jesus. His moment of proclamation, his celebration of the one to come, is accomplished by leaping and dancing for joy in his mother's womb.

What we learn in the Visitation carries forward into the third play, the birth of John and the hymn which tells of his place in the divine scheme of things. The final play, enacted by those around the manger, spell out who it is that Elizabeth recognised as Lord and what God's purposes are in the life and times of Jesus of Nazareth. It is a true Christmas.

Conclusions

1. Luke's account of the events surrounding the conception and birth of Jesus has very little in common with the account given to us by St Matthew. It is well-nigh impossible to iron out the differences between them or to explain, from the point of view of the historian, how two accounts of the same event could be so irreconcilable one with the other.

2. It is clear that we can have no historical certainty about the details which Luke presents. For example, the hymns which enrich his text were clearly not composed by the people to whom Luke attributes them: Mary did not sing the *Magnificat* in an *ex tempore* outpouring of joy; Zechariah did not compose the *Benedictus*; Simeon did not compose the *Nunc Dimittis*. Most scholars are agreed that Luke incorporated hymns which were current in Jewish Christian circles into the body of his text.

3. If Luke's account differs irreconcilably from Matthew's, his methods do not. He has searched the scriptures and he has seized on what he found there to help him explain the meaning of Jesus and the significance for humanity of his mission on earth. If God's will is to be known, it will be found in the scriptures. That is the firm conviction of Luke, of Matthew, and, indeed, of all the first Christians. If Luke is to come to the heart of Jesus, he knows he must grapple with the heart of God laid out before him in his Bible. That is why the people and events in his story are presented in the light of, and often in the precise language of, the record of God's great deeds in shepherding his people Israel.

4. People of faith must look to St Luke, and to St Matthew, for faith's understanding of Jesus. As Luke himself says, we must try to decipher what is written, not by a human hand, but by the finger of God *(Gospel of Luke 11:20)*.

AND THE POINT IS …

Luke's Gospel never uses the noun 'gospel'. Luke likes to use a verb, a doing-word. For that is what he is doing, gospelling his readers.

CHAPTER TWO

Ground Clearance

Christianity is an historical religion. That is to say, Christians claim that their religion is founded on historical events, particularly on an historical figure, Jesus of Nazareth, and on what he did and what he said. That Jesus existed, that he was an itinerant preacher, that he was put to death by crucifixion, and that his disciples claimed that he was raised from the dead, are historically verifiable facts. What Christians do not claim is that the foundational texts of their faith, the Gospels according to Matthew, Mark, Luke, and John, or, indeed, other writings which make up what is called the New Testament, provide them with biographies of Jesus. The writings which Christians hold sacred are acclaimed in churches as The Word of the Lord. They are not honoured as models of historical research.

Yet history mattered to the first disciples of Jesus. They were concerned that he lived, that he taught, that he died. Jesus was no phantom, no figment of their imagination, no product of wishful thinking. If the centre of their faith was a belief that Jesus had been raised from the dead by God, then two things must be beyond denial: Jesus was a real human being; Jesus really died. There is plenty of historical evidence, both inside and outside the New Testament, that Christians concerned themselves with these matters and that they were entirely satisfied that Jesus was truly human and that he was crucified by command of the Roman prefect, Pontius Pilate.

The Gospels, and, indeed, the other New Testament writings, are not concerned with historical research. The gospels were written for people who believed in the Christian message, for people who had come to a religious faith centred on the death and resurrection of Jesus. The Gospels were written, as far as we know, to sustain, support, and reinforce Christians in their faith that Jesus was their Risen Lord. No doubt different circumstances called each Gospel into being but all concern themselves with two over-riding issues: who is Jesus in our life now and what does he demand of us as we journey in faith and hope and love?

Gospel-makers were preachers, not historians. They sought to interpret for their readers/hearers the meaning of Jesus in their time and in their place, with their concerns and expect-ations. A preacher must speak to the world of his community. A preacher must address the concerns of the people in the pew. A Christian preacher, in every age, must translate what Jesus means in the circumstances which beset the lives of those who listen. That is what Matthew, Mark, Luke, and John sought to do. What we have from them is their interpretation of Jesus, trimmed to the circumstances of the people for whom they wrote.

Thus it is that, in approaching the Gospels, readers must be aware of what it is they will find there. There is, at the end of the day, only one Christian question: *Who do you say I am?* Each gen-eration of Christians must confront that question and no one generation can speak for all. But Christians believe that the in-terpretations of Jesus to be found in the Gospels have a defini-tive, non-negotiable understanding of Jesus, against which all other understandings must be tested. To be sure, the four gospel-makers were interpreting Jesus to their time and their place. But over the first few centuries of their existence, Christians came to see that the Gospels written by Matthew, Mark, Luke and John must be held to be definitive for Christian faith in the same way and for the same reasons that the books of the ancient prophets, Isaiah, Jeremiah, and the rest, were to be regarded as the word of the Lord. The writings which came to make up the New Testament were held to have come into being under the guidance of the Holy Spirit in the same measure as the books which Jesus held sacred, the books of the Jewish Bible. It is for this reason that the answers the Gospels make to the question, *Who do you say I am?*, are regarded as definitive for Christian faith.

Of course, Christians cannot prove that the Holy Spirit in-spired the creation of the books which make up the Bible. Jews cannot prove that the Spirit of God inspired the books which they hold sacred and which form the basis of their faith. The followers of Islam cannot prove that the Koran is divinely inspired and comes from the mouth of God's angel. To say that the Bible, the Old Testament and the New Testament, or to say that the Koran come from God is a matter of faith. Thus, the answers given in the Gospels to Christianity's one question, *Who do you say I am?*, are a matter of faith, not of historical analysis, no matter how firmly rooted such answers are in historical realities. The Gospels are faith speaking unto faith, not history underpinning belief.

Stilling a Storm at Sea

An example will help. In the *Gospel according to Mark*, we read of Jesus calming a fierce storm:

> And, that same day, when evening had come, he [Jesus] says to them [disciples], 'Let us go over to the other side.' And leaving the crowd, they took him as he was in the boat. And there were other boats with him. And there comes a great tempest of wind, and the waves were breaking upon the boat so that in that moment the boat was filling up. And he is sleeping on a cushion in the stern. They wake him and say to him, 'Teacher, don't you care that we are perishing?'
> And waking up, he rebuked the wind and he said to the sea, 'Hush! Be still!' And the wind dropped and there was a great calm. And he said to them, 'Why are you so cowardly? How is it you have no faith?'
> And they feared a great fear and they were saying to one another,
> 'So who then is this, that the wind and the sea obey him?'
> *Gospel of Mark 4:35-41*

The historian who believes in miracles will have to research the nature of storms on Lake Kinnereth, the kind of boats which were used on the lake, the skill of local fishermen, such as Simon and Andrew, James and John, the fishermen who followed Jesus, to cope with storm conditions. And the answers to these questions will be next to no help in understanding what St Mark is trying to tell us.

The historian who does not believe in the possibility of miracles will simply say so and let us all go home to tea. If, however, one wishes to understand what is going on in the *Gospel of Mark*, and why this strange story is so important to him, one will have to work very hard indeed. Prepare your soul.

The lake's name is Yam Kinneret, which means 'the harp lake' because of its shape. The Jewish historian, Flavius Josephus, calls it 'the lake of Gennesareth'. When Mark tells of the calling of the fishermen, he speaks of the Sea of Galilee *(1:16-20)*. As far as we know, he is the first writer ever to call the lake by that name. In other words, he invents a new name.

First, he confers on the freshwater lake the status of a sea. He highlights the importance of this new 'sea' in the ministry of Jesus. Jesus calls his first disciples, Peter, Andrew, James, and John, on the shoreline of the Sea of Galilee. There he teaches the crowds and heals those who come to him. There are six dramatic crossings of the 'sea' in the course of which the disciples are given the opportunity to learn who Jesus is, to understand the nature and source of his power.

Secondly, Mark names the new 'sea' the Sea of Galilee. Galilee, the northern province of Palestine, in the *Gospel of Mark*, is the place where the enterprise begins. It is where Jesus carries on his preaching, teaching and healing. It is where the crowds flock to Jesus and where he feeds them with the care and attention of a devoted shepherd. To be sure, there is opposition in Galilee but it makes no headway. It will have its time in the south, in Jerusalem, where Jesus heals no one and is beset by enemies who put him to death. Significantly, the risen Jesus does not show himself in Jerusalem. The promise of the angel at the empty tomb, as he reminds the women of the words of Jesus himself, is quite explicit: *Go, tell his disciples, and Peter, I go before you into Galilee (Gospel of Mark 14:28; 16:7).*

Thirdly, and underpinning the two observations just made, Mark turns the lake into a sea because it gives him the opportunity to bring into play all that imagination in the Bible has explored in the symbiosis between God and the sea.

Stilling the Storm and an Identity Crisis
The boat which first appeared in Mark's story at 3:9, and which was turned into a pulpit at 4:1, will continue to play its role as a

place of teaching. When Jesus finishes his teaching beside the sea, he proposes to go across to the other side. What is of great moment here is that Jesus is determined to go into a pagan land, to leave the Holy Land of Palestine and set foot on unholy ground. What will happen as he journeys to take his message and his healing to an unhallowed land? And how will he be received in the world of pagans?

Though Jesus instigates the journey across the lake, Mark says that they took him as he was in the boat. This may mean no more than that the disciples cast off and Jesus is resting in the stern. But there may well be more to it than that. Mark may be hinting that the disciples take Jesus with them to a pagan land, just as later they will take the gospel of Jesus to the whole world after the resurrection. The Teacher the disciples take to the pagan territory of the Gerasenes on the other side of the lake is the Teacher they will one day take to the whole world. Read the next chapter to learn the extraordinary events which occur when Jesus is confronted by demons in a Godless land.

Great storms are fairly common on Yam Kinnereth. But Mark's storm takes place on the Sea of Galilee and it is the Old Testament to which we must turn if we are to discover the meaning of his storm. The Jewish people, as many ancient peoples, believed that, in the beginning, the whole earth was submerged under water. In order to overcome this watery chaos, God had to put the waters in their place and to watch so that the cruel sea did not rise up and overwhelm the earth:

> And God said, 'Let the waters under the heavens be gathered together in one place, and let dry land appear.'
> *Book of Genesis 1:9*

The *Book of Job* speaks of God as the one who created the sea and keeps it within its allotted confines:

> Who shut in the sea with doors,
> when it burst forth from the womb;
> when I made clouds its garment,
> and swaddled it with thick darkness,
> and prescribed boundaries for it,
> and set bars and doors,
> and said,

'Thus far shall you come,
and no farther,
and here shall your proud waves be stayed'.
Book of Job 38:8-11

But the sea, while it remains under God's rule, has the power to return the world to primeval chaos. God must be vigilant and keep watch. Those who go down to the sea in ships must trust that God is at his post:

O Lord, the floods have lifted up,
the floods have lifted up their voice,
the floods lift up their clamour.

But creation is safe in God's hands:

Mightier than the thunder of many waters,
mightier than the waves of the sea,
the Lord on high is mighty!
Psalm 93:3-4

So dangerous is the sea that the *Book of Daniel* sees it as the source of those evils with which imperial powers will enslave the world before they are toppled to make way for the kingdom of God (about which Jesus had been speaking as he sat in the prow of the boat).

The agents of evil who dwell in the deep waters of the sea were sometimes given names such as Leviathan and Rahab and the Old Testament writers loved to sing of the ease with which God controls such powerful adversaries. At the end of the *Book of Job*, the fertile imagination of the poet pictures God pointing out to Job that the human mind cannot probe the mystery of God. In a rather mocking tone (sometimes God is a pain), God points out that, unlike powerless Job, he can play with the demons of the deep as if they were little fish: *Can you land Leviathan with a fish-hook, or pull against his tongue with a fishing line? (Book of Job 41:1)*. Isaiah imagines that the great escape from Egypt was made possible by God slaying the dragon of the sea:

Was it not you who cut Rahab to pieces,
you who pierced the dragon?
Was it not you who dried up the sea,
the waters of the great deep;
you who made the depths of the sea a pathway

for the redeemed people to pass over?
Book of Isaiah 51:9-10

It is against this background that Mark constructs his telling of the Storm at Sea. For him the storm is as much a challenge to the power and authority of Jesus as that waged by Satan and his minions or the religious powers who ascribe the source of his power to Beelzebul.

Peaceful and untroubled sleep is a sign of confident trust in God's protective care:

I lie down to sleep;
I wake again,
for the Lord sustains me.
Psalm 3:5

In peace I will lie down and sleep;
for you, O Lord, ensure I dwell in safety.
Psalm 4:8

If the sleeping Jesus radiates confidence and trust in God, the same cannot be said of his disciples. The poets of Israel often spoke of the care God expends on those who go down to the sea in ships:

When you pass through the waters,
I will be with you;
and through the rivers –
they shall not overwhelm you.
Book of Isaiah 43:2

But there were times in Israel's history when God was felt to be far distant and it seemed that he had abandoned his people. At such perilous moments, the religious imagination of the people pictured God as having fallen asleep and, in urgent prayers, begged him to bestir himself on their behalf:

Awake, awake, put on strength,
O arm of the Lord.
Awake, as in the days of old,
the generations of long ago.
Book of Isaiah 51:9

God is invited to wake up, to shake off the pins and needles in his arms, and come to the rescue as he did generations ago in the days of the Exodus from Egypt. When the psalm-writer contemplates the destruction visited on his people by the Babylonians in 587 BC, he cries out,

Rouse yourself!
O Lord,
why are you sleeping?
Awake!
Do not cast us off forever!
Why do you hide your face?
Why do you forget our afflictions and our oppression?
For our soul is bowed down to the dust;
our body is stuck to the ground.
Rise up!
Come to our aid!
Deliver us for the sake of your steadfast love!
Psalm 44:23-26

Thus the religious tradition of the frightened disciples in the storm everywhere encourages them to turn, as Jonah did, to *the Lord, the God of heaven, who made the sea and the dry land (Book of Jonah 1:9)*. But they do not do so. They turn to their teacher: *Teacher, don't you care that we are perishing?* Who is this teacher, this carpenter *(6:3)*, whose help is sought to save from the dangers of a great storm of wind? The question of the identity of Jesus is the linchpin of the story.

As if in answer to the ancient cries of the psalm-writers, Jesus wakes up and rebukes the wind, and commands the sea, *Hush! Be still! And the wind dropped and there was a great calm!*

The tale is nearly done. By his language, his choice of words, Mark directs our steps to the great storehouse of Israel's words so that we can find the key to what he about. Consider carefully:

Some went down to the sea in ships,
doing business on the great waters;
they saw the deeds of the Lord,
his wondrous works in the deep.
For he commanded, and raised the stormy wind,
which lifted up the waves of the sea.
They mounted up to heaven,
they went down to the depths;

their courage melted away in their terrible plight;
they reeled and staggered like drunken men,
and were at their wits end.
They cried to the Lord in their trouble,
and he delivered them from their distress;
he made the storm still,
and the waves of the sea were hushed.
Psalm 107:23-29

Clearly, Mark tells his story of the stilling of the storm in the style and even the very words of Psalm 107. But whereas the rescuer in the psalm is the Lord, the rescuer in the Gospel is Jesus of Nazareth. Notice, too, that Jesus does not pray to God for the storm to end. He creates the great calm by the authority of his own word. Who is this man?

And, note, too, that Jesus rebukes the wind, just as he rebukes demons *(1:25; 9:25)*, and will rebuke Peter whose thoughts come from Satan and not from God *(8:33)*. God's power over the forces opposed to his authority in the world is revealed in the authoritative word of Jesus.

In the *Gospel of Mark*, as in the other Gospels, the mighty works of Jesus are there for all to see. But does everyone see? In Mark's telling of the story, the disciples indeed see the healing of the halt and the lame. A great storm, then, should hold no terrors for Jesus is with them. But yet: *Why are you so cowardly? How is it you have no faith?* Throughout his Gospel, Mark highlights the constant failure of the intimate companions of Jesus to understand him, to trust him, to be guided by him. Why?

The community for which Mark wrote his Gospel had suffered from a persecution instituted by Nero. We know from the Roman historian Tacitus, who wrote soon after the events, that Christians were responsible for betraying fellow Christians to the imperial police. Mark knows that the closest friends of Jesus were the ones who betrayed him, denied him, cursed him, and ran away in a final act of abandonment. Yet people without faith, people filled with fear, people who do not prove strong when strength is needed, are not abandoned by Jesus. Jesus does not leave his frightened friends to the terrors of the storm, be they ever so faithless. Even utterly faithless disciples in Rome can take heart. There is hope for us all.

So who then is this, that the wind and the sea obey him? That is not just a question to be answered when the boat pulls in safely on the other side of the lake. It is a question to which every generation of Christians must turn. The church, battered by storms and fearful for its very life, must join the frightened disciples in the boat and, with them, turn to the Lord who may seem to be asleep but is ever watchful of the little craft as it makes its way on the turbulent waters of the world.

Who then is this … ?
This is not a question. It is *the* question. For the identity of Jesus is the secret each of the four Gospels seeks to reveal. Of each Gospel, and of each story in each Gospel, we must ask, 'What does this Gospel, this Gospel story, tell me about who Jesus is?' Here are two questions:

Who WAS Jesus?
Who IS Jesus?

Gospels do not concern themselves with the first question, though they provide much material which allows historians to engage their skills. It is the second question which concerns gospel-makers. Who IS Jesus? What does Jesus mean for the people for whom I am writing? That is their question. That means, of course, that gospel-makers were not writing for us, since we do not belong to their time and their place. But through the centuries Christians have come to believe that the Lord who emerges from the four Gospels we hold sacred is not only a man for their time. He is, indeed, a man for all seasons.

CHAPTER THREE

Luke and Herod: Religion and Politics

Now Herod the tetrarch heard of all that was done, and
he was utterly perplexed because some people were saying that John had been raised from the dead, other people
that Elijah had appeared, and yet others that some
prophet from the olden days had risen. But Herod said, 'I
myself beheaded John; *who then is this man* about whom I
hear such things?' And he was seeking to see him.
Gospel of Luke 9:7-9

Our search is for the Jesus who is. We will begin with Herod. We
will join him in perplexity and surmise. However, unlike Herod,
we will have St Luke as our guide, and we will be aware that our
guide was a Christian, that he had a committed point of view,
that he was, in all probability, trying to confirm his readers/lis-
teners in their understanding of the true significance of Jesus in
the world in which he inhabited. We will watch our backs.

To join Herod in his perplexity, to commit ourselves to Luke
in his persuasive rôle as mentor and guide, we need to know
who Herod was, who Luke was, and what both were about.

Herod
We have met Herod the Great in Matthew's infancy presentation. When he died in 4 BC, his Roman overlord, the mighty
Emperor Augustus (30 BC-14 AD), sought to maintain stability
in a volatile province on the eastern edge of the empire. Many of
Herod's family hastened to Rome to stake a claim in the carve-
up. Augustus took his time. He decided that none of the heirs to
Herod the Great should be allowed to use the title king and that
the old man's kingdom should be divided. There was much unrest and brutal retaliation in Palestine but Augustus forced his
settlement on the country.

The lands in the south of Palestine, including Jerusalem,

went to Herod Archelaus (4 BC-6 AD), who proved as despotic as his father but without the brains (he is mentioned in the Gospel of Matthew 2:22). He was deposed and Rome imposed direct rule. Thus the territories of Judaea, Samaria, and Idumaea, were ruled directly by Rome from 6 AD to 41 AD, with intermittent regime change down to the outbreak of the Jewish war against Rome in 66 AD. Rome's administrators during this period were called prefects, sometimes procurators, the best known of whom is Pontius Pilate (26 AD-36 AD). It is very important for readers of the New Testament to be aware that the presence of Rome was felt directly and immediately in the south of Palestine, including Judaea, with its capital Jerusalem, and in the homeland of the Samaritans, the region of Samaria.

Not so Galilee. Herod Antipas, the brother of the hapless Archelaus, was given the northern region of Galilee and the eastern region of Transjordan (Perea). He was not permitted to adopt the title of king; instead, he was named a tetrarch, which means 'ruler of a fourth part', in recognition that his father's kingdom had been carved into bits. But Antipas ruled from 4 BC to 39 AD, until he was deposed by Caligula because he sought to be called king. For forty-three years he ruled Galilee. Throughout the whole lifetime of Jesus of Nazareth, Antipas was the political ruler and this meant that there was no direct Roman rule in Galilee, no direct Roman taxation, no Roman soldiers, no Roman coinage, none of the many and immediate symbols of Roman might which afflicted Jews in the south. Herod Antipas had sufficient Jewish blood in his veins to employ his diplomatic skills when dealing with local Jewish sensitivities. He instigated many building projects which gave employment. One such project, the restoration and fortification of the city of Sepphoris, the region's capital, a few miles from Nazareth, provided many jobs in the area. Jesus probably grew up on the building sites of Sepphoris. Of course, the reconstruction of Sepphoris, and later the town of Tiberias, had an economic downside. Cities drew away produce from the countryside to the urban economy and created an incentive to establish large country estates at the expense of the peasant population. These economic shifts are fairly obvious in the Galilee which emerges from our Gospels.

On the other hand, he beheaded John the Baptist. It will be instructive to listen to two accounts of what happened. The first is from the *Gospel of Mark:*

And King Herod heard of it; for his name [Jesus] had become well-known, and he was saying, 'John the Baptist has been raised from among the dead, and on this account these powers are at work in him'. But other people were saying, 'It is Elijah'; yet others were saying, 'A prophet, like one of the prophets.' But when he heard, Herod was saying, 'The one whom I beheaded, John, has been raised.' For Herod had sent out and seized John and had him chained up in prison on account of Herodias, the wife of Philip his brother, whom he had married. For John was saying to Herod, 'It is not permissible for you to have your brother's wife.' Herodias resented him and wanted to kill him but she couldn't. For Herod was afraid of John, knowing that he was a righteous and holy man, and he protected him. When he listened to him, many things puzzled him, and yet he listened to him gladly.

But an opportune day came when, on his birthday, Herod gave a feast for his nobility, his military commanders, and the leading people of Galilee. The daughter of Herodias came in and danced, and pleased Herod and those at table with him. The king said to the little girl, 'Ask me anything you wish and I will give it to you.' And he swore to her, 'Whatever you wish, I will give you, as much as half my kingdom.' And going out, she said to her mother, 'What will I demand?' And she said, 'The head of John the Baptist.' Going in quickly to the king, she made a request, saying, 'I wish that you give me immediately the head of John the Baptist on a dish.' The king was deeply distressed but on account of his oaths and those at table with him, he didn't want to refuse her. Immediately, the king, sending out a guard, gave orders to bring in his head. And, going out, he beheaded him in prison, and he brought in his head on a dish and gave it to the little girl, and the little girl gave it to her mother. His disciples, hearing about it, came and took his body and laid it in a tomb. *Gospel of Mark 6:14-29*

We need not dwell on the improbabilities of this story. Mark seems to think that Herod Antipas was a king. He wasn't. He thinks that Herodias, who was Antipas' niece, was married to Philip, the tetrarch of Trachonitis and Gaulonitis (the Golan Heights area), who was also Herodias' uncle. Herodias' daughter, Salome, was married to Philip. Nor is it at all likely that a young girl of the royal family would have danced before Antipas and his merry friends. The whole episode looks very like a down-market version of the *Book of Esther*. Of course, it could be that there was another Philip in the Herodian family. And, perhaps, Mark intended to mock the royal pretensions of Antipas by calling him a king. But consider the account of the Jewish historian, Flavius Josephus, Jerusalem-born and a contemporary of Saint Mark. Antipas was defeated in battle by his father-in-law, King Aretas of Arabia, the quarrel arising from the fact that Antipas attempted to dismiss his wife, the daughter of Aretas, and marry Herodias. This is how Josephus describes the outcome:

> Now some of the Jews thought that the destruction of Herod's army came from God, and that very justly, as a punishment for what he did against John, who was called the Baptist; for Herod slew him, who was a good man, and commanded the Jews to exercise virtue, both as to righteousness towards one another, and piety towards God, and so to come to baptism; for that the washing would be acceptable to Him, if they made use of it, not in order to the putting away of some sins, but for purification of the body; supposing still that the soul was thoroughly purified beforehand by righteousness.

> Now when many came in crowds about him, for they were greatly moved by hearing his words, Herod, who feared lest the great influence John had over the people might put it into his power and inclination to raise a rebellion (for they seemed ready to do anything he should advise), thought it best, by putting him to death, to prevent any mischief he might cause, and not bring himself into any difficulties, by sparing a man who might make him repent of it when it should be too late. Accordingly, he was sent a prisoner, out of Herod's suspicious temper, to Macherus [in modern Jordan] ... and was there put to death. Now the Jews had an opinion that the destruction of this army was sent as a

punishment upon Herod, and a mark of God's displeasure against him. *The Antiquities of the Jews, Book 18, ch.5, section 2*

This is an altogether more plausible explanation for the execution of John the Baptist. Herod's policy of not going out of his way to offend his Jewish subjects would not prevent him taking action against any possible threat to his security. He owed it to himself and to his Roman overlords to keep the lid on.

Luke

Luke was not a Jew. He was an educated Greek, a native of God knows where, perhaps of the city of Antioch in the Roman province of Syria, but pagan-born, and, according to some, a doctor, and most certainly an accomplished writer with wealthy friends. He may have converted to the Jewish faith, subsequently becoming a Christian. He may, or may not, have been a companion of St Paul at some point in his life. As the writer of the Gospel which bears his name, and of the *Acts of the Apostles*, he is the only non-Jew whose writings made it into the New Testament. Luke knew the world of the eastern Empire well. As a Roman citizen, he was not opposed to Rome's domination of the world but he knew that imperial power was exploitative, coercive, and cruel. He had little truck with imperial haughtiness, especially of the kind which usurped what belonged to God and only to God. His attitude to the seriously rich and powerful of this world was that, in the end, they got no more than they deserved (read the *Magnificat* and *Gospel of Luke 6:24-26*).

Luke does not recount the death of John the Baptist in detail, contenting himself to supply the bare bones of the story *(Gospel of Luke 3:19-20)*. But he is interested in John, as his infancy presentation clearly shows, and, indeed, he gives a whole section to an account of the ministry and preaching of John. For Luke, John is the greatest of the prophets, but he no more than a prophet. John is not Jesus, and for that reason they never meet except in the Visitation story. Luke rather skips around the fact that Jesus was baptised by the Baptist. But it is entirely in keeping with Luke's strategy that the question of the identity of Jesus should be raised by the political ruler who put John to death and who ruled over the homeland of Jesus of Nazareth. We shall see later why speculation concerning the identity of Jesus should embrace John the Baptist, Elijah, or a prophet like the prophets of old. But, for the moment, we have noticed Luke's interest in the political map of the world. He placed the birth of Jesus, and the revelation of his identity and mission, in the reign of Caesar Augustus and his minions in the Middle East. The context for the eruption of John the Baptist on the scene is equally political:

> In the fifteenth year of the reign of Tiberius Caesar, when Pontius Pilate was governing Judaea, and Herod was tetrarch of Galilee, and his brother Philip tetrarch of the region of Ituraea and Trachonitis, and Lysanias tetrarch of Abilene, in the high priesthood of Annas and Caiaphas, the word of God was with John the son of Zachariah in the desert ...
> *Gospel of Luke 3:1-2*

So it is that the birth of Jesus and the beginning of the preaching of John the Baptist are set within the political contexts of their day. Luke calls careful attention to the realities of the world, not divorcing what God is doing in John and Jesus from the world of oppression which characterised Roman imperial might. It is of great interest that Pilate, Herod, and Caiaphas are placed at the inauguration of the preaching of John and Jesus, and in Luke's Gospel, and only in Luke's Gospel, Pilate and Herod are accomplices in the condemnation of Jesus. The following extraordinary incident is recorded only by St Luke:

> Then the whole assembly [of the chiefs priests and scribes] arose and took him to Pilate. And they began to accuse him, saying, 'We found this man perverting our people and opposing paying taxes to Caesar, and saying that he is Messiah King.' And Pilate asked him, saying, 'Are you the King of the Jews?' Answering him, he said, 'So you say.' Then Pilate said to the chief priests and the crowds, 'I find no guilt in this man.' But they were insistent, saying, 'He stirs up the people, teaching throughout the whole of Judaea, from Galilee even to here.'
>
> When Pilate heard this, he asked whether the man was a Galilean. And when he heard that he was from Herod's jurisdiction, he sent him to Herod, who was in Jerusalem at the time.

Herod, seeing Jesus, was very pleased. For a long time he had wanted to see him on account of hearing about him, and he hoped to see some sign done by him. He questioned him at great length. But he answered him not a word. The chief priests and the scribes stood by and vigorously accused him. And Herod and his soldiers belittled him and mocked him; and throwing around him a splendid cloak, he sent him back to Pilate.

And Herod and Pilate became friends on that day, for before that they had been enemies.

Gospel of Luke 23:1-12

A strange friendship. A friendship between two politicians founded on the callous disposal of an innocent man. *Plus ça change, plus c'est la même chose.*

Making Some Sense of it All

Luke seems to have wanted his readers to be alert to the political realities concerning the time and ministry of Jesus. He seems to have so organised his presentation that his readers would understand quickly that Jesus and his message did not and do not seek a hearing in weekend seminars. Jesus is with the people, with the crowds; Jesus is where people, like John the Baptist, get killed on the remotest suspicion of rocking the boat. How dangerous it is that Herod is the one who asks the question: *Who is this man?*

Another thing. Notice Luke writes that Herod *sought to see him* in the quotation at the heading of this chapter and, again, *he wanted to see him*, in the account of the Jerusalem interview. This is strange, for a number of reasons. First, the Herod who kept a close eye on every goings-on in Galilee, the Herod who picked up John the Baptist, could easily have apprehended Jesus, who, after all, carried out most of his preaching within a few miles of where Herod lived. Luke records that some Pharisees even warned Jesus that Herod wanted to kill him *(Gospel of Luke 13:31)*. Secondly, Herod seems strangely totally unaware of who Jesus is and he is dependent on what he hears from others. He knows nothing of the momentous events leading to the murder of the Bethlehem babies in the last days of his father's life.

Strange, because Antipas was one of the very few of his many children trusted by Herod the Great. With Archelaus, he was named in his father's will as heir.

What we must conclude is that Luke places his key question – *Who is this man?* – on the lips of the political potentate, Herod Antipas, the one who held power of life and death over Jesus, in order to impress on his readers that the answer to the question is a matter for the world of power politics, the world of imperial and royal coercion, the world in which the only good news comes from Bethlehem, not Rome. Luke's political agenda is to debunk Herod as he had debunked the great Emperor Augustus in his infancy presentation.

That is why it is important to attend to how Luke answers the question. Of course, it is true, as we have seen already in his infancy presentation, that Luke is everywhere concerned to identify who Jesus is. Every page he writes tells who Jesus is. *Who is this man?*, Herod's question, is answered in every line of his story. But the thirty or so sentences that follow Herod's question in chapter 9 are worth close attention because they provide Luke's immediate answer to Herod's question. In 9:51 we are told that Jesus sets his face to go to Jerusalem, the city of crucifixion and death. Before he sets out on the way that will take him to the Place of the Skull (23:33), Luke tells his readers who it is that makes the journey and why. Not only that, but Luke, in drawing a portrait of a man on his way to death, draws a portrait of all who would take up a cross and follow him. *Who is Jesus?* becomes *Who am I?*

CHAPTER FOUR

Jesus Welcomes People

And the apostles, on their return, reported to him what they had done. And taking them along, he withdrew privately to a city called Bethsaida. but the crowds, knowing of it, followed him. And *welcoming them*, he was chatting with them about the kingdom of God and he was healing those who needed healing. *Gospel of Luke 9:10-11*

Between the question of Herod Antipas and beginning of the journey of Jesus to Jerusalem, St Luke places his answers to the politician's question. It is not, of course, all that he has to say about Jesus. To garner all his rich insights into Jesus and his mission, we need to read his Gospel and his other book, *Acts of the Apostles*. But he gives us enough in these thirty sentences or so to equip us for the journey with Jesus. Enough to understand with whom we are travelling, where we are going, and why.

In chapter 6, after a night on the mountain, out of the many who followed him, Jesus chose twelve, *whom he named apostles*. In chapter 9, he sends them out *to preach the kingdom of God and to heal*, the identical tasks undertaken by Jesus himself. They embarked on what was a temporary work experience, an initial learning curve, gospelling and healing people in the villages around. When they return to report to Jesus, Luke again calls these apprentices apostles. Very flattering, but they still have much to learn and the journey which will begin at 9:51, when Jesus turns his face to Jerusalem, will be a journey for them into the more arduous demands of apostleship, a journey which will end and begin for hardened apostles at Calvary. To become the genuine article, they will need all that Pentecost has to offer. But, for the moment, they are back from the gospelling and healing and, like Luke's readers, will have to attend to the immediate answers to Herod's question.

Jesus Welcomes People

Though the instinct of Jesus is to take the Twelve apart into a quiet village (Luke keeps calling villages cities!), the crowds flock to him and he welcomes them. First, we will ask whether it is true. Did Jesus welcome people? Before judging the question to be impious, we must keep firmly to the forefront of our minds that Jesus is not the answer to our needs, our dilemmas, our tragedies, our complexities. Jesus does not come, if he comes at all, as an answer to frightened cripples who cannot face the world without heavenly props. Jesus comes to us with questions. Together with him we seek to find. But we engage in the search together. We are invited to journey with him, not to hand over the map to him and content ourselves to be no more than mindless tourists in the back of the bus.

Did Jesus welcome people? Here is some evidence from the *Gospel of Luke:*

A Mission Statement
The Spirit of the Lord is upon me;
therefore he anointed me
to gospel the poor;
he has sent me
to announce freedom to captive people,
sight to the blind,
to liberate the oppressed,
to proclaim a year of the Lord's welcoming.
Gospel of Luke 4:18-19

A Day's Work
When the sun was setting, all those people who had anyone who was sick with whatever diseases, brought them to him; he laid his hands on every one of them and healed them.
Gospel of Luke 4:40

A Welcoming Hand
He happened to be in one of the cities,
and, take note,
a man full of leprosy!
Seeing Jesus, he fell at his feet

and begged him, saying,
'Lord, if you wish,
you can clean me'.
And he stretched out his hand,
and touched him ...
Gospel of Luke 5:12-13

Two Kinds of Welcome
One of the Pharisees asked him to eat with him, and, going into the house of the Pharisee, he reclined at table.

And, take note, a woman who was a sinner in the city, when she learned he was dining in the house of the Pharisee, took an alabaster jar of perfume, and, standing behind him at his feet, weeping the while, she began to wet his feet with her tears, and wipe them with the hair of her head, and she kissed his feet, anointing them with the perfume.

When the Pharisee who had invited him saw it, he murmured to himself, saying, 'If this man were a prophet, he would know who and what this woman is who is touching him, for she's a sinner'.

Answering him, Jesus said, 'Simon, I have something to say to you'. He said, 'Teacher, speak!'

'A money-lender had two debtors. One owed him five hundred denarii, the other, fifty. Not being in a position to pay up, he let them off. Now which of them will love him more?'

Simon answered and said, 'I suppose, the one he let off more'. And he said, 'You have judged rightly'. Turning towards the woman, he said to Simon, 'Do you see this woman? I came into your house. You gave me no water for my feet. She has wet my feet with her tears and wiped them with her hair. You gave me no kiss. Since I came in, she has not ceased to kiss my feet. You didn't anoint my head with oil; she has anointed my feet with perfume.

For this reason, I say to you, her sins, her many sins, are forgiven, because she loved much ...'
Gospel of Luke 7:36-47

Shunned for Twelve Years

A woman who had been haemorrhaging for twelve years, and could not be healed by any one, coming up behind him, touched the hem of his cloak; and the haemorrhage stopped in that instant.

And Jesus said, 'Who touched me?' When everyone denied it, Peter said, 'Teacher, the crowds hem you in and press upon you'. But Jesus said, 'Someone touched me! I know that power has gone out of me!'

When the woman saw that there was no hiding, with trembling she came and fell down before him and declared before all the people why she had touched him, and how she was instantly healed.

And he said to her, 'Daughter ...'
Gospel of Luke 8:43-48

Begrudgers

Now the tax collectors and the sinners were all drawing near to listen to him. The Pharisees and the scribes complained, 'This man welcomes sinners and eats with them'.
Gospel of Luke 15:2

A Tree Climber on the Look-out

He entered Jericho, and was passing through. And, take note! there was a man named Zacchaeus and he was a chief tax collector, and rich. And he wanted to see who Jesus is, but, because of the crowd, he couldn't, because he was a small person. So he ran on ahead, climbed a sycamore tree, in order to see him. When he came to the place, looking up, Jesus said, 'Zacchaeus, make haste, come down ...'
Gospel of Luke 19:1-5

Even Babies

They were bringing babies to him that he might touch them. But when his disciples saw this, they rebuked them. But Jesus called the babies to him, saying, 'Let the children come to me and do not hinder them; for to such as these the kingdom of God belongs.'
Gospel of Luke 18:15-16

Even a broad sweep through Luke's story makes it plain that Jesus welcomes people. But other questions present themselves. What kind of people are embraced by the welcome of Jesus? And why are some people deeply disturbed by the welcome Jesus gives to these people?

It is critical to our enterprise to know who Jesus welcomes. Mary's *Magnificat* is very black and white and offers, at first sight, little for those who limp along, not very successful saints but not very successful sinners either. Mary praises the Lord, rejoices in God the Saviour, because,

> He has shown strength with his arm,
> he has scattered the proud-hearted,
> he has put down the mighty rulers
> from their thrones,
> and exalted lowly people.
> He has filled hungry people
> with good things;
> the rich he has sent away empty.
> *Gospel of Luke 1:51-53*

Apart from the political overtones ('mighty rulers'), there is an uncomfortable feeling of revenge about these lines, an absence of forgiveness and an exclusion of the possibility of repentance. But if we notice that these verses are in the past tense, that the unseating of the mighty, the proud, and the rich, speak of what God has done in ancient times to the great empires which are no more, we begin to see that there is a new agenda. The birth, life, death and resurrection of Jesus are seen as a fulfilment of promises made to Abraham. Mindful of his mercy, God is now, in the person of Jesus, about to bring to pass what was said to the ancient patriarch: *I will bless those who bless you ... by you all the families of the earth will be blessed (Book of Genesis 12:3)*. What Jesus brings is blessing, not curse, mercy, not retribution. It is as if, in the daring vision of the poem, God has remembered that it is mercy, not revenge, which is needed, if humanity is to be saved. Long ago, in the mythological days of the Flood, when Noah came to land, God came to repentance:

> I will never again curse the earth because of humanity, for the imagination of the human heart is evil from its youth; nei-

ther will I ever again destroy every living creature as I have done. *Book of Genesis 9:21*

This is what is known as repentance with a firm purpose of amendment. What God is doing in Jesus is not slamming doors in people's faces; what is proposed in Jesus is God's offer to accompany human beings on a journey to some kind of wholeness, some kind of peace and rest.

The Welcome List in Full

Luke's infancy presentation has an array of the unexpected:

Zachariah and Elizabeth, old, barren.

Mary, unmarried.

Shepherds, shifty lot.

Simeon, old.

Anna, old.

Why the preponderance of old people? Why a young girl? Why shepherds, not kings?

Moving into Luke's story, we find that a welcoming acceptance is given to a ragbag of odd people:

A mother-in-law (4:38-39).

Demon-possessed (4:39-41).

A leper (5:12-16).

A paralysed sinner (5:17-26).

Levi, a tax collector (5:27-32).

A man with a withered right hand (6:6-11).

A Roman soldier (7:1-10).

A woman of the town (7:36-50).

A madman (8:26-39).

A bleeding woman (8:42-48).

Which brings us up to our chapter 9. Beyond that, the story does not change; the list merely grows longer:

A demon-possessed dumb man (11:14-23).

A bent woman (13:10-17).

A man who had dropsy (14:1-6).

Ten lepers (17:11-19).

Babies (18:15-17).

A blind beggar (18:35-43).

A wee small little fellow (19:1-10).

What is intriguing about this motley collection of people is that they are, for the most part, outsiders of one kind or another. Women were blamed for childlessness and the pregnant Elizabeth, with more than a sigh of relief, can hold her head up: *This is what the Lord has done for me when he took away my disgrace among the people.* An angel must assure Mary, and Luke's readers, that her pregnancy is not a matter for condemnation and public contumely, with Mary herself only one step ahead of the gossip: *I have no husband.* Preachers of the new ways of God, Simeon and Anna, are an unlikely pair of gospellers. Shepherds are shepherds.

The mother-in-law, the demon-possessed people, the lepers, the paralysed, the man with the withered hand, the madman, and the woman with the haemorrhage, all are unclean. This is no small matter; nor is it a question of public health or human revulsion. Demons caused sickness, sickness indicated sinfulness, sinfulness entailed rejection by God. Whatever one's views on ancient (and not so ancient? what of churching of mothers?) ignorance and fears, the Bible understood and enshrined uncleanness as 'unacceptable to God'. Whether one became unclean by touching that which was itself unclean (a corpse, for example), by eating unclean animals (pigs) or meat with blood in it, by bodily functions (menstruation; an emission of semen), by sickness of any kind, and a whole host of other taboos, the unclean were deemed to be unacceptable to God. To become unclean is to forfeit that holiness which is demanded of those who would be near to God: *You shall not defile yourselves ... For I am the Lord your God who brought you out of the land of Egypt, to be your God; you shall therefore be holy, as I am holy (Book of Leviticus 12:45).* Approach to God is banned to any unfortunate priest who is deemed defective:

> For no one who is defective shall draw near [God's altar], a man blind or lame, or one who has a mutilated face or a limb too long, or a man who has an injured foot or an injured hand, or a hunchback, or a dwarf, or a man with a defect in his sight or an itching disease or scabs or crushed testicles ... he shall not come near the veil or approach the altar ... because he has a defect ... for I am the Lord who makes them holy. *Book of Leviticus 22:16-23*

Whatever we may think of such biblical commands, their effect on the lives of ordinary people who did not have the means of avoiding what was forbidden or the cost of satisfying a demanding God, was that many, temporarily or permanently, were outside God's camp, outside God's people.

Tax collectors, like Levi and Zacchaeus, (collaborators, because they worked for Rome, and sinners because they gave the produce of God's holy land to pagans), the pagan Roman soldier, and the woman of the town, are, in Jewish estimation, simply outside God's concern. Children, as St Paul's tells us, were little better than slaves (*Letter to the Galatians 4:1*).

Who, then, is this Jesus who welcomes people who are on the outside, who are unclean, branded as sinners, of no account in the sight of God or in human estimation? The answer, as with so much in Luke's Gospel, is to be found in the parables. Parables are subversive stories. They subvert our cherished ideas; they undermine the *status quo* of social, political, and religious certainties. Parables get under the skin and confront complacency, question the acceptable, and demand an alternative to the way we are now. Luke's parables are about God. Many of them are, in effect, journey stories. But then all the world's great stories are journey stories. For now, we will look at two.

The first parable journey is from Jerusalem to Jericho, recounted in what we call The Parable of the Good Samaritan (*Gospel of Luke 10:25-37*). The context is important. A lawyer puts a test question to Jesus concerning what he must do in order to inherit eternal life. Jesus throws the question back to the lawyer: What does the Law of Moses, the Torah, say? The lawyer replies with an unusual (for the time) but clever summary of the six hundred and thirteen laws which make up the Torah. With great insight and perception, he advocates that the whole of God's demands may be summarised in two quotations:

1. You must love the Lord your God with all your heart, with all your soul, with all your might, and with all your mind.
Book of Deuteronomy 6:5
2. You must love your neighbour as yourself.
Book of Leviticus 19:18

Jesus agrees: one's attitude towards God should be the same as one's attitude towards one's neighbour. However, the lawyer, as lawyers sometimes do, put his finger on the crucial point: *Who is my neighbour?*

His supplementary question is not merely clever. 'Neighbour' in the second quotation refers to a fellow Jew. There were even some Jews who believed that one must love only members of their own community (at Qumran) and hate everyone else, other Jews and the rest of wicked humanity. Jesus replies with a parable. You will, of course, notice that he does not directly answer the lawyer's question, *Who is my neighbour?*; rather, he explores altogether more profound questions, *How can I be a neighbour?* and, *Are there any limits beyond which neighbourliness need not go?*

Taking up his point, Jesus said:

A man was travelling down from Jerusalem to Jericho, and he fell among robbers. They stripped him, beat him up, and left him half-dead. By chance, a priest was going down that same way, and seeing him, passed by on the other side. In the same way, a Levite, coming to the place, looked and passed by on the other side.

But a Samaritan, as he journeyed, came across him, and what he saw moved him to pity. Approaching, he bound up his wounds, pouring on oil and wine, and, putting the man on his own animal, brought him to an inn, and there attended to him. The next day, he took out two denarii, gave them to the inn-keeper, and said, 'Look after him, and whatever it costs you over and above, I will reimburse you on my return.'

Which of these three, in your opinion, proved to be a neighbour to the man who fell among robbers? He answered, 'The one who did the kindness to him'. So Jesus said to him, 'Go and do the same yourself'.

Gospel of Luke 10:30-37

The question, as Jesus sees it, is not who is one's neighbour. It is not about a neighbour's identity but about human need. It is human need which determines neighbourly action. Wherever there is human distress of any kind, it imposes on all the obligation to heal, to put things to rights.

The parable cuts to the heart. The hero is a Samaritan, the

villains belong to the priestly class. A man is beaten up and left for half-dead. A priest and a Levite (a minor Temple official responsible for duties related to public worship), see the half-dead man and keep to the other side of the road. Two respected members of the Jewish community pass by and one can hardly blame them. Their passing-by is to avoid contamination by contact with or even nearness to a dead, or apparently dead, body. God's command in the the *Book of Numbers 5:2* is that anyone who becomes unclean through contact with the dead is to be shunned to prevent spread of the contamination of uncleanness which makes people unacceptable to God. Through Moses, God issues a special warning to priests:

And the Lord said to Moses,

'Speak to the priests, the sons of Aaron, and say to them that none of them shall defile himself on account of the dead among his people, except for his nearest family, his mother, his father, his son, his daughter, his brother, or his unmarried sister ...' *Book of Leviticus 21:1-3*

Returning from the holy city of Jerusalem to Jericho, one can appreciate the weighty religious reasons which motivate the priest and Levite not to arrive home unclean and unacceptable to God. A little detail stands out. The priest and Levite happened to be on the way 'by chance'. Are we to understand that they just happened to be there and reacted to the situation, casually falling back on instinctive religious taboos?

The Samaritan, on the other hand, is on a journey. The man seems full of purpose and business-like. Jews kept clear of Samaritans and Samaritans of Jews for all the reasons which prejudice can muster. But both observed the Torah, the Law of God, laid down in the first five books of the Bible. Of course, Jews didn't think much of Samaritan religious understanding and practice (think Catholic and Protestant here, at their worst). And this is the man who, even the lawyer has to admit, is the one who gets it right, the one who actually does the will of God. Bluntly, Jesus tells him to do the same.

The complacent belief of the lawyer that he has got it right is undermined by a parable. His worldview is subverted by an insidious story which calls into question his understanding of

God's demands. The primary consideration is human need, not adherence to religious prescriptions, if they are dead to the pleas of human need. The welcome which Jesus gives to the gallery of human hurt and pain, to lepers and lame, to the deaf and blind, and all the rest, is the welcome that God gives. Jesus takes upon himself to interpret the mind of God and to act on what he finds there. The welcome which Jesus gives is rooted in the being of God. Luke's catalogue of outsiders turns out to be God's guest list. So who is Jesus, who is this man who goes around inviting people to God's table? Who is this man who says that, in God's book, the victim writes the script?

The next parable is a long story and an unfinished one and it, too, is a story of journeys. Having told a parable about a man who loses a sheep and another about a woman who loses some money (Luke is good at balancing men and women), he tells what has become the most famous parable of all:

A man had two sons. And the younger of them said to the father, 'Father, give me the share of the property that's coming to me.' He divided the estate between them.

Not many days later, the younger son gathered everything and went to live in a distant country. There he squandered his property, living dissolutely.

When he had spent all he had, a severe famine hit that country, and he began to feel the pinch. And he went and hired himself out to one of the citizens of that country, and he sent him to his estates to feed pigs. And he longed to satisfy his hunger with the carob pods the pigs got to eat, but nobody would give him anything.

Then he came to his senses and said, 'How many paid servants of my father have more than enough food, while here I am dying of hunger. I will get up and go to my father and I will say to him, "Father, I have sinned against heaven and against you; I am not worthy to be called your son; treat me like one of your workers".' So he got up and went back to his father.

While he was still a long way off, his father saw him, and was moved with compassion; running, he hugged him and kissed him.

The son said to his father, 'Father, I have sinned against

heaven and against you; I am not worthy to be called your son.' But the father said to his slaves, 'Quickly, bring out the best robe and put it on him, and give him a ring for his finger, and sandals for his feet, and bring out the fatted calf and kill it, and let us eat and make merry, for this, my son, was dead, and has come back to life; he was lost and has been found.' And they began to make merry.

Now the elder son was in the field. As he approached the house, he heard music and dancing, and calling one of the lads, he asked him what it was all about. And he said to him, 'Your brother has come, and your father has killed the fatted calf because he has got him back safely.' He became angry and didn't want to go in.

So his father came out and pleaded with him. He said to his father, 'Look, this many a year, I have slaved for you, and I never disregarded one single command of yours; yet you never gave me a goat to make merry with my friends. Now that son of yours, who has wasted your livelihood on prostitutes, when he comes, you kill the fatted calf for him!'

But he said to him, 'My child, you are always with me, and all I have is yours. But it was necessary to make merry and rejoice, because your brother was dead and has come to life, was lost and has been found.

Gospel of Luke 15:11-32

Why did Jesus tell the parables of the lost sheep, the lost money, the lost son? Luke explains:

All the tax collectors and sinners were drawing near to [Jesus] to listen to him. And the Pharisees and the scribes murmured constantly against him, and they were saying, 'This fellow welcomes sinners and eats with them'.

Gospel of Luke 15:1-2

There is more to this than meets the eye. We have met the Pharisees and the scribes murmuring to Jesus' face because he was eating with tax collectors and sinners *(Gospel of Luke 5:30)*. When Jesus decides to eat in the house of that notorious and wealthy tax collector, Zacchaeus, the bystanders murmured because, in their view, he had gone in to be a guest of a sinner *(Gospel of Luke 19:7)*.

When Moses was leading the people of God out of Egypt and through the desert to the promised land, he had much to cope with. Not least, he was faced with murmuring, grumbling, complaining people. They murmur against God and his servant Moses, longing for the flesh pots of Egypt. Listen to these whinges and whines:

The whole gathering of the people of Israel murmured against Moses and Aaron in the desert, and said to them, 'Would that we had died in the land of Egypt, when we sat by the flesh pots and ate to the full ... *Book of the Exodus 16:2-3*

So Moses and Aaron said to all the people of Israel, 'At evening you shall know that it was the Lord who brought you out of the land of Egypt, and in the morning you shall see the glory of the Lord, because he has heard your murmuring against the Lord. *Book of the Exodus 16:6-7*

And the people murmured in the hearing of the Lord about their misfortunes; when the Lord heard it, he was angry ... *Book of Numbers 11:1*

And the Lord said to Moses and to Aaron, 'How long shall this wicked people murmur against me? I have heard the murmuring of the people of Israel, which they murmured against me'. *Book of Numbers 14:26-27*

Luke uses exactly the same Greek word for murmuring as the old texts and for good reason. He wants to make the startling claim that murmuring, complaining, whining against Jesus is exactly the same as murmuring and whingeing against God. By welcoming the kind of people we have listed, Jesus is welcoming precisely those people God wants at his table. The Parable of the Prodigal Son is a telling riposte to those begrudgers who would draw a line in the sand when it comes to mercy.

There is a long list of begrudgers in Luke's gospel:
Angry people (4:16-30)
Pharisees (5:17 *et passim*)
Teachers of Torah (5:17; famously 10:23-37)
Scribes (5:21)

Simon, a Pharisee (7:36-50)
Fearful citizens (8:37)
A synagogue officer (13:10-17)
A fox (13:31-35)
Grumpy old men (15:2)
Grumpy young man (15:28)
Money-loving Pharisees (16:14)
Scoffers (16:14)
More grumpy people (19:7)
Plotting chief priests and scribes (20:19)
Mocking theologians (20:27-40)
Elders of the people (22:66)
A stupid thief (23:39)

And that is why the Parable of the Prodigal Son is unfinished. The reader is invited to complete the story. What will the elder son do next? Will he go in? Will he accept a father who is celebrating because one who was lost has been found? And who is this father who welcomes home a lost child? And who is the brother who refuses to welcome, to rejoice, to celebrate?

The door is not closed to begrudgers, any more than the elder son is barred from the feast. God's welcome in Jesus is always on the mat. It is clear, however, that God has a lot to put up with and much to do to get people to understand how much they are loved and appreciated.

We are beginning to know who it is who is welcoming in Luke's Gospel. Jesus is the one who is extending God's hand of welcome and friendship to sinners, to sick people, to cast-offs, to unclean people, to the halt and the lame, to children, to any one, indeed, who is lost. To be lost is to qualify for God's especial concern. And we are all lost in one way or another.

One last question: if people are lost, who lost them? The shepherd who loses a sheep stands for the God who must leave the ninety-nine and go looking for the one he has lost. The woman who sweeps the house from top to bottom stands for God who has lost a valuable silver coin. A father who loses a son stands for a God hoping someone will turn up. It looks as if God has been very careless.

CHAPTER FIVE

Chatting ...

And the apostles, on their return, reported to him what they had done. And taking them along, he withdrew privately to a city called Bethsaida. But the crowds, knowing of it, followed him. And welcoming them as usual, *he was chatting with them* about the kingdom of God and he was healing those who needed healing. *Gospel of Luke 9:10-11*

And welcoming them, what then? Your English translation of the next phrase probably says that Jesus spoke to them of the kingdom of God. Actually, Luke didn't write 'spoke to them'. The Greek verb he uses *(lalein)* means to chatter, to pratter, even to gossip. The word cluster semantically attached to Luke's verb relates to the babbling of water, the chirping of birds, and, in the context of human conversation, embraces prattlers, babblers, and gossips. To translate the word as 'to speak to them', rather than 'chatting/talking with them', is to identify the speaker as the sole source of information, the know-all who is imparting knowledge to ignorant people. It is to adopt a strategy of all-knowing condescension, of talking down to people. This is known as filling empty buckets.

Chatting, talking also defines a strategy but it is a strategy rooted in gossip, in conversation, in the exquisite sharing of thoughts and feelings, hopes and expectations. It's about 'Well, I never!', 'She wouldn't!', 'He didn't!', and 'Would you believe it!' Everyone has a say. Here is common ground, shared interest, delicious confluence, and an eternal, atavistic, human demand to know what happens next. Chatting is part of welcoming, welcoming people's opinions, respecting other people's views, willing to be persuaded by other people's experience. *Did you hear the one about the kingdom of God?* That is Jesus' welcoming, engaging style. The big words for this positive, affirming acceptance of people where they're at are *covenant* and *incarnation*. It is the promise of God come alive in God-in-Jesus talking to people about what they know and feel and hope about the God who is their Father. Luke's Gospel is a lifelong journey of an engaging Jesus welcoming, chatting, healing and feeding, kaleidoscoped into a few months.

To list the people with whom Jesus chats and talks is to gather together outsiders (really insiders) and begrudgers alike. Nobody is excluded from the excitement of digging up the kingdom of God. That is why the conversations of Jesus with crowds and disciples, gainsayers and begrudgers, are littered with questions. Questions engage. Questions provoke reflection and open the heart to persuasion. To meet the Jesus who comes to talk with us, to question us, to engage with us in our search for love and hope, is to meet with one who honours human dignity, respects human freedom, shares our stories. To understand what religious convictions ran through the veins of Jesus and the people with whom he chatted and talked, we need to dig around the bedrock of Jewish faith, to identify some of the fault-lines which run through all attempts to know the mind of God. By doing so, we will come to share the common ground which Jesus shared with those with whom he chatted and talked and the kinds of futures they envisaged to heal the pain of the world.

Covenants Unilateral and Bilateral

When reading the Bible we have to be careful. The Bible may be the word of God but it is written in human words. Take the word 'covenant'. This is one of the Bible's big words but the meaning shifts according to the circumstances in which it is used. At the Last Supper, Jesus inaugurates of 'a new covenant in my blood'. To understand what he means, we need to follow the word from one circumstance to the next. We will begin with the Flood.

According to the Bible, violence provoked God to destroy humanity with the exception of Noah, Mrs Noah, and their three sons and daughters-in-law. After the deluge, when God had thought better of a somewhat impetuous action, God establishes a new bond with all creation, an unreserved commitment to a new policy which he announces to Noah and family:

> Behold, I establish my covenant with you and your descend-
> ants after you, and with every living creature that is with
> you, the birds, the cattle, and every beast on earth with you,
> as many as came out of the ark. I will establish my covenant
> with you, that never again shall all flesh be cut off by the
> waters of a flood, and never again shall there be a flood to
> destroy the earth. *Book of Genesis 9:8-11*

This covenant is a unilateral promise on God's part. No obligation is imposed on Noah nor on his descendants. God's commitment is without reserve. It is a promise to human beings and
to animals alike. The only person bound by this promise is God
and the rainbow is its sign. As long as it continues to appear in
the clouds, God will remember.

The reason for God's conversion from a policy of destruction
to one of everlasting protection is plainly stated:

> I will never again curse the earth because of human beings,
> for the human heart is inclined to evil from its youth. Nor
> will I ever again destroy every living creature as I have done.
> *Book of Genesis 8:21*

If humanity is to be saved from its violence, using violence as
the means of salvation is a failed policy. Even God learns from
mistakes. A new policy is enshrined in a new covenant, a new
promise of protection, based, not on human goodness, but on
God's.

Another such covenant/promise is made to Abraham but it
is not unilateral. A condition is attached. At first, the promise
seems to be entirely without reciprocal obligation:

> On that day the Lord made a covenant with Abram [=
> Abraham], saying, 'To your descendants I give this land,
> from the river of Egypt to the great river, the Euphrates, the
> land of the Kenizzities, the Kadmonites, the Hittites, the
> Perizzities, the Rephaim, the Amorities, the Canaanites, the
> Girgashites, and the Jebusites.' *Book of Genesis 15:17-21*

There is no mention here of any obligation on Abraham's part;
the land is a free gift. The peculiar rite which accompanies the
covenant/promise makes this clear. Animals are slaughtered
and solemnly cut in half. If this were a bilateral treaty, each

party would walk between the animal sides, promising to abide by the terms agreed. But in the ritual carried out to underpin God's promise to Abraham, the Lord alone, represented by 'a flaming torch' passes between the divided carcasses and, therefore, only God is bound by his word. The gift of the land has no strings attached.

Matters are modified somewhat the next we hear of a covenant/promise, in a chapter in which the word covenant occurs seventeen times. God makes a demand: *I am God Almighty; walk before me, and be blameless (Book of Genesis 17:1)*. But whether failure to live up to the demands of blamelessness in God's sight means an end to the promises is, as yet, unclear. Once again, God spells out the covenant/promise:

The Lord appeared to Abram, and said to him,

'I am God Almighty; walk before me and be blameless. And I will make my covenant between me and you, and will multiply you exceedingly.'

Then Abram fell on his face; and God said to him,

'Behold, my covenant is with you, and you shall be the father of a multitude of nations. No longer shall your name be Abram, but your name shall be Abraham, for I have made you the father of a multitude of nations. I will make you exceedingly fruitful; and I will make nations of you, and kings shall come forth from you. I will establish my covenant between me and you and your descendants after you throughout their generations for an everlasting covenant, to be God to you and your descendants after you.

And I will give to you, and to your descendants after you, the land of Canaan, for an everlasting possession; and I will be their God.' *Book of Genesis 17:1-8*

The covenant/promise in this quotation would appear to be attached to a general obligation to walk blameless before God but it is not clear that what God promises – to be God for Abraham and his descendants, to give them secure possession of the land – is dependent upon Abraham's goodness. However, a definite commandment emerges in the next few lines:

And God said to Abraham,

'As for you, you shall keep my covenant, you and your

descendants after you throughout their generations. This is my covenant, which you shall keep, between me and you and your descendants after you:

Every male among you shall be circumcised. You shall be circumcised in the flesh of your foreskins, and it shall be a sign of the covenant between me and you. ... So shall my covenant be in your flesh an everlasting covenant. Any un-circumcised male who is not circumcised in the flesh of his foreskin shall be cut off from his people; he has broken my covenant.' *Book of Genesis 17:9-14*

It is quite clear that a very special bond is being created between God, on the one hand, and Abraham and his descendants, on the other. Just as the rainbow is the sign of the covenant with Noah, circumcision is the sign of the covenant/promise to Abraham. But circumcision depends on a human decision. Those who do not bear the mark of circumcision will be cut off from the people, cut off from the inheritance that otherwise would be theirs. The bond between God and his people can be broken by human choice. However, nothing is said here about leading a blameless life. The bond between God and those who would benefit from God's promise is a physical mark, not a moral life.

Covenant is at the heart of the experience of those who were slaves in Egypt and were led to freedom by God. The beautiful image of the mother eagle carrying her little ones to safety springs from the mind of God:

And Moses went up to God, and the Lord called to him out of the mountain, saying, 'Thus you shall say to the house of Jacob, and tell the people of Israel:

"You have seen what I did to the Egyptians, and how I bore you on eagles' wings and brought you to myself. Now therefore, if you will obey my voice and keep my covenant, you shall be my possession among all peoples; for all the earth is mine, and you shall be to me a kingdom of priests and a holy nation."

These are the words you shall speak to the children of Israel.'
Book of the Exodus 19:3-6
The covenant, from the people's point of view, is not now

based solely on choice but on an effect of that choice: God chooses Israel, God saves Israel. It is this momentous act of saving which forever binds the people of Israel to God. But here an obligation is placed on those who have been saved, if they are to continue to enjoy the blessings promised by the Lord. To be sure, God's covenant confers status. The people, God's treasured possession, shall be separate from profane, unclean humanity, as priests are intended to be separate from all that contaminates; they are to be part of God's holiness, inoculated against all that paganism implies. But now guarantees of well-being come hand-in-hand with obligations. Obedience to God's voice is now a stipulation of covenant living. It is not that God will renege on promises made; rather, the people, if they are to experience the bond of covenant must commit themselves to gratitude and fidelity. A life lived in gratitude and fidelity is a life lived in accord with all the commandments which hedge around God's people with holiness.

What follows the great deliverance from Egyptian slavery is not obedience but infidelity. Golden calves begin to dominate the religious landscape. But God's bond, God's promised care of this people is never irrevocably annulled. From the beginning the people of Israel tended to unfaithfulness but God's steadfast love responded to restore awareness of the covenant, the promise to be there even for a recalcitrant people.

King David was not the kind of man to bother canonisation tribunals. Even on his deathbed he planned the murder of old enemies. Colourful might be the word to describe him, like the curate's egg, good in spots. But God made a covenant with David and his successors which, lucky for him and them, resembled that made with Noah and Abraham. It did not depend on clean living. The eternal covenant made with the royal family was an unconditional promise. A hymn written some hundreds of years after the time of King David (c. 1010-970 BC) recalls the old promise and its relevance to present and future kings:

I have found David, my servant;
with holy oil I have anointed him;
so that my hand shall ever abide with him,
my arm also shall strengthen him.
...

I will make him the first-born,
the highest of the kings of the earth.
My steadfast love I will keep firm for him for ever,
and my covenant will stand firm for him.
I will establish his line for ever
and his throne as the days of the heavens.
If his children forsake my law
and do not walk according to my ordinances,
if they violate my statutes
and do not keep my commandments,
then I will punish their transgression with the rod
and their iniquity with scourges;
but I will not remove from him my steadfast love,
or be false to my faithfulness.
I will not violate my covenant,
or alter the word that went forth from my lips.
Once and for all I have sworn by my holiness;
I will not lie to David.
His line shall endure for ever,
his throne as long as the sun before me.
Like the moon it shall be established for ever;
it shall stand firm while the skies endure.
Psalm 89:20-37

As with Noah, the promise to David and his royal descendants is unconditional, a covenant which cannot be broken. If David's successors do not walk blameless before the Lord, God will punish them as a father punishes his children. But God will not take back the promise. Like God's steadfast love, the covenant goes on forever. So the perspective here is very different from that of the covenant made with Moses and the people, where divine favour is conditional on human obedience to the commandments.

All of which, of course, leaves us with two difficulties. First, the people of Israel were not able to live up to the covenant demands spelled out to Moses on Mount Sinai. Like most western Christians today, most ancient Israelites were not breaking down the doors of the local temples of worship. The prophets believed that infidelity led to national disaster, that God's rod was often on the back of Israel because of disobedience. Foreign domination, exile, impoverishment, to the outsider, may be nothing but the calamities of history. But to Isaiah, Jeremiah and the rest of the prophets, looked at from God's point of view, they were punishments for forsaking covenant obligations and walking away from that holiness which God sought from his people. No matter how faithful God is, no matter that God's steadfast love endures for ever, God's love will always be rendered null and void by stiff-necked people.

Secondly, the promise to David and his heirs didn't come to much. The kingship of David's descendants came to an end in 587 BC and the future of the royal House of David was bleak.

Pregnant Pause

Before grappling with the conundrums posed by covenant, obedience, kingship, infidelity, tragedy and loss, we need to remind ourselves what we are doing. What we are doing is trying to understand the mind of God with fallible human language. Words like covenant are only a human way of trying to express the relationship which we think God has with humanity. As with all human concepts which try to explore the mind of God, covenant is an imperfect expression of the relationship between God and the world's inhabitants. The simplest statement about covenant is this: *I will be your God and you will be my people (Book of the Exodus 6:7)*. But this cannot be understood to mean that God and humanity have agreed on a bilateral contract, a treaty with the terms to be observed by either side spelled out, because God cannot be subjected to human obligation. We cannot, as human beings, commit God to doing what we want. Being good doesn't cut much ice with God, not if you're in it for what you can get out of it. All we have is a mouthful of human words by which to explore the mind of God. If we walk with the idea of covenant a little further, we will begin to see how fallible it is but, at the same time, how strong it is in turning our thoughts to God.

Here is a list of some of the books which make up the Jewish scriptures:

Book of Joshua
Book of Judges
First Book of Samuel

Second Book of Samuel
First Book of the Kings
Second Book of the Kings.

These books contain some of the best stories, the most intriguing men and women, and the most contentious historical details in the whole of the Bible. What is certain is that all the material contained therein was subjected to a single editorial policy and presented in such a way as to convey an overriding religious point of view. All these books give an unqualified negative judgement on God's people from the time they entered the land flowing with milk and honey to the day, eight hundred years later, when they lost everything, land, Holy City, and Temple, in the disaster known as the Babylonian Exile (587 BC). The whole people, including their kings, with few exceptions, according to these tragic books, were unfaithful to the God of the covenant; they took to themselves the gods of pagan neighbours, they flouted the demands of justice among themselves, walking on the faces of the poor as brazenly as any cruel pagan, and they worshipped and prayed with a hypocrisy that beggared belief. And all that, say these books, brought about the catastrophes which were visited upon them in the shape of Babylonian invaders.

The *Book of Jeremiah* is a heartfelt reflection on the crisis visited upon God's people in the destruction of Jerusalem in 587 BC, on the deportation of the people, and the loss of the land. The prophet realised that his people's failure to keep the covenant of Moses was not due to a lack of commitment, a lack of fidelity, on God's part. It was, as ever, a problem of unfaithful people. What was needed was a new beginning. As I see it, this is how Jeremiah worked it out:

The Problem:
We are the victims of aggression from the Babylonian jackboot. Our God's holy land is devastated, Jerusalem is in ruins, the Temple is destroyed, and the king and many thousands of our people have been exiled and scattered to the four winds. To the casual observer, we are suffering what hundreds of thousands of people are enduring as victims of continuous warring between the superpowers of the Middle

East. But to the eyes of faith, we, the People of God, have the added burden of knowing that we brought all this misery on ourselves. God is our God. We are God's people. God gave us this land to be our land. God has been good to us. God has cared for us for God is faithful. With God, promises made are promises kept. But we have not walked with our God. We have abandoned faithfulness and thrown the covenant back in God's face. Our sufferings are self-inflicted and God is punishing us for our hardness of heart, not to mention our stupidity.

Solution 1

We, the people, will repent of our infidelity, turn back to God, and make a firm purpose of amendment. God will forgive us and we will return to the land, rebuild our cities and towns, restore our Temple in holy Jerusalem, and live happily ever after.

This solution is for the birds. I know (says Jeremiah), and you know that we wouldn't be back five minutes before the old infidelities and the disgrace of the old days will be back. We have been here before. We simply haven't got what it takes.

Solution 2

God must change the plot. If we can't be faithful, then there is no point in God sticking to the old script laid down on Mount Sinai. Punishing the people to bring them into line with the covenant is a waste of time. What God must do is change the basis of the covenant relationship. This is how I imagine future developments:

Behold, the days are coming,
says the Lord,
when I will make a
NEW COVENANT
with the house of Israel
and the house of Judah.
Not like the covenant
which I made with their ancestors
when I took them by the hand

to bring them out of Egypt,
my covenant which they broke,
though I was their husband,
says the Lord.
Book of Jeremiah 31:31

These are the terms:
This is the covenant
which I will make
with the house of Israel
after those days,
says the Lord.

I will put MY LAW
within them,
I will write it
on their hearts;
I will be their God;
they will be my people.

Now longer shall anyone
teach a neighbour,
or a brother or sister,
'Know the Lord',
for everyone will know me,
from the most lowly to the highest,
says the Lord.

FOR I WILL FORGIVE
THEIR INIQUITY,
and
I WILL REMEMBER
THEIR SIN
NO MORE.
Book of Jeremiah 31:33-34

Plan B it is, then.

Notice that the Lord compares the old relationship to a marriage. God had married Israel. Israel had proved unfaithful, time and again. This marriage is not going anywhere because of serial infidelity. A new beginning is called for, new marriage vows, new terms of endearment. After the Babylonian nightmare is over, there will be reconciliation of the spouses and a new plan for the future. For the sake of the children.

For the sake of the children. If the future is to hold promise, then a new beginning is necessary. God's fidelity to the people of Israel must be shown in a new way, which, says the Lord, *will not be like the covenant that I made with their ancestors when I took them by the hand to bring them out of Egypt; a covenant that they broke (Book of Jeremiah 31:32).* First, God will cause a more personal engagement. God's goodness, God's graciousness, God's love, will reach into the human heart and affect a change. God will not change; the sacred Torah will not change; people will be changed and they will be changed by a new policy whereby forgiveness and pardon will become the effective instruments of God's rule.

God's covenant, God's determination to be God for people even when people turn their backs on God, will bring to light in the world the true character of God, always there but not always understood, or, when understood, not always believed, and even when believed, seldom trusted. What we are dealing with here is a delicate balancing act. There is enough and plenty in the Bible about a vengeful God who makes short shrift of enemies. *Vengeance is mine, says the Lord (Letter to Romans 12:19,* quoting the *Book of Deuteronomy 32:35).* There can be no doubt that people expect their gods to exterminate enemies, to prove their worth in time of war by inflicting disaster on the other side. Warring nations always believe that God, or the gods, are on their side. However, the matter in the Bible is not so clear cut. A little probing will reveal that vengeance, love, and mercy, are infinitely complicated terms, at least as complicated as the idea of covenant which lies at their biblical roots.

Vengeance is mine …
No one can doubt that the Bible is full of divine vengeance. If you are of a nervous disposition, look away now:

Vengeance is mine, and I will repay!
Book of Deuteronomy 32:35

I will take vengeance on my adversaries.
I will get my own back on those who hate me.

I will make my arrows drunk with blood,
and my sword shall eat human flesh!
Book of Deuteronomy 32:41-42

Be strong!
Fear not!
Behold,
your God will come with a vengeance,
with divine retribution.
He will come and save you.
Book of Isaiah 35:4

I will take vengeance,
and no one will be spared.
Our Redeemer – the Lord of hosts is his name –
is the Holy One of Israel.
Book of Isaiah 47:3

The Lord saw that there was no justice …
He put on righteousness as a breastplate,
and a helmet of salvation upon his head;
he put on garments of vengeance for clothing,
and wrapped himself in a cloak of anger.
Book of Isaiah 59:14-17

The Lord is a jealous God, an avenger!
The Lord is avenging and full of wrath!
The Lord takes vengeance on his enemies,
and stores up wrath for his adversaries,
The Lord is slow to anger and of great might,
but he will by no means spare the guilty.
Book of Nahum 1:2-3

Revenge would seem to be a prominent aspect of God's character. But it is important to notice that the enemies of God are of
three kinds. First, there are people who act with callous disregard for the poor and who career through this world with
scant regard for justice or mercy. Secondly, there are those nations
who oppress weaker peoples, such as Israel, inflict tyranny

upon them and reduce them to slavery. Thirdly, in the midst of God's holy people, there is a rump, a festering sore, of unholy people who thrive on exploitation, who batten on the poor and the needy: men and women who get rich by violence and thuggery; people who lie and cheat, who bribe and corrupt, people who model themselves on petty tyrants like Omri and his son Ahab, husband of Jezebel (for all this, see the *Book of Micah* 6:9-16 and all of the *Book of Amos*).

In the midst of all these statements about vengeance, the insistence that divine vengeance is not an end in itself runs side by side with God's determination to confront human depravity. A commitment to right wrongs runs hand-in-hand with a pledge that, at the end of the day, saving people is at the heart of God's covenant to be God for people.

The Bible does not present just one image of God. While one can identify the God of revenge, the Almighty God, the jealous King, who brooks no opposition, one must also identify the Bible's insistence that it is love, not avenging power, which defines the heart of God. Almost all books in the Jewish Bible present a vision of God for whom love, not revenge, is the ultimate and unconditional characteristic. There is in the Bible a tension between the image of the God of mercy and the God of might. Remember Jonah?

Jonah and Castor Oil

The *Book of Jonah* is about more than a man-eating fish. Like every line in both Jewish and Christian scriptures, it is about God. The book was written, I believe, after the Babylonian Exile (587 BC) at a time when some exiles had been allowed to return to Jerusalem to begin the task of rebuilding and resettlement. It was a time of bitterness and narrowness. Bitter, because of the sufferings imposed on a tiny nation by a cruel succession of imperial tyrants. Narrow, because a ghetto mentality sought to close off contact with the outside world and ignore the call to be a light to the nations, a beacon of God's presence for all peoples. The fictional short-story we enjoy as the *Book of Jonah* is a protest against the narrow religiosity that seeks to confine God's love to one chosen people. It is a fierce statement that you can't keep

God locked inside your church, no matter how strong your doors and how high your rood screens.

Here is the background to Jonah and the castor-oil plant. Nineveh was, for a time, the capital city of the Assyrian people who lived in what is now Iraq but whose empire extended to Egypt, Cyprus and Asia Minor (Turkey). In the many wars fought by this aggressive and cruel empire, the tiny land of Israel was frequently involved, either forced to pay crippling tribute tax or pressured into disastrous alliances against the might of the empire. Indeed, in 724 BC, the king of Israel revolted against Assyria but the imperial troops swept in and, by 721 BC, had reduced it to rubble. The Assyrians deported much of the population and scattered them to the four corners of its empire where they disappeared from history. None was left but the tribe of Judah only, laments the *Second Book of the Kings (17:18)*. The tiny southern province of Judah struggled to keep its land, its faith, its identity.

When news came over the mountains that Nineveh had been destroyed by the Babylonians in 612 BC, not many tears were shed in Jerusalem, as the song of revenge which is the *Book of Nahum* gloatingly records. The prophet Nahum sings of God who is revenged on his enemies, a God who utterly destroys on the principle that your enemy is my enemy. When the messenger arrived with the news that Nineveh had been destroyed, this was the song in the Jerusalem charts:

Look!
There on the mountains!
The feet of the one bringing good news [gospel!]!
The one proclaiming peace!
Judah!
Celebrate your feast-days,
fulfill what you swore!
Never again will the wicked invade you!
They are annihilated!
Book of Nahum 1:15

But, of course, the Babylonian were no different than the tyrants they replaced and they came south and destroyed Jerusalem, its Temple, and deported its people (587 BC).

At last! A Messiah! King Cyrus II, of the Medes and of the Persians, conquered the Babylonians, and, would you believe, allowed a trickle of Jews to return to the little land of Judah and begin to rebuild Jerusalem and its temple. Most Jews didn't want to go back and the few who did were fired by the old religion, a sense of identity, and a determination to keep out of trouble. The order of the day was to keep your head down, as the rather drab *Book of Ezra/Nehemiah* recommends. One can understand the zeal of these people by reading the middle chapters of the *Book of Isaiah*. There the writer states that the whole Middle Eastern imperial upheavals had been engineered by God solely for the purpose of bringing about the return of a few Jews from the banks of the Tigris and Euphrates. God had created international mayhem just to save Israel! Cyrus was none other than God's Messiah, anointed by God to subdue all the nations in order to be in a position to free a few Jewish exiles. Cyrus II is praised as God's good shepherd who fulfils God's purpose by seeing to it that the Jewish people are shepherded home safely (*Book of Isaiah* 44:24-45:7).

All this was ancient history when the *Book of Jonah* was written. Nineveh had been in ruins for years. But the narrow racial and religious outlook of those who rebuilt Jerusalem seemed to one imaginative poet to reduce God to a local god, a tribal deity, with no interest in anything beyond the city walls. The *Book of Jonah*, by presenting God as the saviour of Nineveh and its people, the most hated pagans a Jew could imagine, rescues God from obscurity. After all, if God saves the Ninevehites (and their cows), who does God not save?

All the best stories about God are works of fiction, that is, they are conceived in our imagination and nurtured in our hearts. The *Book of Jonah* is a work of fiction. It is a powerful statement about God. Its hero, the reluctant prophet Jonah, is forced to admit that the God who saves his people saves all people, even the most hated of all peoples. Jonah had to stomach what he knew in his heart-of-hearts to be true:

I knew that you are a gracious God, a merciful God, slow to anger, abounding in steadfast love, and that you repent of evil.

Book of Jonah 4:2

What Jonah wanted for Nineveh was death and destruction. What God did was to have mercy on a people who didn't know their right hand from their left *(Book of Jonah 4:11)*. And don't forget the cows.

The character of God is what is at stake here. Is our God a God of vengeance? Or is God a God of mercy? If we are honest, we want both: a God who destroys our enemies, a God who loves us. And when God creates a castor-oil plant to provide shade from the desert sun for Jonah and then takes it away, Jonah must reluctantly admit that a gift is always in the hand of the giver. The Lord gives, the Lord takes away. Blessed be the name of the Lord!

Throughout the Jewish Bible there is an unresolved ambiguity. On the one hand, God is a God of everlasting, merciful love; on the other hand, love is not freely given:

The Lord passed before [Moses] and proclaimed:
'The Lord, the Lord,
a God merciful and gracious,
slow to anger,
and abounding in steadfast love and faithfulness,
keeping steadfast love for thousands,
forgiving iniquity and transgression and sin,
but who will by no means clear the guilty,
visiting the iniquity of fathers on their children
and the children's children,
to the third and forth generation.'
Book of the Exodus 34:6-7

Moses sees the ambiguity here: how can love be steadfast if it does not extend to the guilty? When unfaithfulness appears in the desert, he appeals to God:

Now I pray you,
let the power of the Lord be great
as you have promised, saying,
'The Lord is slow to anger,
and abounding in steadfast love,
forgiving iniquity and transgression,
but he will by no means clear the guilty,
visiting the iniquity of fathers upon children,

upon the third and upon the fourth generation'.
Pardon the iniquity of this people,
I pray you,
according to the greatness of your steadfast love,
and according as you have forgiven this people,
from Egypt even until now.
Book of Numbers 14:17-19

Others, like Moses, appeal to God to lean towards love rather
than punishment:

You are a God ready to forgive,
gracious and merciful,
slow to anger
and abounding in steadfast love,
and did not forsake them.
Even when they made a molten calf ...,
in your great mercy,
you did not forsake them ...
Book of Nehemiah 9:17-19

The *Book of Jeremiah 32:16-44* tries to balance God's steadfast love
and a punishment which seeks to reform the offender. The *Book
of Psalms*, which, of course, is a collection of prayers, and prayers
usually get things right, makes a determined case for love without end and without conditions attached, but it cannot get away
from the conviction that there are commandments to be met and
kept:

Bless the Lord,
O my soul,
and all that is within me,
bless his holy name!

Bless the Lord,
O my soul,
and forget not all his benefits,
who forgives all our iniquity,
who heals all your diseases,
who redeems your life from the Pit,
who crowns you with steadfast love and mercy,
who satisfies you with good as long as you live,
so that your youth is renewed like the eagle's.

The Lord works vindication and justice
for all who are oppressed.
He made known his ways to Moses,
his acts to the people of Israel.
The Lord is merciful and gracious,
slow to anger,
and abounding in steadfast love.

He will not always chide,
nor will he keep his anger for ever.
HE DOES NOT DEAL WITH US
ACCORDING TO OUR SINS,
nor pay us back for our iniquities.
For as the heavens are high above the earth,
so great is his steadfast love
toward those who fear him;
as far as the east is from the west,
so far does he remove our transgressions from us.
As a father pities his children,
so the Lord pities those who fear him.
For he knows how we are made,
he remembers that we are dust.

As for human beings,
their days are like grass;
they flourish like a flower of the field;
for the wind blows over it,
and it is gone,
and its place knows it no more.
But the steadfast love of the Lord
is from everlasting to everlasting
for those who fear him,
and his righteousness to children's children,
to those who keep his covenant
and remember to do his commandments.
Psalm 103:1-18

Psalm 136, on the other hand, sings of a God who, from the moment of creation, through every vicissitude, and, in the face of every human turmoil, remains constant: *his steadfast love en-*

dures forever. Twenty-six times the refrain is repeated: *his stead-fast love endures forever*. It is a psalm for slow learners.

The conundrum is at the heart of Jesus' conversation. When Jesus talked with his people, the question in all hearts was how people can experience the presence of God's steadfast love in their lives, how can they hope that God is there for them, how can they believe that all will be well? All faith is a matter of trust and we and our fathers and mothers in faith have but one question: *Can we trust God?* All of this talking and discussion, agreement and disagreement, is centred on an enduring symbol which brings together all the questions and some of the answers: the kingdom of God. If our God reigns, is it a reign of terror, is it a reign of vengeance, is it a reign of total indifference to what goes on in the life of the poor man at the gates? Can God cope with sin without resorting to violence? We may anticipate the answer in a story, a parable, which many Jewish rabbis told and continue to tell:

A notorious sinner died and found himself prostrate before Almighty God. The Almighty sat on the Seat of Judgement as the Recording Angel read from the book the long litany of the man's sins. Page after page, the multitude and variety of the man's sins were laid bare. As Almighty God listened to the endless catalogue of the man's evil ways, he said, 'If I sit here on the Seat of Judgement, I shall have to destroy this wretched man.' So God got up and moved over to sit on the Seat of Mercy.

We shall have to attend closely to these matters. But, for now, the kind of God in the parable is the kind of God Jesus talked about, the kind of God whose presence in him came to our world. When Jesus chatted about the kingdom of God to anyone who cared to join in the conversation, he was chatting about the place of God in human hearts, about the possibility of transforming hearts of stone into hearts of flesh.

CHAPTER SIX

About the Kingdom of God

And the apostles, on their return, reported to him what they had done. And taking them along, he withdrew privately to a city called Bethsaida. But the crowds, knowing of it, followed him. And, welcoming them as usual, he was chatting with them *about the kingdom of God* and he was healing those who needed healing.
Gospel of Luke 9:10-11

Translating the Jesus who was, the Jesus who lived and died long ago and far away, into our time and our place, is the task of every generation of Christians. The Jesus who is is the Jesus each generation creates for itself. Each generation looks at the Jesus who lived and died, and the past wisdom garnered by the church, and tries to make sense of what it learns in order to make Jesus present now, in our time and in our place. We read the Jesus of the Gospels, the Jesus of previous generations of Christians, and we translate what we read into the language of our time and our place. The Jesus who is, the Jesus for our world, is the Jesus we say he is. This is known as carrying the can.

When St Luke wrote that Jesus was chatting about the kingdom of God, he was translating. He wrote in Greek. Jesus spoke in Aramaic. In his own language, Jesus would not have spoken of the kingdom of God. He would have spoken of the kingdom of heaven. As a Jew, Jesus would have been sparing in using God's name and would, like everyone with whom he conversed, have avoided the divine name by using roundabout substitutes. It is noticeable that Matthew's Gospel, a very Jewish text, employs the phrase 'kingdom of God' sparingly. For that Gospel, as for Jesus, it was preponderantly the 'kingdom of heaven' (see *Gospel of Matthew 12:28; 19:23-24* – where both forms are used interchangeably; *21:31; 21:43*). Heaven, in our creative imagination, is God's 'space'; heaven is where God 'reigns' and 'sits on a throne', with all the paraphernalia of a royal court; heaven is where we all want to go (but not yet). But when Jesus and Matthew's Gospel speak of the 'kingdom of heaven', they do not mean what we mean by 'heaven'. They mean what the Bible means by the word 'God'. By translating the Jesus phrase 'kingdom of heaven' as 'kingdom of God', Luke, the gospel-maker, like St Paul and St Mark before him, is translating Jesus into his language, into his time, into his place.

Already, then, in the very first days of Christianity, we find people translating and, therefore, interpreting the words of Jesus. And not just the words. The thought patterns and ideas of Jesus had to be broken down and rebuilt to make sense to would-be disciples drawn from the pagan world. Even the person of Jesus and the details of his life, death, and resurrection, had to be reconstructed and made understandable to people who did not have the rich traditions about God inherent in the Jewish Bible and in Jewish faith. We are accustomed to speaking of Jesus as Jesus Christ. But 'Christ', as we shall see in later chapters, is little more than a surname, an addition to the name Jesus that means little. When did you last pray to the Messiah? The term Messiah, or Christ, with all the connotations which the Jewish Bible and, more particularly, Jewish traditions and expectations, had placed on the word, had little meaning for even the earliest Christians who came to belief in Jesus from the pagan world. Consequently, the designation Messiah or Christ quickly lost its Jewish implications and became another name for Jesus, rather than the forceful description of his destiny which it had and has in its native home. Again we need to remind ourselves of the responsibility which lies on the shoulders of every generation of Christians. Every generation has to translate not only what Jesus said but who Jesus was for its own time and its own place. Otherwise, the Jesus who was remains the Jesus who was: interesting and irrelevant.

Chatting About What?
If you were to ask, 'What is the teaching of Jesus?', you would get no marks for answering, as many do, 'Love God and love

your neighbour'. Admittedly, when a lawyer suggested a rather unusual summary of the whole of God's teaching to the Jewish people, Jesus approved of the man's insight:

> You must love the Lord your God with all your heart, with all your souls, with all your might, and with all your mind; and you must love your neighbour as yourself.
> *Gospel of Luke 10:27*

It is, of course, true that we must love God with all the passion and concern that we have for our neighbour, and our neighbour with all the passion and concern that we have for God. But the lawyer was simply quoting two passages from the Jewish Bible (*Book of Deuteronomy 6:5* and the *Book of Leviticus 19:18*) and that is hardly a claim to originality. After all, we do not need the life and death of Jesus to teach us what we could have found out by looking up a couple of books, do we?

Nor would marks be awarded to any clever-clogs who answered 'Christianity'. For Jesus was, by race and religion, a Jew, not a Christian. And, if the heart of the Christian message is that the death and resurrection of Jesus accomplish the salvation of the world, Jesus never said that. Nor, indeed, can one imagine him doing so. No, at the heart of what Jesus talked about day in, day out, is the kingdom of heaven, or, as Luke translates it for Christians for whom he wrote, the kingdom of God. We can be certain that the Jesus who was spoke endlessly about God's kingdom. The Gospels are full of his magnificent obsession. In a word, if you are asked what the message of Jesus was, and, indeed, is, the answer was and is *The Kingdom of God*. To get to the heart of Jesus, we must get to the heart of the kingdom. And where better to start than with our most familiar prayer? We shall examine Luke's Lord's Prayer in detail in Chapter Ten. For now, what it has to say about the kingdom of God is our concern.

Thy Kingdom Come!

The very kingdom for which we are bidden to pray in *The Lord's Prayer* is at the heart of what Jesus teaches. So – whatever it is – the kingdom of God is something about which Jesus can chat and talk and raise for discussion again and again, yet its coming is problematical and must be at the heart of our prayer. What is the kingdom of God?

God's kingdom is not a place; it is not a country. God's kingdom is all hearts of stone replaced by hearts of flesh. It is an implanting of God's spirit, the making of a new creation, the straightening of human crookedness. Ezekiel spent his life in exile from Jerusalem in far off Babylon (Iraq) and at a time of fierce international wars and conflicts, wrack and ruin, in the Middle East. His hopes were for a clean sweep of the world's evils and for a settled, quiet, peaceful, and, therefore, holy world, for all its warring inhabitants. Usually, his imagination stretched to the bizarre and beyond. Here his eloquence is in simplicity:

THUS SAYS THE LORD GOD:
On the day that I cleanse you from all your iniquities,
I will cause the cities to be inhabited,
and the waste places shall be rebuilt.
And the desolate land shall be tilled,
instead of being the desolation
seen by all who passed by.
And passers-by will say,
'This land that was desolate has
become like the Garden of Eden!
The waste and desolate and ruined cities
are now inhabited and secure!'
Then the surrounding nations about you
shall know that it is
I, THE LORD,
who has rebuilt ruined places,
and replanted that which was desolate.
I, THE LORD,
have spoken.
AND I WILL DO IT!
Book of Ezekiel 36:33-36

God brings his holiness to bear on our world when God makes his presence felt. God's kingdom is in every heart transformed and set beating by God's spirit. To pray for God's kingdom is to pray that we may be where God is present. It is to pray, as we do in St Matthew's version of The Lord's Prayer: *thy will be done on earth, as it is in heaven.* May God see to it that the world knows its God, experiences the presence of its God in a transformed God-like people. It is a consummation devoutly to be wished.

The Our Father provides the perfect definition of God's kingdom. The first three petitions of our daily prayer all mean the same:

Hallowed be thy name!
is the same as
Thy kingdom come!
is the same as
Thy will be done on earth!

And this doing on earth of God's will must be so perfect, so complete, that it will be as it is in heaven! So one thing is crystal clear immediately: men and women can't be kingdom-builders. They haven't got in them; hearts of stone can't change themselves. As Jesus chatted with people about the doing of God's will, people will have wondered how it might come about, and what a world transformed by God might look like. They might have wondered how we might recognise the kingdom's coming, and, most of all, when we could expect it to arrive. This is where Jesus, the one-liner and storyteller, tries hardest. We must now enter the imaginative world of Jesus, engage with his stories, and discuss with him to our heart's content. But, since the God who spoke to and through Jesus was no stranger to Jewish people, in order to join in the conversation of Jesus and his friends, we must learn what they had learned at their mothers' knees. We have to think our way into their mind-set.

Back to Basics
We spent much ink looking at the idea of covenant and we left some difficult questions hanging in the air. We will have to spend more ink and delve deeper into undusted nooks and crannies.

We encountered conflicting views about the covenant in Jewish thoughts about God as they are enshrined in the Bible. We might summarise the various viewpoints by asking and answering two questions. The questions are the same but the answers are profoundly different. These questions and answers may appear to be about the experiences of the Jewish people throughout history and about the conclusions they drew from those experiences. In fact, they are about God and whether there is any point in believing in God. It is one thing to listen to God's word proclaiming *I will be your God and you will be my people;* it is quite another if God fails to deliver the goods.

Question 1:
If we are God's people, why do we suffer from foreign aggression, generation after generation? Why have we no peace in this land which God is supposed to have given to us?

Answer:
We have disobeyed God's commandments. Our sinfulness has brought about all our calamities. God is using the powers of this world to punish us for our infidelities, our unwillingness to be worthy of all that God has given and all that God has promised.

Question 2:
Why? Does this incessant divine punishment have any purpose? Is there a future, other than endless suffering?

Answer:
Yes! God's punishment is reformative. It is intended to bring us to our senses. God is inflicting the rod of his anger in order that we repent. We must turn from our evil ways and return to God's ways. Then we shall live in security, in harmony, and in peace. It's up to us!

Now, an alternative vision:

Question 1:
If we are God's people, why do we suffer from foreign aggression, generation after generation? Why have we no peace in this land which God is supposed to have given to us?

Answer:
God is all-powerful. But there are evil, demonic forces in the world who are opposed to God and, consequently, seek to overcome God by overcoming God's people. All the afflictions of our history have been due, not to our sins, but to the fact that we are

caught up in a cosmic battle between good and evil. We are the victims of forces beyond our control. Only God can rescue humanity from the satanic chains which bind us.

Question 2:
Why? Does this incessant punishment have any purpose? Is there a future, other than an endless suffering?

Answer:
Yes, there is a future but it lies in God's hands. God will intervene on behalf of battered and broken humanity and will directly confront and destroy the cosmic forces of evil and their human agents. What poor humanity must do is to remain as faithful as possible and wait for God to put everything to rights.

The difficulty with the first solution is that the possibility of Jewish people, and, for that matter, the rest of humanity, turning away from the sins and deceits which beset us all is nil. If the people of God have to earn their salvation (to put the matter in churchy language), then there is no hope. Anyone who lives in the real world knows that human beings cannot so reform themselves that a new heaven and a new earth is ours for the making. And, another thing. If we manage to pull ourselves together and turn away from all the evils which beset humanity, then we would have saved ourselves. We would have forced God's hand and constrained God to pursue a policy dictated by our agenda. It is difficult for Christians to grasp this simple truth: you can't buy your way into God's world, even when the price you are willing to pay is a saintly life.

The second solution is simple: it's up to God! And that is the solution which is embodied in the teaching and life's work of Jesus of Nazareth. What we hear and see in Jesus is the inauguration of the second solution. In short, the second solution is the kingdom of God. It is the solution we have seen proposed by Jeremiah and the writer of the *Book of Jonah*. This is the heart of the teaching of Jesus and the essence of all he tried to say in his discussions with those who had ears to hear, and even with those who had not. To turn the Jesus who was into the Jesus who is, we have to listen. On the mountain of the Transfiguration (which we shall climb before journey's end), the voice from the cloud shouts out, *Listen to him!* We will be transfigured by listening.

Kingdom Talk
Listen especially to the parables. Parables are subversive stories. They subvert our complacencies. They shatter our religious certainties and call in question our unquestioned beliefs. Parables are beguiling. As you are nodding your head in agreement with the story, suddenly it jumps up and bites off your head.

As well as presenting many parables about the kingdom of God, Luke supplies snippets of crucial information which we need to garner as gold nuggets before we are exposed to the explosive parables which lie like minefields along the way of our thinking about God. Jesus peppers us with one-liners which are tantalising, exasperating, and liberating. What he does is lead us in one direction, up the garden path, if you like, and then he creates an almighty diversion. And what diverting diversions!

John the Baptist, quoting Isaiah the prophet, promised that, in the coming of Jesus, all humanity will see the deliverance of God *(Gospel of Luke 2:6)*. When Jesus opened the scroll to read to the congregation gathered for prayer in his home village of Nazareth, deliberately he turned to the place where it was written:

The Spirit of the Lord is upon me,
because he has anointed me
to gospel the poor;
he sent me
to announce freedom to captive people,
and new eyes for blind people;
to send into freedom oppressed people,
and to shout out like a town-crier
the welcoming year of the Lord.
Gospel of Luke 4:18-19

To counter those villagers who were slow to be impressed by (as they saw him) a jumped-up local odd-job man claiming to be a prophet, Jesus pointed to two occasions in the past when God intervened to rescue two people. One was a widow-woman, a pagan famine victim who lived in Lebanon; the other was a leper, a pagan general who led the enemy armies of Syria. Outsiders both: a woman (how outside can you get?), a pagan, a foreigner, an enemy, unclean, unacceptable to God; a leper, a pagan, an army commander, a foreign and ancient enemy, unclean, unacceptable to God. To these 'unworthy', unclean, despised pagan enemies, God, without so much as by-your-leave from pious prigs, dispatches two top-notch prophets to feed the one, and heal the other. The time of God's welcoming has arrived, says Jesus, a welcoming for pagans, enemies, sinners, ne'er-do-wells, chancers, backsliders, indeed, a welcoming for anyone who is lost in whatever hell-holes men and women dig for themselves or are thrown into. What Jesus shouts out in Nazareth is a Hundred Thousand Welcomes, or, if you will allow me, *Céad Míle Fáilte*. Welcome to the kingdom! The time of God's welcoming is now! All God's chillun got wings! Everyone wins, everyone gets a prize!

As he went through his native province of Galilee, by word and action, Jesus kept saying the same thing: *I must gospel [you] about the kingdom of God (Gospel of Luke 4:43)*. Where God reigns, the just, the unjust, the saint, the sinner, lost sheep, lost coins, lost children, are sought out, found, and given a seat at the feast. On one occasion Jesus said to his friends, *If you love those who love you, what thanks from God do you deserve? (Gospel of Luke 6:32* and see *8:1)*. If God loves only those who love God, where does that leave God? Or us? If, on this earth, we have to love our enemies, and God, in heaven, doesn't have to love God's enemies, then … why bother?

Kingdom One-Liners

Meditate on the following one-liners:

1. *Blessed are you poor, for the kingdom of God is yours (Gospel of Luke 6:20).*

Who are the poor? Apart from being poor, do these people have to do anything to be with God?

2. *The least in the kingdom of God is greater than he [John the Baptist] (Gospel of Luke 7:28).*

But how do you get in? If you have lost your way, who is looking out for you?

3. *When he called the Twelve together, he gave them power and authority over all demonic forces and to heal diseases; and he sent them out to herald the kingdom of God and to heal the sick (Gospel of Luke 9:1-2).*

So their mission is the same as that of Jesus? Must they be and say and do in their time and place what Jesus was and said and did in his?

4. *Let the dead bury their dead! Let you run out and proclaim the kingdom of God! (Gospel of Luke 9:60).*

What could be more urgent? And why?

5. *The kingdom of God is close to you! (Gospel of Luke 10:10).*

How close is close?

6. *Truly I tell you, there are some people standing here who will not taste death before they see the kingdom of God (Gospel of Luke 9:27).*

Lucky for them!

7. *But if I drive out demonic forces by the finger of God, the kingdom of God has indeed come to you (Gospel of Luke 11:20).*

If God so much as lifts a little finger against those cosmic terrors … then what?

Is Jesus the finger of God?

If God's finger is a cross … what then?

8. *Your Father has determined to give you the kingdom (Gospel of Luke 12:32).*

Free gratis and for nothing?

9. *They will come from east and west, from north and south, and will sit at table in the kingdom of God (Gospel of Luke 13:29).*

Some party!

10. *When asked by the Pharisees when the kingdom of God was coming, he answered them, 'The kingdom of God does not come while you watch for it. People won't say, "Look, here it is!", or "Look, there it is!" In fact, the kingdom of God is among you' (Gospel of Luke 17:21).*

You're looking at it!

11. *Let the children come to me. Do not stop them, for the kingdom of God is of such as these. Amen, I am saying to you, that whoever does not receive the kingdom of God like a child, shall not enter it (Gospel of Luke 18:16-17).*

Like children? How? Why children?

12. *How exasperatingly difficult it is for those who have wealth to enter the kingdom of God! (Gospel of Luke 18:24).*

Like getting a camel through the eye of a needle?

13. *Amen I say to you, there is no one who leaves house, or wife, or brothers, or parents, or children, for the sake of the kingdom of God, who will not receive many times as much in this present time, and, in the age to come, everlasting life (Gospel of Luke 18:30).*

Hyperbole, certainly. But many times as much NOW? And what is everlasting life, anyway?

14. *I have earnestly desired to eat this Passover with you before I suffer; I tell you, I shall eat it no more until it is fulfilled in the kingdom of God (Gospel of Luke 22:15-16).*

Take this [cup] and share it among yourselves; for I tell you, from now on I shall not drink of the fruit of the vine until the kingdom of God has come (Gospel of Luke 22:18).

There is, after all, a price. There will be a death, a time when the bridegroom will be taken away, a time when freedom is not gained by crossing the waters but by crossing from life into death.

15. *You are those who have stood by me throughout my testing. Therefore, I give to you a kingdom as the Father gave to me in order that you may eat and drink at my table in my kingdom, and you shall sit on thrones judging the twelve tribes of Israel! (Gospel of Luke 22:30).*

Take a chance on me!

16. *Jesus, remember me when you come into your kingdom! (Gospel of Luke 23:49).*

What started out as the kingdom of God is about to become the kingdom of Jesus. When God remembers, safety is at hand. Remembering is now a Jesus task. We have heard John the Baptist promise that, in the coming of Jesus, *all humanity will see the salvation of God (Gospel of Luke 2:6).* The burden of remembering, of seeing to all humanity's safety, seems now to rest on the shoulders of Jesus. The kingdom has passed from Father to Son. Born to be King – that's the way of the world. Die to be King – that is new under the sun; that is the way of God, the Way of the Cross!

Kingdom Parables

The *Gospel according to Matthew* almost everywhere introduces parables with the catch-phrase, *The kingdom of heaven may be compared to ...* Luke does the same but not so often. He, too, has, *What is the kingdom of God like, and to what shall I compare it? (Gospel of Luke 13:18)* but many of Luke's parables are presented without a stereotypical introduction. Nonetheless, all are about the kingdom, what it is, how you get in, what it's like when you're there, what kind of people you'll meet there, what values are cherished and promoted there, what fun you'll have there, and, depressingly, how you might not recognise it if it hit you over the head. In short, the kingdom parables are a revelation.

Three Gospels, those of Matthew, of Mark, and of Luke, tell of Jesus giving to his disciples *the mysteries [or secrets] of the kingdom (Gospel of Matthew 13:12* and *Gospel of Luke 8:10)* or *the mystery [secret] of the kingdom of God (Gospel of Mark 4:11).* The context of these statements is the same in each gospel. Great crowds (Matthew), a very large crowd (Mark), a great crowd (Luke), have just heard Jesus tell the parable of the sower who went out to scatter seed on his fields. However, the interpretation of the parable (a rarity in the Gospels) is given only to *the disciples* (Matthew and Luke), or *those who were about him with the Twelve* (Mark). The explanation as to why Jesus does not share his interpretation with the crowds is, to say the least, puzzling:

> When his disciples asked him what this parable might be, [Jesus] said, 'To you it has been given to know the mysteries of the kingdom of God; but to the others they are in parables, in order that seeing they may not see, and hearing they may not understand. *Gospel of Luke 8:9*

At the risk of over-simplifying what is a deeply perplexing problem for the most perceptive of scholars (Does God deliberately complicate matters in order to exclude some people from divine well-being?), we might find some enlightenment if we approach the matter step-by-step.

Step 1: We must ponder why God chooses one person, one tribe, one people over others. Why Sarah, not Hagar? Why Jabob, not Esau? Why Jews, not Greeks? When it comes to divine choice, there is always a question of being called for a purpose. The call is always made on behalf of humanity but always made to what appear to be inadequate, insignificant people. When it comes to 'converting the world', God seems always to begin small. Think Mary.

Step 2: Our four Gospels all record the call of disciples such as Peter, James, Philip, Nathanael, at or very near the beginning of the preaching ministry of Jesus. In these men, and in the women disciples, Mary Magdalene, Joanna, Susanna, and Mary the mother of James, who were part of the enterprise from the beginning (*Gospel of Luke 8:1-3* and *24:10*), Jesus invested much time and care. They were schooled to know and understand what he was about, to grasp his message of the kingdom of God in order that they might spread the gospel.

Step 3: These men and women were entrusted with the message. But, more essentially, they were called to be with Jesus to come to know who he was and is. They were called, not simply to understand his message, but to fall passionately in love with a man. They were invited to throw in their lot with a carpenter and discover God. *Who is Jesus?* had to become for them *Who are we?* They had so to understand Jesus that they could faithfully relay his every word and deed; much more than that, they had to be other Christs, to be in their day what he was in his. Not that they were to leave Jesus in a tomb; rather they were to be raised with Jesus to be the Body of Christ to the world. As St Paul was very fond of saying, they were to be so immersed in Christ that they could say with Paul, *It is no longer I who live, but Christ who lives in me (Letter to the Galatians 2:20)*. Language is a bit difficult here. It's not easy to put the mystery of it into words. You have to feel it. It's called passion.

Step 4: The parables are a way into this mystery. And, in the words of the prophet Isaiah (which Luke quotes), some get it and some don't: *Seeing, they may not see; hearing, they may not understand (Book of Isaiah 6:10)*. Parables start the learning process. The clearest parable of all is the Cross. So parables it is then.

The Sower (Gospel of Luke 8:4-15)

What is exciting about the Parable of the Sower is that the sower is God. If there is to be a human harvest, God must scatter seed. It is God who must act to cause the kind of rejoicing in human hearts that only a plenteous harvest can inspire. People who hold fast to what is sown in their hearts (and it will take patience) will live to bear much fruit.

Mustard Seed (Gospel of Luke 13:18-19)

The kingdom of God is like a single grain of mustard dropped into the ground by a man (God) which, without so much as a shovel of manure from any human gardener, becomes a tree. Everyone is invited to nest in its sturdy branches. Think Jonah. Think castor-oil plants.

Leavening a Big Batch (Gospel of Luke 13:20-21)

The kingdom of God is like when God (a woman, this time) puts leaven into the whole human dough and sits back to watch it rise! How many echoes of the *Book of Genesis* 18:1-8 can you find in Luke's Gospel?

A Lost Sheep (Gospel of Luke 15:3-7)

A friend, Tom Hamill, told me this parable:

A certain man had one hundred sheep, secure in a sturdy sheepfold. A ring fence guarded the flock from foxes and wolves. But a very curious sheep, wondering what the great world outside the sheepfold was like, dug a hole under the fence and romped off into the alluring adventure beyond. And it was so exciting! Bright lights! Star attractions! Round-the-clock rock and roll! Suddenly a wolf, a stalker, moved in for the kill. But just as the wolf pounced, the shepherd grabbed the sheep, lifted the frightened little thing on to his shoulders, and brought him safely home. For the shepherd had been stalking, too. And although all his friends said, 'You better mend the hole in that fence!', he never did.

Compare and contrast.

Losing Money (Gospel of Luke 15:8:10)

A woman (God again) turns out every corner to find what she has lost. What is lost, the sheep and the coin, are lost by God and God must seek diligently to find. Rejoicing all around.

Lost Children (Gospel of Luke 15:11-32)

Father-God in this parable must look out for head-strong young ones who run off to the bright lights and come a cropper. But the story ends with a challenge to the goody-two-shoes at home. A reminder that we can see and not see, hear and not understand. The kingdom of God is a challenge to do an about-turn and try to see things from a God's eye point of view. This is known as conversion, and, if you find conversion hard going, it's called repentance.

Beaten-up (Gospel of Luke 10:30-35)

Religious types, for good reasons (we always have good reasons!), walk by on the other side. The Samaritan, taking the part of God, is the one to watch.

So Far …

So far we have a picture of the God whose kingdom is at the heart of the gospel of Jesus. It is as if God has been away in a far country and comes home to discover that lots of his people have got lost, and realises that the lost have got to be found. A great programme of searching for lost people is immediately put in place. This programme is called Jesus of Nazareth.

Consequences

While all the parables are God stories, some have an edge which caution that in the kingdom of God it's not all cakes and ale. Being found by God, being welcomed into the kingdom, imposes consequences and demands that guests become hosts, that the attitude of the host must become the attitude of all who have been invited to the feast. The very magnanimity of God changes hearts. To find the kingdom within you (plural) is to discover that you have the energy to say, 'We can be like that!'

Bigger Barns (Gospel of Luke 12:16-20)

When the rich farmer beholds an amazing harvest, his thoughts do not turn to God in thanksgiving; nor do they turn to the poor, the dispossessed, the destitute who, by God's command, have gleaning rights:

> When you reap the harvest of your land, you shall not reap your field to its very border, neither shall you gather gleanings after your harvest. And you shall not strip your vineyard bare, neither shall you gather the fallen grapes of your harvest; you shall leave them for the poor and the migrant-worker: I am the Lord your God.
> Book of Leviticus 19:9-10

As every farmer knows, once the seed is sown the harvest is in the lap of the gods. A mighty harvest is an answer to prayer, not to husbandry. Beautiful barns though. Pity about the funeral.

Seeing and Not Understanding (Gospel of Luke 16:19-31)

The Rich Man and Lazarus. All that purple and fine linen; all that feasting sumptuously. All those sores; all those licking dogs. The parable is not about heaven in the conventional sense. After all, how big a bosom does Abraham have? Surely, it is about the realisation that, if you are inside the gates, if blessings have been showered upon you, if you are experiencing the kingdom, you must look to those lying in the streets. Or, if you insist on conventional terms, you can't enter the kingdom on your own. You enter with other people or not at all.

Going it Alone (Gospel of Luke 18:10-13)

Two men went up to the Temple to pray. One man has twenty-nine words in his prayer and 'I' five times. The other has six words and not a single 'I'. Work it out for yourself.

A Slow Fig Tree (Gospel of Luke 13:6-9)

A slow and hesitant response to God's tender, loving care, is tolerable, and everything will be done to ensure that all is well. But, at some point, the owner will look to see a healthy crop. To live the kingdom is to endorse its values, delight in its ways, and rejoice in its God. Sooner. Or later.

Bringing it together ...

The one-liners and parables of Jesus create an ethos, an atmosphere. They invite people who meet Jesus, who are welcomed by him, who converse with him, to embrace an alternative world. They subvert received notions of how life should be lived. They demand that we do a re-take on our notions of God. They offer an adventure into the unknown of selfless love, the embrace of steadfast love which endures as nothing else endures. As we listen, we see a man who lived the kingdom, whose life is the kingdom, a man who embodies God-with-us. There is the implied invitation to allow this Jesus who was to be the Jesus who is in our lives. There is a name for all of this. It's called the church, God help us!

CHAPTER SEVEN

And he was healing ...

And the apostles, on their return, reported to him what they had done. And taking them along, he withdrew privately to a city called Bethsaida. But the crowds, knowing of it, followed him. And, welcoming them, he was chatting with them about the kingdom of God and *he was healing those who needed healing.*
Gospel of Luke 9:10-11

Did the Jesus who was have miraculous powers? Did Jesus perform miracles in Galilee and Judaea? Did the blind see, the deaf hear, the lame walk? Were storms stilled and bread and fish multiplied? Did Jesus walk on water? Was water changed into wine? Were devils expelled from possessed people? Did fig trees wither at a word? Did Lazarus come out of the tomb? Did the daughter of Jairus return to life and happiness? Did God raise Jesus from the dead?

The answer, of course, is no. Miracles are simply impossible. They cannot happen. People who claim to perform miracles are charlatans and people who believe in miracles are fools. Again and again, over the last three hundred years, eminent thinkers have emphasised that the very idea of a miracle is repugnant to human reason. To believe that someone, acting as an agent of divine power, in the sight of reliable witnesses, has performed an action that is beyond reasonable explanation and beyond any force or power which is known to our world, is itself unreasonable. We understand enough science to know that water does not change into wine because someone tells it to; we know cripples don't walk because someone shouts, 'Get up and walk!' We know that it is a sad waste of time to stand at a graveside and bellow 'Lazarus, come out!' Miracles are not possible because they are impossible.

Ancient people may not have had the advantage of our extensive scientific grasp of the realities governing our universe. They may have lived in what we like to call a pre-scientific world. That does not mean they were gullible. When you buried a man today and the next day the body had vanished, you shouted, 'Tomb-robbers!', not, 'Resurrection!' (Consult the *Gospel of Matthew 27:62-66*, if you want evidence.) Ancient writers, such pagans as Epicurus, Lucian, Lucretius, and Cicero, wrote scathingly about claims that the gods endowed people with miraculous powers, or, indeed, that the gods themselves were capable of doing the impossible. It is mistakenly condescending to think that ancient people were more gullible, more credulous, than we are.

Even those who granted the possibility and even the fact of Jesus performing some miraculous events did not see his actions as signs of God's work. The gospels themselves present a cogent argument against such a claim:

He [Jesus] was driving out a demon which was dumb. When the demon went out the dumb man spoke, and the crowds were astonished. But some of them said, 'He drives out demons by Beelzebul, the ruler of demons'.

To which Jesus replied:

If I drive out demons by Beelzebul, by whom do your people drive them out? Therefore they will be your judges. But if I cast out demons by the finger of God, then the kingdom of God has, indeed, come upon you.
Gospel of Luke 11:14-20 passim

An early critic of Christianity, the philosopher Celsus, whose writings have partly survived, made the same revealiong point. His Christian opponent, a man named Origen (185-284 AD), records what Celsus wrote about the year 180:

Christians get the power they seem to possess by pronouncing the names of certain demons and incantations … it was by magic that Jesus was able to do the miracles which he appears to have done.
Origen, *Contra Celsum* 1.6

What we have, then, are two charges, coming to us from our

world and from the world of Jesus and the first Christians. First, miracles are impossible. Secondly, even if they are possible, the so-called miracles of Jesus are not the work of God as all the Gospels claim, but are acts of the devil who possesses and empowers Jesus. People who believe that Jesus went about healing the halt and the lame by his merest word are deluded. If they are to escape the charge, they must show that (a) miracles are possible; (b) that Jesus performed miracles; and (c) that Jesus healed through the power of God and was not a demon-possessed magician. And, of course, it can't be done, can it?

I believe in miracles.

Wise as Serpents

We must be as wise as serpents. If we are venturing forth like sheep among wolves, we had better be *(Gospel of Matthew 10:16)*. First, then, the claim that miracles are impossible because they violate what we know about the way the universe works. But most people in the world believe that miracles are possible and that they do not run counter to the universe as they know it. People who believe in God, believe that God created all that exists and that God's activity within creation is not a violation of creation but a participation within the created world. To prove that miracles are impossible, it is necessary to prove that God does not exist, that creation simply came to be as a result of accidental chemistry. Many people, most people, do not believe that. However, their belief is belief, not scientifically verified data. When the magicians of Pharaoh were confronted by the miraculous activities of Moses and Aaron, they said, *This is the finger of God (Book of the Exodus 8:19).* There is no way an historian, or scientist, or biblical scholar, can assert that the magicians were right in their estimation of what they saw before their eyes. Indeed, the magicians do not manage to convince Pharaoh of their claim; nor do they convince us. They can be certain of what they have seen but they can only assert that God was responsible if, in fact, they have come to believe in Moses' God. In other words, when we declare that a miracle has happened, we are declaring that we believe in a God who is concerned to participate in our world. That is an act of faith. A scientist may say that he believes that God created the world but he can do so, not as a scientist, but as a believer.

There are seventeen accounts of healings in the Gospels, including three reports of Jesus bringing people back to life; there are six accounts of Jesus healing people by exorcism, and there are six other miraculous events which include turning water into wine, calming storms, multiplying loaves and fishes, and walking on water. As well as these, there are numerous summary accounts of Jesus going about the countryside healing all the sick who were brought to him. All of the Gospels, independently of each other, record that Jesus was a miraculous healer.

A fair assessment of the evidence would have to conclude that at least some people (Gospel writers and their informants, for example) believed that the stories they were told about Jesus were accounts of what happened. Not only did they affirm that Jesus healed miraculously but they confronted objections made by Jewish authorities and others who denied or doubted the veracity of what they recorded. Not only that, but the Gospels affirm that the person of Jesus, his preoccupation with the kingdom of God, and his healing work are all of a piece. Jesus welcomed people, conversed with them about the the kingdom of God, healed all who were in need of healing, for one purpose and as one grand design: *to seek and to save that which is lost (Gospel of Luke 19:10)*. They believed that the person of Jesus, the words of Jesus, the doings of Jesus, were all of a piece. The man, his words, and his deeds, proclaim that God remembered.

Whether the claim is true or not is a matter of faith. That is what is at stake in the controversy about Beelzebul. The worldview which Jesus and many (but by no means all) of his fellow Jews shared was, as we have seen, black and white. Cosmic forces of evil were drawn up against the forces of God and the peoples of the world suffered from the ravages of these demonic powers which sought to crush humanity, all God's people, in their war with God. To allege that Jesus overcame evil through the power of Beelzebul, is to assert that Jesus is on the side of the demons, a mere tool used by them to destroy the good and enthrone the bad. Listen to and ponder on the full defence which Jesus made against such a charge:

> He was driving out a demon which was dumb. When the demon departed the dumb man spoke, and the crowds were astonished. But some of them said, 'He drives out demons by

Beelzebul, the Ruler of Demons'. Others, putting him to the test, sought a sign from heaven. Knowing their thoughts, he said to them, 'Every kingdom divided against itself is laid waste, and house after house collapses. And if Satan is divided against himself, how can his kingdom stand? – for you are saying that I drive out demons by Beelzebul. If I drive out demons by Beelzebul, by whom do your sons [= associates] cast them out? Therefore they will be your judges. But if I drive out demons by the finger of God, the kingdom of God has indeed come upon you. When a strong man who is fully armed guards his palace, his possessions are in peace; but when a stronger man than he attacks him and conquerors him, the stronger man takes away the armour in which he trusted, and divides the spoils.
Gospel of Luke 11:14-22

Jesus is the stronger man because the source of his strength is God and he is empowered to defeat his weaker opponent, to destroy all those cosmic, demonic powers who bear arms against God. The stronger man storms the citadel of Satan, routs the enemy and frees all who are enslaved therein. The evil kingdom of Satan must give way to the kingdom of God. Jesus is God's warrior. Or, to put it as Luke does, *the power of the Lord was with him for healing (Gospel of Luke 5:17).*

Who Were Healed?
The answer is pretty well everybody. Consider:
   A man possessed by a demonic spirit (4:31-37)
   A mother-in-law (4:38-39)
   A man full of leprosy (5:12-14)
   A man who was paralysed (5:18-26)
   A sick slave (7:1-10)
   A man infested by a legion of devils (8:26-39)
   A woman with a haemorrhage (8:43-48)
   A crowd of hungry people fed (9:12-17)
   An epileptic boy (9:37-43)
   A bent woman (13:10-17)
   A man with oedema (14:1-5)
   Ten lepers cleansed (17:11-19)

A blind beggar (18:35-43)
A dead son restored to his mother (7:11-17)
And a dead daughter to her father (8:40-56)

Then there are six accounts scattered throughout the four Gospels of miraculous events which demand control over natural forces:
Cursing of a fig tree (*Gospel of Matthew* 21:18-20)
A miraculous catch of fish (*Gospel of Luke* 5:1-11)
Walking on water (*Gospel of Mark* 6:45-52)
The stilling of a storm (*Gospel of Luke* 8:22-25)
Changing water into wine (*Gospel of John* 2:1-11)
Multiplying bread and fish (*Gospel of Luke* 9:12-17)

To these must be added numerous summary passages where Luke reports that healing the sick was an everyday occurrence:

When the sun was going down, all those who had people suffering from various diseases brought them to him. He laid his hands on each one of them and healed them. Demons, too, went out from many, shouting out, 'You are the son of God.' *Gospel of Luke 4:40-41*

News about him spread more and more, and great crowds gathered to listen and to be healed by him of their illnesses. *Gospel of Luke 5:15*

There was a great crowd ... who had come to hear him and to be cured of their diseases, and those who were troubled by unclean spirits were being healed. All the crowd were seeking to touch him, because power was coming out from him and curing them all. *Gospel of Luke 6:17-19*

Hearing and healing were the order of the day. Jesus welcomed people, he talked with them, and he healed those who had need of healing. The historian will have to admit that the people who wrote the Gospels were convinced that Jesus of Nazareth was a miracle-worker. But that is as far as historians can go. To go the extra mile, and see in the healing activities of Jesus the finger of God, demands an act of faith.

Welcoming, Chatting, Healing: A Must
The welcome which Jesus gave to people, the animated discussions about God, and the healing of all who needed healing, are

all of a piece. The purpose of the welcoming, the chatting, the healing, is to define what the kingdom of God is all about. To understand what Jesus means when he says, *I must be gospelling the kingdom of God (Gospel of Luke 4:43)*, we need to analyse his sentence with all the care we can muster.

I must be gospelling the kingdom of God. The 'I' in Jesus' sentence is, as we shall see, the Messiah of God, the Son of God, the man of prayer, the Son of Man, the crucified and risen Lord. As we explore what these designations might mean, we will be drawn into the God-with-us who comes to us as the man from Nazareth. But the fulness of his identity will emerge only when we have walked with him on the way of welcoming, chatting, healing, and feasting – and much else besides. And we must walk, too, to the place of the cross. And we must stand at the empty tomb.

I must be gospelling the kingdom of God. The 'must' in the sentence of Jesus is a revelation in itself. Just posting before our eyes the sentences in which we find the word in Luke's Gospel is a revelation. You really MUST work your way through these passages of God's holy words to grasp the enormity of what is happening, and the astonishing revelation that is been made to you:

Why is it that you are seeking me? Did you not know that I MUST be in my Father's house? *Gospel of Luke 2:49*

I MUST be gospelling the kingdom of God in other cities also. *Gospel of Luke 4:43*

The Son of Man MUST suffer many things, be rejected by the elders, the chief priests and the scribes, and be put to death and rise again on the third day.
Gospel of Luke 9:22 and look up 17:25

When they bring you before synagogues, before rulers and authorities, do not be anxious how you will defend yourselves, or what you will say, for the Holy Spirit will teach you at that time what you MUST say. *Gospel of Luke 12:11-12*

Whereupon [after Jesus had healed a woman] the synagogue officer, angry because Jesus had healed on the Sabbath, said to the crowd, 'There are six days on which work MUST be done; so come and be healed on them, and not on the

Sabbath'. But the Lord answered him and said, 'You hypocrites! Does not everyone of you on the Sabbath release his ox and his ass from the stall and bring them to water? MUST not this woman, a daughter of Abraham, bound by Satan for eighteen years, be released from this imprisonment on the Sabbath Day?' *Gospel of Luke 13:14-16*

Yet I MUST continue my journey today and tomorrow and the next day, because it is impossible that a prophet should die outside Jerusalem. *Gospel of Luke 13:33*

It was a MUST that we rejoiced and were glad, because this brother of yours was dead and has come to life, he was lost and has been found. *Gospel of Luke 15:32*

He told them a parable about how they MUST pray continually and not be discouraged. *Gospel of Luke 18:1*

When he came to the place, Jesus looked up and saw him, and said to him, 'Zacchaeus, make haste and come down; today I MUST stay in your house.' *Gospel of Luke 19:5*

But when you hear of wars and disruptions do not be frightened. These things MUST happen first, but the end is not at hand yet. *Gospel of Luke 21:9*

The day of the Unleavened Bread came, on which the Passover MUST be sacrificed. *Gospel of Luke 22:7*

I tell you this, that which has been written [by God] MUST still be fulfilled in me. *Gospel of Luke 22:37*

Why are you seeking among the dead him who is alive? Remember how he said to you while he was still in Galilee that the Son of Man MUST be delivered into the hands of sinful men, be crucified and on the third day rise again.
Gospel of Luke 24:7

Oh how lacking in understanding you are! How slow of heart to believe all the things of which the prophets spoke! WAS IT NOT NECESSARY [MUST] for the Messiah to suffer these things and to enter into his glory?
Gospel of Luke 24:25-26

> These statements which I made to you while I was still with
> you, saying that all that is written concerning me in the Law
> of Moses, the Prophets and the Psalms, MUST be fulfilled.
> *Gospel of Luke 24:44*

Every MUST here describes a divine necessity. Each states what
must be and what *must* be done and what *must* be said because
that is what God has determined. Jesus must be in the Temple
because that is where God wanted him to be. Jesus must take up
his cross because that is what God wanted him to do. Jesus must
heal the disfigured woman because that is God's will. Jesus
must stay in the house of the great sinner Zacchaeus because
God has determined that salvation must visit that family on the
day that is the today of Jesus. Jesus must do all that he does and
say all that he says because that is what the holy words of God,
written in the scriptures, have shown to be the will of God. Jesus
must be who he was and who he is because God said IT MUST
BE SO!

The miracles of healing are intended to reveal the nature of
the God who has remembered the plight of humanity over-
whelmed by evil. The cruel world of Israel's history is not unique.
Whether we share the ancient view that demonic powers deface
the image of God in creation is neither here nor there. That our
world is full of good people, that there are many saintly people
going about doing good does not disguise the fact that, individ-
ually and collectively, human beings need God's steadfast love
if men and women, and all creation, are to be what they are
meant to be. To know God in this life is to know that we are
loved. That is what God's work of healing reveals to us in the
man from Nazareth. The kingdom of God is the healing of the
halt and the lame, the deaf and the blind. The kingdom of God is
peopled with broken hearts who know that they are mended,
who know that they are loved, unconditionally, steadfastly. The
kingdom is where lost are found and dead come to life again.
The kingdom of God, and the healing that is its hallmark, is a
MUST for God.

Welcoming, Chatting, Healing: Gospelling
I must be gospelling the kingdom of God. Of course, there is no such English word as 'gospelling'. But I have invented it in order to emphasise that Luke (writing in Greek) always used a verb to characterise what Jesus was doing in his preaching. He was good-newsing people. A look at the background to the word 'gospel' and my new word 'gospelling' will help us to grasp what an extraordinary message Jesus was discussing with the crowds who flocked to hear him on the hillsides of Galilee.

The Greek noun from which we derive our English 'gospel' and from which Luke's verb is derived comes from a word meaning 'good messenger'. The good messenger was the one who brought news from the battlefield that victory had been achieved and celebrations could begin. When the messenger proclaimed the good news of victory over enemies, he was said to be 'gospelling' the anxious crowds and signalling the festive celebrations to begin. After twenty-six and a bit miles, the messenger from the battlefield of Marathon proclaimed the gospel that we've won and the celebrations can begin. In the Roman world, an *evangelium* (the Latin version) might be the good news of the emperor's birth, his coming of age, and, of course, his accession to the imperial throne. All were celebrated with public holidays and official festivities. Rome did not neglect the business of spin and propaganda.

We find much the same use of the words 'gospel' and 'gospelling' in the Bible. When messengers arrive from the field to announce a victory to King David, the welcome report is called 'gospel'. As we have seen, when the prophet Nahum called for festivities to celebrate the news that the hated city of Nineveh had been destroyed, he was, of course, working on the principle that my enemy's defeat is a victory for me, no matter who caused it. The word he used to characterise this longed-for military victory over an old enemy was 'gospel'. To remind ourselves:

Look!
There on the mountains!
The feet of one bringing gospel!
The one proclaiming peace!
Judah!

> Celebrate your feast-days,
> fulfil what you swore!
> Never again will the wicked invade you!
> They are annihilated!
> *Book of Nahum 1:15*

Then something new happened to the word. The prophet Isaiah took over the word but used it in an altogether new way. The word retains the sense of a report of a victory in battle but the victory has moved from the human plane to the divine. We can grasp what Isaiah has done by remembering our confirmation.

When Christians are confirmed, that is, when the fulness of the gifts of the Holy Spirit are conferred on those who affirm their faith (if that is what confirmation is all about), some words of Isaiah spell out what is at the heart of the matter:

> There shall come forth a shoot
> from the stump of Jesse,
> a branch shall grow out of his roots.
> And the Spirit of the Lord
> shall rest upon him,
> the spirit of wisdom,
> and understanding,
> the spirit of counsel,
> the spirit of might,
> the spirit of knowledge,
> and the fear of the Lord.
> And his delight shall be in the fear of the Lord.
> *Book of Isaiah 11:1-3*

There are six gifts of the Spirit here but later (Greek) editions of the *Book of Isaiah* added another, piety, thus completing the Seven Gifts of the Holy Spirit, familiar to devotees of catechisms. What Isaiah was praying for was that a descendant of Jesse (a shoot from the stump of Jesse), the father of King David, would appear to lead the people of God to safety and peace, and to a time of justice and contentment. Such a kingly figure would possess God's gifts in abundance and so be a fit shepherd for a people who were lost in the storms of a chaotic world. When we move to a more confident part of the *Book of Isaiah*, hope has given way to the certainty that God has acted and the longed-for

shoot from the stump of Jesse has arrived and is about to begin
to rescue God's people from all the vicissitudes of foreign domination and the calamities of exile. We do not know to whom the
prophetical words refer but Isaiah's pictures of a glorious delivery certainly resonate with a Christian imagination:

> The Spirit of the Lord God is upon me,
> because he has anointed me
> to gospel the poor;
> he has sent me to heal the broken of heart,
> to shout out like a herald liberty to captive peoples,
> and sight to the blind,
> and to proclaim a year of God's welcoming.
> *Book of Isaiah 61:1-2 (Greek Version)*

There is, says Isaiah, or at least there will be, a day of God's victory over all the forces which enslave God's people, a victory
over all powers and dominions which bind and fetter and enslave. Isaiah has moved the field of battle from the earthly do-
main to the cosmic spheres, to that realm where good confronts
evil and carries off the spoils. You will recall that in Luke's
Gospel Jesus appropriates the words of Isaiah as his mission
statement *(Gospel of Luke 4:18-19)* and claims that *Today this scripture has been fulfilled in your sight (Gospel of Luke 4:21).* Jesus is
claiming to be the one who fulfills the hopes long ago expressed
by the optimistic prophet.

Gospelling, Demons, and Healings

Gospelling, announcing to people that a great victory has been
won, that their fears are at an end, is most clearly affirmed in the
casting out of demons. To many in the ancient world, illnesses
and diseases were the work of demonic spirits, spirits who
struck people down with every kind of misfortune. We may be
more sophisticated in our understanding of all the frailties that
flesh is heir to but the devastation visited upon us by illness is no
less real. Jesus confronted evil spirits with authority and power
and restored people bound by Satan to well-being and peace.
The very first healing after Jesus had announced his mission is
brought about by casting out an unclean demon:

> He came to Capernaum, a city of Galilee, and taught them on

the Sabbaths. They were amazed at his teaching for his word carried power. And in the synagogue there was a man with the spirit of an unclean demon, and he cried out with aloud voice, saying, 'Ah! What is there between us, Jesus of Nazareth? You have come to destroy us! I know who you are, the Holy One of God!' But Jesus stopped him in his tracks, saying, 'Be silent! Come out of him!' The demon threw him down in the midst of them and came out of him without doing him any harm. They were all struck with amazement, and they were saying to one another, 'What word is this? For with power and might he commands unclean spirits and they depart.' And the report about him echoed in every place throughout the region. *Gospel of Luke 4:31-37*

A summary account follows almost immediately:

When the sun was setting, all those who had people suffering from various diseases brought them to him. He laid his hands upon each one of them and healed them. Demons, too, went out from many, shouting out, 'You are the Son of God!' But he checked them and did not allow them to speak, because they knew that he was the Messiah.
Gospel of Luke 4:40-41

There is much here to grasp. Immediately on announcing his purpose under God, Jesus storms the citadel of the enemy. The stronger man takes the attack to the enemy and sets about freeing one of God's creatures from demonic imprisonment. The supernatural beings know well who the enemy is, the Holy One of God, the Son of God, the Messiah. And they know, too, that he has come to destroy them, to shatter the kingdom of evil and build the kingdom of God. In their defeat, the demons recognise who Jesus is, where he comes from, what his power is, what his mission is, and what the inevitable outcome will be.

At root, this is what the healing miracles are about. To be sure, people are healed. But each healing is a battle in a wider war, a war in which God has at last engaged and in which there can be only one outcome. The kingdom of God is not a temporary respite; it is a new and secure home for all who are saved from the demonic powers which seek, not to save, but to destroy. This is power on behalf of people and the crowds flock to welcome the one who embodies all the hopes of the prophet Isaiah.

And notice what might pass as a tiny detail as the crowds rush with their sick to the man from Nazareth: he laid his hands on each one of them. Even lepers: *He stretched out his hand and touched him (Gospel of Luke 5:13).* To those who are unclean, who are, so it is said, unacceptable to God, Jesus reaches out, touches, and, in taking on their status of uncleanness, he confers on them his status of sonship.

Curing, Healing, Saving

There is more. Jesus does more than cure people. He heals them. The paralysed man has his sins forgiven as his legs are strengthened *(Gospel of Luke 5:17-26).* The sins of the woman of the town are forgiven and on her is conferred the status of peace *(Gospel of Luke 7:36-50).* The poor woman with the haemorrhage touches him, and, not only is she made clean again, but her status as a true daughter of Abraham is proclaimed and she, too, is at peace *(Gospel of Luke 8:43-48).* Ten lepers are made clean but it is the one who comes back to Jesus to give thanks to God (!) who recognises what has really happened: he has been made whole, saved, brought to contentment and peace *(Gospel of Luke 17:11-19).*

And finally ...

There is no *finally* when it comes to kingdom coming and the healing touch of the finger of God. The kingdom of God is on earth as it is in heaven. But it is still coming to us. It is present to us and yet it lies ahead. When John the Baptist sought reassurance that his prophetic instincts about Jesus were right, Jesus sends the answer:

> Go tell John what you have seen and heard: the blind recover sight, the lame walk, lepers are made clean, the deaf hear, the dead are raised, and the poor are gospelled, and those who take no offence at me are blessed. *Gospel of Luke 7:22*

These are the signs. Where is the evidence? One can't help wondering about the Jesus who did his healing on the hillsides and in the villages of Galilee. Where is he? – this Jesus who was so close that the woman could reach out and touch him. Is he so near now? Is the Jesus who *is* quite so near, quite so accessible as the Jesus who *was*? Where is the finger of God casting out our demons?

CHAPTER EIGHT

Feeding People ...

The day began to wane. The Twelve came and said to him, 'Send the crowd away in order that they may go into the villages and farms around to lodge and to find food, for we are in a desert place'. But he said to them, 'You give them to eat'. They said, 'We have no more than five loaves and two fish, unless we are to go and buy food for all this people'. Now they were about five thousand men. He said to his disciples, 'Have them recline in groups of about fifty'. They did so and and made them all stretch out [on the ground]. He took the five loaves and the two fish, looked up to heaven, said a blessing over them, and broke them, and gave to the disciples to set before the crowd. *And all ate and were satisfied.* What was left over after them was collected, twelve baskets of left-overs. *Gospel of Luke 9:12-17*

Why is it that the only miracle story told in all four Gospels is the the Feeding of the Five Thousand? Why is it that the Feeding of the Five Thousand (or Four Thousand), is told six times in the four Gospels? Why did St Matthew *(Gospel of Matthew 14:1-21* and in the very next chapter, *15:32-39)* and St Mark *(Gospel of Mark 6:32-44* and *8:1-10)* tell the story twice? And why do all the Gospels take up so much precious space on a writing-scroll to record that Jesus was eating and drinking? Why is there so much eating and drinking in the urgent gospelling of the kingdom of God that Jesus and his crowd become a byword for partying (a glutton and wine-drinker, a friend of tax collectors and sinners!)? And why does Jesus revel in the accusation? Why does he insist that eating and drinking is at the heart of his coming, with all that that word implies *(... has come to seek and to save that which is lost)*? And why, at the death, when he wanted to leave a remembrance that spoke of his very being, a sign that went to the very heart of the man, he left a table, and bread and wine?

First, be struck by the weight of it all, and that means ploughing through it. We need to post every sentence which mentions eating and drinking. This is known as doing your homework:

Full of the Holy Spirit, Jesus returned from the Jordan and was led by the Spirit into the desert for forty days, being put to the test by the devil. And he ate nothing during those days, and when they were completed he was hungry. The devil said to him, 'If you are the Son of God, tell this stone to turn into bread'. But Jesus, in answering him, was saying, 'It is written, *A man does not live by bread alone*'.
Gospel of Luke 4:1-2

After these things [After *what things?* Look it up, please!], he went out and saw a tax-collector named Levi sitting at the receipt of custom, and he said to him, 'Follow me'. He left everything, and rose and followed him. Levi gave a great party for him in his house. And there was a large crowd of tax-collectors and others who reclined with them. The Pharisees and their scribes carped at his disciples, saying, 'Why do you eat and drink with tax-collectors and sinners?'
Gospel of Luke 5:27-31

They [=The Pharisees and their scribes] said to him, 'John's disciples fast frequently and offer prayers, and so do associates of the Pharisees, but yours eat and drink'. He said to them, 'Can you make the friends of the bridegroom fast while the bridegroom is with them?'
Gospel of Luke 5:32-34

Blessed are you who hunger now, for you shall be satisfied!
Gospel of Luke 6:21

Woe to you who are full now, for you shall go hungry!
Gospel of Luke 6:25

John the Baptist has come neither eating bread nor drinking wine, and you were saying, 'He is demon-possessed!' The Son of Man has come eating and drinking, and you are saying, 'Look, a glutton and wine-drinker, a friend of tax-collectors and sinners!' *Gospel of Luke 7:33-34*

One of the Pharisees asked him to eat with him. He entered the Pharisee's house and reclined at table. And, behold, there was in the city a woman of a certain kind, a sinner. Knowing that he was eating in the house of the Pharisee, she brought an alabaster jar of perfume … *Gospel of Luke 7:36-50*

Taking her by the hand, he cried, 'Little girl, get up!' Her spirit returned and she got up at once. He gave orders that she be given to eat. *Gospel of Luke 8:53-54*

Lodge in that house, eating and drinking what they provide. *Gospel of Luke 10:7*

When he had spoken, a Pharisee invited him to a meal with him. He went in and sat down. The Pharisee, seeing this, was astonished that he had not washed before the meal. *Gospel of Luke 11:37-38*

Life in more than food, and the body than clothes. Consider the crows; they do not sow, nor do they reap; they have no store-room nor barn; yet God feeds them. *Gospel of Luke 12:23-24*

Blessed are those slaves whom the master, when he comes, will find keeping watch. Amen I say to you, he will put on an apron, recline them at table, and come and attend to them. *Gospel of Luke 12:37-38*

Someone said to him, 'Lord, are those who are being saved few in number?' He said to them, 'Strive to enter by the narrow door, for I tell you, many try to enter and will not be strong enough. When the householder gets up and shuts the door, and you stand outside and knock at the door saying, "Lord, Lord, open up for us!", he will answer, saying to them, "I don't know where you are from!" Then you will say, "We ate and drank with you, and you taught in our streets." But he will say, I tell you, I don't know where you come from; depart from me all you workers of injustice. There will be weeping and gnashing of teeth there, when you see Abraham, Isaac and Jacob, and all the prophets in the kingdom of God, but you yourselves thrown out. They will come from east and west, north and south, and recline at table in the kingdom of God!' *Gospel of Luke 13:22-29*

When he entered the house of one of the chief men of the Pharisees on the Sabbath to eat, they were watching him for in front of him was a man suffering from dropsy ...
Gospel of Luke 14:1-2

These upholders of Torah and the sacred traditions of their ancestors, these chief men of the Pharisees, Luke tells us quite bluntly, were suspicious and, indeed, appalled at the attitudes struck by Jesus of Nazareth. They were indignant at his searching questions: *Is it lawful to heal on the Sabbath or isn't it?* They kept silent, for the most part. So Jesus, (I can't help feeling), with a delicious mischievous smile on his face but with steel in his voice, told very uncomfortable stories, uncomfortable then, and uncomfortable now:

He spoke a parable to those who reclined at table as he watched how they were choosing the top places. He said to them:

'When you are invited by anyone to a wedding feast do not recline in the top place, in case a more important person than you has been invited by the host, and he who invited both of you comes and says to you, "Give place to this man", and then with shame you will go to take the bottom place. But when you are invited, go and sit in the bottom place so that when he who has invited you comes he will say to you, "Friend, go up higher." Then you will have honour before all who are at table with you. For everyone who raises himself high will be humbled, and he who humbles himself will be raised high.'

He said also to his host: 'When you give lunch or dinner do not ask your friends or your brothers or your relatives or rich neighbours, lest they invite you back and you are repaid. Whenever you give a party invite rather the poor, the crippled, the lame, the blind; and you will be blessed, because they have not the means to repay you; for you will be repaid at the resurrection of the righteous.'

When one of those who were reclining at table with him heard this, he said to Jesus: 'Blessed is the one who eats in the kingdom of God!' But Jesus said to him:

'A man was giving a great feast and invited many guests. At the time of the feast he sent his slave to tell those who had been invited, "Come, for everything is now ready." All of them, with one accord, began to make excuses. The first said, "I have bought a field and I really must go out to see it. Please excuse me." Another said, "I have bought five pair of oxen and I'm on my way to try them out. Please excuse me." Another said, "I have married a wife, and so I can't come." The slave came and told his master these things. Then the master of the house became angry and said to his slave, "Go out quickly into the streets and alleys of the city, and bring in here the poor, the crippled, the blind, and the lame." The slave said, "Sir, I've done what you ordered, and there is still room." Then the master said to the slave, "Go out into the roads and hedges and make them come in, that my house may be filled. I tell you that none of those who were invited shall taste of my feast!"'
Gospel of Luke 14:15-24

We have met some of these stories before. But we must hear now the acerbity in the voice of the man from Nazareth; we must listen to the anger of a peasant from Galilee who, brought up far from the niceties of fashionable etiquette, finds himself condescendingly invited to recline at table with the rich, and with the hostility of host and guests scarcely disguised: *they were watching him*. Were they, indeed? The courtesies which traditions of hospitality demand are subverted in the interests of imprisoning God within the confines of convenient doctrine. It is convenient to hide behind *Thou shalt keep holy the Sabbath Day*. It is called mindless religion, disguised as piety. It is quite another to stretch heart and mind to understand that the Sabbath was made by God for humanity's good, not for God's convenience. When Simon the Pharisee insulted Jesus by neglecting even a modicum of common courtesy, Jesus tore into him, telling him, first, that he had no manners, and, secondly, that his closed mind and heart excommunicated him from the world of God's peace to which Jesus has raised the woman (*Gospel of Luke 7:36-50*).

We must press on with the eating and drinking reports which so besmirched the reputation of Jesus with his betters:

The Pharisees and the scribes were murmuring, saying, 'This fellow welcomes sinners and eats with them.'
Gospel of Luke 15:2

'Bring the fatted calf, kill it, and let us eat and rejoice, because this son of mine was dead and has come to life again, was lost and is found.' And they began to celebrate. But ...
Gospel of Luke 15:23-24

There was a certain man and he was rich. Forever clothed in purple and fine linen, he feasted sumptuously every day. A man named Lazarus, a poor man, a man covered in sores, lay at his gate, hoping to be filled with whatever fell from the rich man's table. Not only that, but the dogs came and licked his sores. *Gospel of Luke 16:19-21*

'Zacchaeus, make haste and come down; today I must stay in your house.' He made haste and came down, and welcomed him joyfully. Seeing this, they all murmured, saying, 'He has gone to stay with a sinner!' *Gospel of Luke 19:6-7*

He said to his disciples in the hearing of all the people, 'Beware of the scribes who like to walk about in robes and love greetings in the market-places, the chief seats in synagogues, and the best places at feasts, but who devour widows' houses and for show offer long prayers; they will receive greater condemnation'. *Gospel of Luke 20:45-47*

And then the hour came; he sat down, his apostles with him. And he said to them, 'With great longing I have desired to eat this Passover with you before I suffer. For I tell you that I shall eat it no more until it is fulfilled in the kingdom of God. When he had received the cup, giving thanks, he said, 'Take this and share it among yourselves; **for I tell you, from now on I shall not drink of the fruit of the vine until the kingdom of God has come.' Taking bread and giving thanks, he broke it and gave it to them, saying, 'This is my body, which is given for you. Do this in remembrance of me'. And he did the same with the cup after the meal, saying, 'This cup is the new covenant with my blood, which is poured out for you.** But, behold, the hand of the one who is handing me over is with me at table; for the Son of Man indeed goes in accordance with what has been determined. Yet woe to that man through whom he is handed over!' They began to argue one with another which of them in that case it might be, who was to do this. *Gospel of Luke 22:14-23*

[**–** Readers should be aware that there are serious differences in the earliest Greek manuscripts of the sentences between asterisks. Some of these verses are more doubtfully original than others. Since we have only copies of Luke' Gospel made more than one hundred years after it was written, we cannot establish what Luke wrote at this point. There is the possibility that he himself may have written these sentences differently as he produced copies of his gospel (though we have no evidence of this) or scribes who made copies may have altered Luke's text to comply with the words used in the Eucharist in their communities. The Greek text I have followed reflects the text most widely used among early Christian communities. It is deeply rewarding to reflect on the fact that the exact words spoken by Jesus over the bread and wine are not available to us in any of the Gospels.]

Who is the greater, the one who sits at table or the one who serves? Is it not the one who sits at table? But I am among you as one who serves. You are those who have remained with me in my trials; and just as my Father has assigned to me a kingdom, so I assign to you to eat and drink at my table in my kingdom, and to sit on thrones judging the twelve tribes of Israel. *Gospel of Luke 22:27-30*

He withdrew from them about a stone's throw, and kneeling down he prayed, saying, 'Father, if you wish, take this cup from me; yet not my will but yours be done.'
Gospel of Luke 22:41-42

The soldiers also were mocking him, coming to him and offering him sour wine (vinegar), and saying, 'If you are the King of the Jews, save yourself.' *Gospel of Luke 23:36-37*

Two of them were going that same day to a village named Emmaus … they drew near to the village … he sat down with them and took bread, said the blessing, broke it and gave it to them ... and they recognised him in the breaking of the bread. *Gospel of Luke 24:13-35*

Because of their joy, they were disbelieving and still wondering. Jesus said to them, 'Have you anything here to eat?' And they offered him a piece of broiled fish, and he took it and ate it in their presence. *Gospel of Luke 24:41-43*

There are great riches to be garnered by reflecting on eating and drinking in Luke's Gospel. But the first step to reflection is amazement at the volume of material we have just read through. Then we need to ponder what was happening at meals in Luke's Gospel, how eating and drinking work as metaphors, and why eating and drinking become sacrament.

We must take time out. Eating and drinking is of such profound importance in Luke's Gospel, indeed, in all the Gospels, and in the life of the church, that we must reflect on matters which will help us to understand why. We need to delve into the imaginative past of Israel's people.

Ruth

A woman of worth. The story of Ruth, told as an historical fiction in the *Book of Ruth*, is a passionate love story. But it is told with agonising restraint, with a delicacy that emphasises the passion beneath the everyday struggle for survival. The very ordinariness of its daily tragedies (famine, exile, death, childlessness, widowhood, exile again, poverty) serves to underscore the depth of love and desire which shimmer beneath the calculated plotting to engineer the match which will provide a meal ticket. In a harsh world, the story of Ruth and Boaz sings of the indomitable human spirit that knows what it is to find love and be loved.

By now you will have read the story yourself. A tiny interlude in the intricate web of this harsh romantic tale will serve to set us on our way to understanding:

When it was time to eat, Boaz said to [Ruth], 'Come here, and eat some bread, and dip your bread into the wine.' So she sat down beside the reapers, and he heaped up for her some roasted grain. She ate until she was satisfied, and she had some left over. *Book of Ruth 2:14*

Two people falling in love. Bread and wine. A simple sharing. What is happening here: eating together, dipping a bit of
bread into the same bowl of wine, a man heaping up as much as
the woman could eat, she eating as much as he offered, both satisfied and plenty left over? What is being said, though no words
are exchanged? What is being offered, though no demands are
made? What is being promised, what is being anticipated, what
future has crept into the present in a bit of bread and wine? And
when they next meet, where are they?

Manna

When the manna first appeared, nobody knew what it was.
Moses explained, *It is the bread which the Lord has given you to eat*
(Book of Exodus 16:15). The manna appeared each morning but
only sufficient for each day. No hoarding, no bigger barns. Daily
bread. Anyone who tried to gather more than a day's food
found that the extra was eaten up by worms overnight. Except
for one omer (an omer is a tenth of an ephah, the Bible tells us;
say, about what would fill a decent mixing bowl). This is what
God commanded Moses to tell the people:

> Let an omer be kept throughout your generations, in order
> that they may see the food with which I fed you in the desert,
> when I brought you out of the land of Egypt.
> *Book of the Exodus 16:32*

To his brother, the priest Aaron, Moses said,

> Take a jar, put an omer of manna in it, and place it before the
> Lord so that it will be kept throughout all your generations.
> *Book of the Exodus 16:33*

The jar was placed in the Ark of the Covenant to remind everyone that God fed the people, that God gave them daily bread,
that the covenant promise, *I will be your God,* demanded of God
that people be fed. It was a reminder that what happened in the
past, happens for all generations. God remembers.

Some More Stories
A French Story: Melodies of the Past

One day, the French playwright, poet, novelist and film
director, Jean Cocteau (1889-1963), returned, after a long

absence, to the village where he had grown up. He remembered how he used to walk up the street from his home on the way to school, trailing his finger along the wall that skirted the path.

On his visit to the place of his childhood, the old man walked the once familiar street, trailing his finger along the wall. But the gesture did not summon up for him any sense of the past. Suddenly, he realised that he had been smaller then. So he bent down, closed his eyes, and again traced his finger along the wall – this time at the level of a little boy.

Cocteau later wrote of his experience: 'Just as the needle picks up the melody from the record, I observed the melody of the past with my hand. I found everything: my cape, the leather of my satchel, the names of my friends and those of my teachers, certain expressions I had used, the sound of my grandfather's voice …'

An American Story: Where we used to Be

They straightened up the Mississippi River in places, to make room for houses and liveable acreage. Occasionally, the river floods these places. 'Floods' is the word they use but, in fact, it is not flooding, it is remembering. Remembering where it used to be. All water has perfect memory and is trying to get back to where it was. Writers are like that: remembering where they were, what valley we ran through, what banks were like, the light that was there and the route back to our original place. *Toni Morrison*

An English Story: Gifts of Healing

Claire decided to run away. She had spent all her young life in Local Authority care, moved from one unsuccessful fostering to another. The one she was in now was hopeless: a husband and wife with no children of their own. They quarrelled endlessly – argument and acrimony filled the air of every day. Claire felt that she was the cause of the bickering and back-biting. So she ran away.

Then she thought that this was not the thing to do. If she were the cause of so much pain, surely she should have stayed to try to explain, to try to heal, to tell that love is not like that. She could, perhaps, help them to love each other and, then, maybe her. So she decided to go back. On her way, she went into Woolworths and bought a few trinkets. When the husband and wife answered the door, she held out the little things in her hands: 'I brung these.' *ITV Play: Claire*

An Islamic Story: Making Brothers
Saladin the Magnificent, the Khalif of Cairo, ruler of all the peoples of Islam, the greatest military commander of his day, decided to end, once and for all, Christian meddling in the Middle East. He would destroy these European infidels who, on the pretext of guarding the holy places in Palestine of their prophet Jesus – peace be upon his name – marauded and pillaged the land. He moved his army against the Crusaders and managed to surround their huge army at a place called the Horns of Hattin, overlooking Lake Kinnereth (the Sea of Galilee). It was June, 1187. Saladin sealed off all means of escape and let the European army, with its bulky armour and huge shire horses (unlike the nimble Arab horses), sit it out in the heat. The Christians ran out of water. They could see the beautiful fresh water of the lovely lake shimmering below but they could not reach it. Saladin let them sit in the burning sun.

Then, when the wind was right, on July 4, he set fire to the grass and the smoke caused havoc among the horses and soldiers of the invaders. Saladin moved to the attack and cut the enemy to pieces. It was, effectively, the end of Christian Europe's influence in the land of Palestine.

Some knights were taken prisoner and, rather than instant death or slavery, Saladin decided to provide the spectacle of a public execution on the morrow to entertain his victorious troops. On the next morning, Saladin inquired of the officer who had guarded the prisoners: 'Are these men ready to die?' 'Yes, I have fed them with bread and water. They are ready to die.'

When the unfortunate prisoners were marched before Saladin the Magnificent, he said to them, 'Go home, my brothers; you have eaten my bread. Therefore you are my brothers. You cannot kill your brother.'

Jesus feeding people, sitting down and eating with them, whether friends or foes, Jesus speaking love in bread and wine, manna for all generations, doing memory in eucharist, communion, sacrifice, and promise. You can't analyse the how of it. All you can do is listen to the stories. And you will be satisfied. And there will be plenty left over for everyone forever more.

CHAPTER NINE

Time Out: Playing Catch-up

Our task as Christians is to gospel our time and our place with the embrace of Jesus of Nazareth. The task undertaken by St Luke was essentially the same as ours. He never met Jesus; as far as we know, he never set foot in Galilee, nor did he walk the streets of Jerusalem. He was not a Jew. He did not speak the same language as Jesus and he did not share the same cultural background. To find Jesus, he had to delve into the past. Then he had to translate what he found there into his time and his place, to make the then-Jesus a now-Jesus. He had to listen to stories told, and told again; he had to read whatever came his way in an illiterate world; he had to pray his way into the heart of Jesus through the hearts of those who loved the man from Galilee. To do in our time and for our place what Luke did for his time and his place, we must listen to what Luke has to say and we must be attentive to how he goes about his task.

Luke and his problems

Luke was a pagan who became a Christian. He may very well have been converted to Judaism before he took the further step of embracing the kind of Judaism which would emerge as Christianity. It is not difficult to isolate four crucial problems which must have beset Luke on the way to faith in Jesus of Nazareth:

1. How can pagan people, such as myself, be included in God's holy people of Israel on an equal footing and, accordingly, receive the peace which Jesus brought from God to, for example, the Jew Zacchaeus and his family *(Gospel of Luke 19:1-10)?*

2. How can I reasonably entrust my life to a crucified Jewish criminal?

3. How can this Jewish criminal continue to exercise a presence and represent the hope of God, when he has departed from this world? How can Christians justify their claim that an absent and slain criminal was, and continues to be, the very centre of God's work in the world?

4. How must I respond to the call of God-in-Jesus in my time and in my situation so that I may do in my life what Jesus did in his?

These are the conundrums which confronted Luke. How he solved the riddles of his time will enable Christians to unravel the mystery of Jesus in our time and in our place.

Luke and his solutions
Luke was an educated man. He was a writer in a world where few could read or write. And he had an inquiring mind. We do not know all that we would like to know about why he decided to write his books on Jesus and the communities of Christians which grew from the life, death, and resurrection of the man from Nazareth. The traditional surmise, and it is a fairly good one, is that Luke came from the Syrian city of Antioch. That important city had a large and thriving Jewish population and I am inclined to think that Luke came to Christianity there, having first converted to Judaism from paganism. His knowledge of Jewish holy books seems to indicate that he had a good schooling in Judaism before his journey of faith brought him to accept Jesus into his life. His writings, the Gospel and the *Acts of the Apostles*, he tells us, were written for someone named Theophilus, who may have been a rich man who could afford to sponsor the expensive work of research and writing which Luke proposed to undertake. Theophilus must have been a Christian or one who was on his way to embracing faith in the Lord, and, since Luke addresses him in both volumes of his work and speaks of matters fulfilled in us, it is fair to deduce that he found his faith confirmed, as many have since, in the pages laid before him by the doctor from Antioch of Syria.

It is rewarding to reflect on Luke's opening statement where his purposes and his methods of procedure are set forth:
Since many people have undertaken to set down a narrative

account of the those things which have been fulfilled in us, as those who were eyewitnesses from the beginning and had become servants of the word handed [them] on to us, it seemed good to me likewise, having attended studiously and carefully to everything from the beginning, to write for you in an orderly way, most excellent Theophilus, in order that you may grasp with total confidence the words with which you have been instructed. *Gospel of Luke 1:1-4*

Luke set out to tell a story, his version of what he had heard by word of mouth from those who walked with Jesus from the beginning, and what he learned from many others who had committed themselves to writing about the faith, the empowering word, they had embraced. For Luke this precious word was a fulfilment of all God's words spoken through the ages, words which had finally come to an explanation in the life, death and resurrection of Jesus. To grasp God's holy words is to embrace faith in Jesus. But for a non-Jew, such as Luke, and, presumably, for his friend Theophilus, to come to faith in Jesus is to be confronted with a Jew who was condemned as a criminal and crucified by lawful Roman authority. The two distressed disciples on the road to Emmaus had hoped that Jesus (who, so they believed, *was a prophet mighty in deed and word before God and all the people*) was *the one to redeem Israel (Gospel of Luke 24:21)*, not all those horrible ungodly pagans! But, from the pagan point of view, what had a dead Jew got to do with saving the world? Well, Luke maintained, all *this was not done in a corner (Acts of the Apostles 26:26)*, and his writings set out to show how Jesus grew out of the fertile soil of Jewish faith and overflowed into the whole world. Luke set out to explain how God's concern for the world, mapped out in the story of the people of Israel, came to fruition in the mission and person of Jesus of Nazareth, and spread throughout the world of pagans by the impetus of the Holy Spirit which was outpoured on 'all flesh' on the Jewish Feast of Pentecost *(Acts of the Apostles 2:1-36)*. That is why he began his tale in Jerusalem, the capital of religious Judaism, and ended his story in Rome, the capital of benighted paganism.

Having listened to tellers of tales and read whatever came to hand, Luke took up his pen. But he wrote some sixty years after the death of Jesus when the tale had often been told and had grown in the telling. He wrote when there were already Christians scattered in tiny communities throughout the eastern Mediterranean world and even in Rome itself (think of St Paul's writings to little groups in big cities). He wrote, in other words, when much water had flowed under many bridges, from the Jordan to the Tiber, and all that water, all those babbling brooks, are part of the story. And Luke set out to take into account 'the story so far' in the hope that Theophilus, and, indeed, all his hearers/readers, would take up the telling and sing the song.

All this means is that he is not an abstract historian but a preacher of the word. Luke strove to make the Jesus who *was* into a Jesus who *is* for Theophilus, and for whoever chooses to ponder his words in their hearts. And that is why we must take time out to learn things which Luke's hearers/readers would have taken for granted, to make sure that we are playing on a level playing field. What we must do is to play catch-up.

The Four Pillars of Judaism
It is hardly necessary to remind ourselves that Jesus was a Jew, though there were German scholars in the last century who tried to prove otherwise. The question we need to ask is, rather, what kind of Jew Jesus was. First, all Jews believed in the basic tenets of the religious faith we know as Judaism. All believed in one, and only one, God. All believed that the people of Israel were chosen by God, without any merit on its part, to be God's people, to be, as it were, married to God (remember the covenant catch-phrase: *I will be your God and you will be my people*). Fidelity in this married love was clear to the world in living in obedience to God 's Torah. God's glory before the world was diminished by the beloved's infidelity. While, in the interests of historical accuracy, we must say that the Temple in Jerusalem was not the earthly centre of faith for all Jewish people, it is true to say that, at the time of Jesus, it was the focal point of the worship of God and the centre of pilgrimage for Jews throughout the world. It is, therefore, perfectly in order to see the Temple as a defining symbol of Judaism.

These were the four pillars of Judaism and for many Jews today thus they remain, with, of course, the pain of living without the Temple which was destroyed by Rome in 70 AD. The destruction of the Temple was not a fact with which Judaism alone had to cope; it was a determining fact in the evolution of Christianity. The unimaginable pain of coming to terms with the catastrophe scars the Gospels and the New Testament, just as it traumatised Jewish faith in the years following the disasters of 70 AD.

The First Pillar: God

Judaism's faith in God, the first pillar of its creed, was steadfast. There was no disagreement about God. There was no disagreement that Israel's status before God flowed directly from the kind of God Israel believed God to be: *For you are a people holy to the Lord your God; the Lord your God has chosen you out of all the peoples on earth to be his people, his treasured possession (Book of Deuteronomy 7:6).* God is holy, other, separate, unique. It follows that Israel is called to be, like God, holy, separate, other, unique. But God, though other and separate from creation, was an abiding presence. The God who created the world does not abandon it. If, from one perspective, God is distant, from another, God is with us. To live in the presence of God demands holiness, that is, to live, in St Paul's phrase, unspotted by the world's darkness. Everyone else in the world, despised Gentiles, were simply unclean pagans. To be a Jew was to lay claim not only to an ethnic identity but to a religious identity as well.

Every Jew, then, believed that there is one God and God is one. To question, or appear to question, that foundational belief was to question the very being of Judaism, the essence of being a Jew. This was the faith which nourished Joseph and Mary, their children Jesus, James, Joseph, Judas, Simon and their sisters *(Gospel of Mark 6:3).* The people from the villages of Galilee who listened to Jesus, the fishermen who followed him, the women who ministered to him, all believed the first commandment: *I am the Lord your God … you shall have no other God before me (Book of the Exodus 20:1-3).* The oneness of God never became an issue in the conversations and arguments which we can trace back to Jesus in the Gospels. People might discuss what God demanded in a particular situation but no one questioned God's unique being. All that would change with the resurrection of Jesus.

Christianity would have remained within the arms of its mother Judaism were it not for its belief that God had raised Jesus from the dead. It was not the fact that people were saying that God had raised Jesus, that God had vindicated the life of Jesus, by overcoming his death. Most Jews believed that, one way or another, the resurrection of all those who died loyal to the faith of their fathers and mothers would at some time in the future be vindicated by God who did not abandon faithful people to eternal misery. What makes Christian talk about the resurrection of Jesus so divisive is that it was and is conducted in language which claimed that Jesus possessed and possesses a relationship with the living God that was and is unique, a status that acknowledges the humanity of Jesus yet moves into the sphere of the divine. Christian faith in the resurrection of Jesus was expressed by declaring Jesus to be Lord, as St Peter's address on the Feast of Pentecost concludes:

Therefore let all the house of Israel know with utter certainty that God has made this same Jesus whom you crucified both Lord and Messiah. *Acts of the Apostles 2:36*

We shall have much to say about resurrection and about Jesus the Messiah in later chapters. Judaism did not have insurmountable barriers to declarations that Jesus was a/the Messiah. But, in their experience of the resurrection of Jesus, Christians began to forge a vocabulary to describe Jesus which seemed to call into question the oneness of God and thus to undermine the first pillar of Jewish faith. The Gospels, and, indeed, the whole of the New Testament writings, are shot through with a vocabulary which grows out of belief that God raised Jesus from the dead. Please ponder the following:

Paul, a slave of Christ Jesus, called to be an apostle and set apart for the gospel of God, which he formerly promised through his prophets in the holy scriptures, the gospel about his Son, descended from David according to the flesh, but established as Son of God in power according to the spirit of holiness through resurrection from the dead, Jesus Christ our Lord. *Letter to the Romans 1:1-4*

I have been crucified with Christ; yet I live, no longer I, but Christ lives in me. And the life I now live in the flesh, I live by faith in the Son of God who has loved me and given himself up for me. *Letter to the Galatians 2:20*

In those days it happened that Jesus came from Nazareth of Galilee and was baptised by John in the Jordan. And immediately, on coming up out of the water, he saw the heavens being torn apart and the Spirit, like a dove, descending upon him. And a voice came from the heavens, 'You are my beloved Son; with you I am well pleased.'
Gospel of Mark 1:9-11

[Jesus] said to them, 'But who do you say that I am?' Simon Peter answered and said, 'You are the Messiah, the Son of the living God.' *Gospel of Matthew 16:16*

Mary said to the angel, 'How will this be, since I do not know a man?' And the angel answered her and said,'Holy spirit will come upon you and power of the Most High [God] will overshadow you, and, therefore, that which is born will be called holy, the Son of God.' *Gospel of Luke 1:34-35*

Filled with holy spirit, Jesus returned from the Jordan and was led in the spirit into the desert for forty days being tested by the devil. During those days he did not eat anything, and when they were over, he was hungry. The devil said to him, 'If you are the Son of God, command this stone to become bread'. Jesus said to him, 'It is written that one does not live by bread alone.' *Gospel of Luke 4:1-4*

And John [the Baptist] gave witness, saying, 'I saw the spirit come down like a dove from heaven and remain upon him. I did not know him, but the one who sent me to baptise with water said to me, "The one on whom you see the spirit come down and remain, that is the baptiser in holy spirit." And I have seen and I have borne witness that this man is the Son of God'. *Gospel of John 1:32-34*

While it may very well be true that not one sentence in the whole of the New Testament clearly, unambiguously, indisputably, and beyond any argument, calls Jesus God, there can be no doubt that the Gospels, the writings of St Paul, and other documents which make up what became Christian holy books, in the enlightenment which came with belief in the resurrection, teach that the relationship between God and Jesus was such as no other human being experienced. It was unique and could best be described in human language by the conferring on him an awesome title: Son of God.

Now there is nothing untoward in Judaism in calling people sons and daughters of God. God, we are told, was filled with loathing and anger 'toward his sons and daughters' *(Book of Deuteronomy 32:19)*. A beautiful passage in the *Book of Isaiah* speaks of God determined to bring back to their land the people who languish in exile:

Because you are precious in my eyes,
because you are glorious,
and because I love you,
I will exchange other people for you,
and swap them for your life.
Do not be afraid, for I am with you;
from the east I will bring your descendants,
from the west I will gather you.
I will say to the north,
'Hand them over!
Bring back my sons from afar,
and my daughters from the ends of the earth!'
Book of Isaiah 43:4-6

People who tried to live a decent life and put their trust in God were mocked by ungodly, unclean people:

He [the religious fellow] considers us
to be low-life,
and he avoids our ways as unclean.
He says that the destiny of righteous people is blessed,
and boasts that God is his father!
Well, let's see if his words are true,
Let's see what will happen at the end of his life.
For if the righteous man is
the son of God,
then God will help him and deliver him from his enemies!
Book of Wisdom 2:16-18

The writer of the *Book of Wisdom* was in no doubt that the mockers would have to eat their words when they realised that the person who tried to live a decent life would end up safely in God's hands. They will have to change their tune:

This is the the man we once laughed at,
a man we held to be a laughing-stock.
What fools we were!
Look at him now!
Counted among the sons of God!
Book of Wisdom 5:3-5

Angels were sometimes described as 'sons of God' *(Book of Job 1:6; Psalm 29:1)*. King David and his successors on the throne were sometimes called God's son, as we can see in the *Second Book of Samuel* 7:14 and in Psalms 2:7-8 and 82:6. More striking is a text written in the language of Jesus (Aramaic), probably only twenty-five years before Jesus was born. This fragment of what must have been a longer piece of writing is one of the many discoveries which came to light after an Arab shepherd went in search of a missing goat.

Briefly, the story is this. Mohammed ed-Dhib and two companions were searching for a stray goat in a desert cave in an area called Qumran on the northwest shore of the Dead Sea early in 1947. They found jars filled with ancient scrolls and manuscripts, put them on the market, and initiated years of archaeological activity which has yielded up a great library of Jewish literature which was hidden as Roman soldiers stormed the area during the rebellion which broke out in 66 AD. *The Dead Sea Scrolls*, as these discoveries are called, come from a community who lived a monastic-style life at Qumran from about two hundred years before the time of Jesus and were wiped out by the Roman army in the conflagration following 66 AD. The community formed itself in the desert to prepare for God's final and victorious intervention in the world which would redeem the community at Qumran and bring to an end unfaithful Jews and pagan Gentiles alike. While these zealously devout people waited for the final days, they engaged in minute study of the Torah and prayer. Prayer substituted for worship in the Temple, scrupulous purification rites symbolised inner devotion to God, and study of the Bible and the community's own religious writings ensured that the whole life of these men and women would be stamped with an ardent hope for the final victory of goodness.

A fragment of an Aramaic document discovered at Qumran, and made fully available in translations for the general public between 1992 and 1996, has very interesting references to 'Son of God'. I will quote relevant lines and add some comments:

> He shall be called *Son of God*, and they will call him *Son of the Most High* ...

> His kingdom will be an eternal kingdom, and all his ways in truth.

> The earth shall be in truth, and all will make peace.

> The sword shall cease from the land, and all the cities shall pay him homage.

> The Great God is Himself his might.

> He shall make war for him and give peoples into his hand ... and his kingdom shall be an eternal kingdom ...
>
> 4Q246

[4Q246 means a piece of writing found in Cave Number 4 at Qumran and given the number 246 for identification]

Here we have a fragment of a Jewish document, coming from no more than twenty-five years before the time of Jesus, speaking of someone called the Son of God and the Son of the Most High [God]. Who is this person? Is it possible that people who lived a monastic life no more than twenty miles from where Jesus died, a community which itself was destroyed forty years after the death of Jesus, were living in expectation of one who would bring peace to the world and who could properly be called Son of God? Is there any justification for identifying this hoped-for person with Jesus of Nazareth? The answer to these questions, intriguing as they are, must be a resounding No. There are potent reasons for this negative verdict. The documents found in the Qumran vicinity never mention Jesus. The New Testament documents never mention Qumran or its monastery. Nothing in Judaism before the time of Jesus prepared the world for the claims which Christians made about Jesus. Nothing in Judaism would have any truck with belief which questioned the oneness of God. From the perspective of the faith of Judaism, to call Jesus Son of God, intending to confer on him divine status, was blasphemy. The High Priest at the trial of Jesus judged that such a claim deserved death (*Gospel of Mark 14:61-64*).

It was, nonetheless, precisely the death and resurrection of Jesus which convinced the very first Christians, everyone of them Jews, to believe that Jesus was Son of God, not as King David might be called a son of God, not as any human being might be called one of God's sons or daughters, not even as an angel might be described as God's son, but as a divine Son of God. Once Christians had clarified their thinking about Jesus, and once their fellow Jews were clear on what it was Christians really believed about Jesus, then the parting of the ways was inevitable. The first pillar of Judaism had been undermined and that was that. An acrimonious parting of the ways was inevitable.

The undermining of the first pillar of Judaism by Christianity's developing understanding of the nature and person of Jesus is of immense significance for readers of the Gospels. For the Gospels were written in the light of what was emerging as Christian doctrine about the divine status of Jesus and in the heat of the bitter conflicts which those beliefs engendered. The Gospels reflect both the process of development of Christian thought and the battles which accompanied that development. Most, if not all, conflicts in the Gospels are reported from the perspective of the development of Christian understanding of Jesus in the light of the resurrection and the concomitant controversies which that growing understanding inevitably engendered.

The Second Pillar : The Covenant

Judaism, of whatever hue, believed passionately that God had called the Jewish people to be God's people. Why this unique vocation came about must remain a mystery hidden in God's heart. But the fact of Israel's calling is at the very heart of the Bible. No covenant means no Bible, no Judaism, no Christianity.

The covenant is, as we have noted, simple: *I will be your God and you will be my people.* God's words to Moses as the great man was about to try to wrest the people of Israel from Pharaoh's tyranny encapsulate the elements of the covenant story in brief:

God spoke to Moses and said to him,
'I AM THE LORD.
As God Almighty,
I appeared to Abraham, Isaac, and to Jacob.
But by my name
THE LORD
I did not make myself known to them.
I also established my covenant with them,
to give them the land of Canaan,
the land in which they had lived as outsiders.
I have now heard the groans of the people of Israel,
whom the Egyptians are holding as slaves,
and I have remembered my covenant.
Say therefore to the Israelite people,
'I AM THE LORD',
and I will free you from Egyptian bondage,
and deliver you from its slavery.
I will redeem you with an outstretched arm
and with mighty acts of discretion.
I will take you as my people,
and I will be your God.
And you will know that
I AM THE LORD YOUR GOD,
who freed you from Egyptian burdens.
I will bring you into the land that I swore
to give to Abraham, Isaac, and Jacob;
I will give it to you as your possession:
'I AM THE LORD'.'
Book of the Exodus 6:2-8

God has made his choice. God has freed the people of his choice from slavery. God has given them a land of their own. God will remember them and watch over them. Everything here is down to God; nothing is down to Israel's merit or piety. It is a unilateral covenant, a unilateral commitment to be with and to be for this totally insignificant bunch of navvies.

Over the long and chequered history of this people, one question stands out: Why? What is Israel for? Did God choose this obscure people to the exclusion of everyone else? Or did

God choose this people in order to bring about the inclusion of everyone else. Is it true that God has chosen one people to show that all people are chosen? Is the Jewish vocation to be, as Isaiah put it, a light to every other peoples?:

[My God says],
It isn't enough
that you [alone] should be my servant,
to raise up [only] the tribes of Jacob,
and to restore [only] the survivors of Israel.
I will give you as a light to the nations,
that my salvation may reach the ends of the earth.
Book of Isaiah 49:6

On the other hand, there were those who believed that God's choice was exclusive to Israel and the devil might take the rest. There were even those who believed that most Jews would suffer the same fate at Judgement Day as the rest of unclean, godless humanity (the Qumran Jews believed that they alone would be saved). Some, however, believed that pagan people could enter into the safety of God's covenant by converting to Judaism and undertaking to live the life of a devout Jew.

To which tendency did Jesus belong? Before you rush to the easy answer, consider these statements of Jesus:

Do not cast your pearls before pigs!
Gospel of Matthew 7:6

I was sent only to the lost sheep of the house of Israel!
Gospel of Matthew 15:24

It's not right to take the children's food and give it to pups!
Gospel of Matthew 15:26

Pigs? Pups? Is this what Jesus thought of all pagans? The first Christians struggled with fellow Jews about how far the covenant might be stretched and on what, if any, conditions. The issue left deep scars in the Christian psyche ('Outside the church there is no salvation' became a Christian doctrine and has but lately been painfully discarded). The issue colours many debates in the New Testament, not least in the Gospels. It was an issue which came to the fore on the very first days of the Christian story and deeply affected the way the story of Jesus was told in our Gospels. The controversies which began in the days after the resurrection of Jesus were read back into the days of Jesus himself. This can be seen very clearly in the manner in which Luke reads into the past convictions that were not reached until after the death and resurrection of Jesus. For example, in a remarkable piece of imaginary composition, he has the old and devout man Simeon announce the universal significance of Jesus even as the forty day old baby is presented in the Temple:

Master [= LORD],
you are now dismissing in peace your servant,
according to your word,
for my eyes have seen your salvation,
which you prepared in the sight of all peoples,
a light to enlighten the Gentiles,
and to glorify your people Israel.
Gospel of Luke 2:29-32

In this process of retrospection, where gospel-makers are blessed with hindsight, the second pillar of Judaism, the very covenant itself, is significantly re-interpreted, and, as we shall see, the catalyst of re-interpretation was the death of Jesus.

It is important, in our time and in our place, to realise that Israel, a people of whom God said, *You shall be my treasured possession (Book of Exodus 19:5)*, continues to be in a covenant relationship with God and remains the people to whom the fulfilment of the covenant was promised. Failing to embrace faith in Jesus cannot annul God's fidelity (see *Letter to Romans 9:1-5*, and note that the verbs are in the present tense).

The Third Pillar: Torah

The Torah, the Law, the Teaching, the blueprint for living in the sight of God, is the third pillar of Judaism. The Hebrew word *torah* can refer to instruction, guidance, rule, law, teaching. The Bible's first five books are called the Books of Torah because they contain all the guidance and instructions necessary to live life in the warmth of God's covenant. There are six hundred and thirteen laws in the Books of Torah (that is, the *Books of Genesis, Exodus, Leviticus, Numbers,* and *Deuteronomy*), which can easily give the impression that the Law is the bedrock of Judaism. This is not the case. Torah is living a life of praise to the God who made heaven and earth.

The good order of creation comes from the hand of God. Creation mirrors God's power, God's faithfulness, God's steadfast love. The good order of creation must be sustained by God's faithfulness, by God ever watchful to ward off the threat of chaos. Likewise, the good order of life is maintained by living torah. Thus creation and torah are two sides of the same coin: torah is the ordering of life lived in ordered creation. Ordered creation is God's gift. Torah living is human praise of God's creative goodness. To live torah is to live in harmony with creation and with the Creator who saw that all that came to be at God's creative word – the world and its people – were very good (*Book of Genesis 1:31*). Torah is not a set of rules but is a way of living in God's life-giving presence. For the people of Israel, torah is Israel's obedience to the way creation is; it is singing in harmony with the song of creation. It is a duet sung with God.

Torah or Law defines how to live within the covenant for the covenant is the binding love of Creator and the work of his hand. To live torah is to experience that steadfast love which endures forever. Living in the covenant is how one's life celebrates and proclaims the wonder of God's love. Living the Law, living torah, is a blessing, a benediction of life lived in the joy of God's love. To live according to torah is to declare that one is spoken for, that one is happily married to the greatest love of all, that one is not going to be lured by the blandishments of other gods and their empty promises. It was not easy then and it is not easy now.

While every Jew believed that God's covenant with Israel (*I will be your God and you shall be my people*) was to be lived in accordance with torah, God's blueprint for a blessed life, the many laws which ring-fenced the holiness of God and his holy people were a sure recipe for disagreement and dissension. How are ancient laws to be observed in the here-and-now, in towns and cities, by business people and shepherds, by peasants and the well-to-do, and, more often than not, when people are subjected to foreign powers and their malign influences? How do we live now the way our ancestors lived then?

It is hardly surprising that the interpretation of the torah was a cause of deep divisions in Judaism, divisions which are only too plain in the Gospels inspired by the life and teaching of that most devout Jew, Jesus of Nazareth. We will appreciate these fissures if we try to understand some of the people we meet often in the Gospels: Pharisees, scribes, and Sadducees.

Pharisees

Many of the eating and drinking stories in Luke's Gospel present Pharisees and (sometimes) scribes as bitterly objecting to the practice of Jesus of eating with tax collectors and sinners. When Pharisees, rather surprisingly, invite Jesus to eat with them, each occasion is marred by heated and unappetising exchanges. Who were these people, why did they oppose Jesus, and why did Jesus eat with them so frequently?

Christians know the Pharisees. Their Gospels, their traditions, their dictionaries, and their prejudices, ensure that everyone knows that Pharisees were 'a party among Jews, whose legalistic interpretation of the Mosaic law led to an obsessive concern with the mass of rules covering details of everyday life' (*The Chambers Dictionary*, 2001 edition). Accordingly, we identify as a Pharisee 'anyone more careful of the outward forms than the spirit of religion, a formalist; a very self-righteous or hypocritical person' (*Chambers*). It may come as a surprise to learn that we know very little about the Pharisees at the time of Jesus and that what we think we know is seriously skewed, to say the least.

The Pharisees were a small but influential religious group within Judaism who came on the scene some two hundred years before the time of Jesus. Their origins are obscure but they seem to have emerged during the turbulent days of the Maccabean revolt against foreign domination in the second century BC. Their influence waxed and waned, depending on their luck in backing winners or losers. They had little influence during the reign of Herod the Great (37-4 BC) but may have gained ground when the political situation changed after his death and a Roman prefect, rather than local worthies, ruled Judaea. And it is in Judaea, in the south, and especially in Jerusalem, that the Pharisees, as a religious force, exercised influence. And such weight as they carried was less than that of the aristocratic Sadducees who represented wealthy and priestly interests and power in Jerusalem. The Pharisees had little or no effect on the religious or political landscapes of Galilee, no influence to speak of in a tiny village like Nazareth, where Jesus grew up. Pharisees may have visited Galilee, some may have lived there. But they were not a defining force there and they did not have any controlling influence in the synagogue gatherings, which were presided over by local priests and village elders.

The core beliefs of the Pharisees were those shared by all Jews. They believed in God, in covenant, in torah, in the worship of God by animal sacrifice in God's holy Temple in Jerusalem. They believed in prayer and they hoped that their prayers would one day issue in an outbreak of justice and peace and well-being for all people, especially their own. They were very devout and attentive to the demands of their faith. What distinguishes them from other groups within the rainbow coalition of Judaism may be expressed in three words: tradition, resurrection, angels.

Pharisees believed in the primacy of the covenant. To live in God's holy covenant demanded adherence to God's torah, to the way of life proposed in the laws of Moses expounded in the holy books. But, in order to be faithful to what Moses laid down in his day, one had to pay attention to the traditions which translated the ancient laws into a viable religious life in different times and different places. Pharisees, therefore, hallowed traditional interpretations of the laws, as learned saints and scholars down through the ages sought to ensure that what Moses said in his time and place was sensibly adhered to in their time and place. The written torah would become a dead letter if it were not translated sensibly from one generation to the next. For example, torah lays down what must be done when leprosy breaks out in desert camps because it was during the wanderings in the desert that the ancient laws appear to have their origins. But what happens when people are settled in towns and villages? What happens when nomads become farmers? Just as the church upholds the rôles of scripture and tradition, so did the Pharisee uphold the rôles of written torah in scripture and oral tradition which sought to interpret scripture and apply it to everyday life. Unlike the aristocratic Sadducees and wealthier priests, the Pharisees were liberal-minded, prayerful people, who, though small in numbers, sought to influence ordinary people in their ordinary lives. Where they lived, they were admired and respected for their sincerity and dedication, though their piety will have been seen as over-scrupulousness by some and pretentious by others – quite unfairly, in my view.

Some beliefs of the Pharisees were not shared by all Jews. An aside in the *Acts of the Apostles* is illuminating:

When [Paul] had said this, a dissension arose between the Pharisees and the Sadducees, and the assembly was divided. For the Sadducess say that there is no resurrection, nor angel, nor spirit; but the Pharisees acknowledge them all.
Acts of the Apostles 23:7-8

We shall have more to say on these matters as we proceed on our way. For the moment, it is worth noting that the first use of the precise term Pharisee in this world is in St Paul's *Letter to the Philippians* 3:5, and, similarly, the first precise mention of Sadducess is in the *Gospel of Mark* 12:18. In other words, our earliest written evidence for these tendencies in Judaism come from Christian sources which, we are bound to say, are not unbiased.

History, such as it is, forces some readjustments to our unthinking prejudices. There is little or no evidence that there was a significant presence or influence of Pharisees in Galilee at the time of Jesus. Pharisees were, for the most part, a southern, a Jerusalem phenomenon. It may well be that the kind of religious insight which Pharisees espoused was amenable to the Galilean sensitivities and that matters of torah interpretation, ritual washings, burial customs, and dietary regulations, the day-to-day living of religion which so concerned Pharisees, were equally concerns for Galilean Jews. But evidence, such as it is, hardly justifies a more positive assertion. What we can say is that the areas of controversy, which Luke and the other gospel-makers record, may very well have caused heated debate between Jesus and his fellow Galileans, but we can be certain that Pharisees were not the everyday opponents of Jesus which our Gospels claim.

Consider the following incident:

One day it happened that Jesus was teaching and Pharisees and Teachers of the Law, who had come from every village of Galilee and Judaea and from Jerusalem, were sitting there. And the power of the Lord was with him for healing. Behold, men were carrying in on a litter a man who was paralysed, and they were looking to bring him in and set him down before him. And, finding no way through which to bring him in because of the crowd, going up on the roof, they let him down on the litter through the tiles into the middle before Jesus. And seeing their faith, he said to the man, 'Man, your sins are forgiven you.' Now the scribes and the Pharisees began to dispute the matter, saying, 'Who is this who utters blasphemy? Who can forgive sin but God alone?'
Gospel of Luke 5:17-26

It is simply nonsense to imagine that Pharisees, Teachers of the Law, and scribes, assembled from all over Galilee, from all the villages of Judaea lying sixty to a hundred miles to the south, and from the city of Jerusalem itself, and piled into a house to sit down to observe Jesus. But it is entirely creditable that the issue of the forgiveness of sins was a contentious one between Christians and Jews long after the death and resurrection of Jesus. And it is certain that those Pharisees and Teachers of the Law, and the scribes who supported them in their efforts to rehabilitate Judaism after the disastrous war of 66 AD-73 AD, were opposed to Christian claims about Jesus and to the growing Christian tendency to see in the words and activities of Jesus the very word and action of God. What Luke has done is to recall the story of the healing of the paralytic and the forgiveness of his sins and to read into the past the deadly enemies of his time and his place. The story comes from the days of Jesus and the crowds of Pharisees, Teachers of the Law and scribes come from Luke's. Christian understanding of Jesus undermined the first pillar of Judaism and the issue of who can forgive sin is an example of how Judaism reacted to the Christian enterprise.

Scribes
More re-thinking here, too. The impression given by the Gospels that there was a powerful party within Judaism called Scribes is

misleading. Scribes were people who could write and, in a world where ninety percent of the population was illiterate, they sold their skills in the market-place. Someone in a tiny peasant village such as Nazareth in Galilee could earn a few pence when writing was required. In more populated towns and cities, scribes were necessary to keep the taxation system up to speed and local government administration records in good order. In Judaism there was a special need for literate people. To them were given the task of copying and reading the ancient scriptures which formed the basis of religious faith. At the time of Jesus, the Hebrew language in which the scriptures had been written (for the most part) had died out and people spoke a kindred language called Aramaic. Aramaic was the international language of communication and diplomacy in the Middle East for five hundred years before the days of Jesus and for a considerable time afterwards. The language of the earliest Christians was Aramaic. The entire literary works of Syriac Christianity was written and is preserved in Aramaic and the language is still spoken in pockets throughout the Middle East, including southern Iraq. Jesus, if he could read and write, would not have read the scriptures in Hebrew. He would have had to depend on Aramaic translations, and individual words and phrases of Jesus recorded in the Gospels are in Aramaic (Abba, for example), not Hebrew, and not Greek. Scribes were required to translate the holy books from Hebrew into Aramaic so that they could be read and understood when people gathered in religious assembly. In this way, scribes came to be experts in understanding the Bible and explaining it to illiterate people. What was a professional skill in the rest of the world took on a religious dimension within Judaism because its religion was a religion of books. Luke often calls scribes lawyers because, along with local priests, they would have explained to people what the holy laws demanded, a very important function in the religious life of ordinary but illiterate people. No doubt various factions within the spectrum of Jewish faith employed scribes – they had to – but there was no formal party called Scribes. Of course, people who can read and write, in a society where most people, rich and poor alike cannot, exercise enormous power and influence. It is not surprising, therefore, to find scribes who were well versed in the scriptures arguing with a peasant from Nazareth who may or may not have been able to read and write. By the way, on the issue of whether Jesus could read or write, it is important to note that the ideal father in Jewish tradition from before the time of Jesus was required to teach his children their letters so that they may unceasingly read the Law of God (*Testament of Levi 13:2*, from c.150 BC). It is not impossible that a peasant, a very bright peasant, even from an obscure village in Galilee, would have learned his letters and be called on to read when his neighbours gathered to hear the word of God (*Gospel of Luke 4:16-17*).

Sadducees

Sadducees traced their origins to Zadok, the priest of Jerusalem who served King David and King Solomon (*Second Book of Samuel 20:25; First Book of the Kings 2:27-35*). The Sadducees were well-to-do. That means that they were few in number, disliked by ordinary people and, of course, had their hands in all important pies. Because they were wealthy, they were influential in those areas of life which matter: economics, politics and religion. For the most part, they lived in Jerusalem and its environs. They were close allies of the High Priest and of the important aristocratic priestly families (village priests were peasants). Since the High Priest managed the affairs of the Temple and, under Roman administration, was responsible for political and civil affairs in Jerusalem and Judaea, the Sadducees were at the heart of official Judaism as represented by the Temple and those who controlled it. The Sadducees did not have the affection of the common people (unlike the Pharisees) and, for the most part, supported the *status quo*: they may not have liked the Roman occupation but they liked power and the trappings of comfortable living which Roman culture provided for those who could pay for it and stomach the consequences. Sometimes having an inside loo can cost you your soul.

In religious matters, the Sadducees and the aristocratic priests were conservative. They did not agree with Pharisees that torah had to be constantly interpreted in the light of ancient traditions. They did not believe in the resurrection of the dead for anyone, just or unjust. They had little time for angels. In other words, they tended to believe in the letter of the law, even if they were less committed to its implementation.

However, as people like Nicodemus and Joseph of Arimathea indicate, not all wealthy people in Jerusalem were Sadducees, not all Sadducees were priests, and not all Sadducess were indifferent to religious faith. Yet of the High Priests who ruled the Temple and through it affected the religious lives of Jewish people everywhere during the period of direct Roman rule in Judaea from 6 AD down to the outbreak of rebellion in 66 AD, seven were Sadducees. Caiaphas was one of them (18-37 AD). It was Caiaphas and his Sadducean advisers who handed Jesus into the power of Pontius Pilate.

Historical Distortion

What all this means is that the picture we get in the gospels of Pharisees and scribes implacably opposed to Jesus and his teaching is somewhat distorted. To be sure, confrontation may often be presented as a dramatic device to highlight the issue under discussion. A 'them and us' presentation is a useful dramatic device to bring out what is at stake in an argument. But there is a more forceful historical reason for the distortion apparent in the Gospels and it is a tragic one. After the destruction of the Temple in Jerusalem (70 AD), some forty years after the death of Jesus, the influence of the clergy vanished and was replaced by those who stressed that a Jew could live in God's covenant by faithfully obeying torah, God's holy way of living. People who had stressed this, like the Pharisees, and people who could explain the demands of torah, like those scribes whose work had always involved transcribing the word of God, began to come into their own and to wield profound influence in the way Judaism developed after the catastrophic war (66-73 AD). Judaism was being re-formed, a new religious understanding was taking shape which attempted to deal with catastrophic new realities, and over the next few centuries of its gestation, Pharisees and scribes, with saints and scholars, sought to bring to birth a religious identity that was faithful to tradition and flexible enough to roll with the punches. In this courageous struggle to save the Jewish people and their religious identity there was no room for a subversive interpretation of Judaism which sought to break down boundaries, to identify Jew and pagan as the same before God, to abandon hallowed traditions and practices such as circumcision and food laws. In short, in the new Judaism, there was no room for Christianity. The attempt to rebuild Judaism after the disasters meant a parting of the ways for mother and child. Judaism could not endure internal factions and Christians had already moved beyond what traditional Judaism could tolerate. Around about 85 AD disputes and dissensions between those who sought to redeem Judaism from the mess and Jewish Christians, who sought (in the eyes of their opponents) to re-write the entire script, came to a head and Christians were formally banned from the synagogues. The parting was acrimonious, as such family partings always are, and the consequences were disastrous for both, as history tragically records.

The years of acrimony, which began in Jerusalem in the very first days of Christianity, continued in the clashes between St Paul and St Peter (read Paul's *Letter to the Galatians*), and came to a parting of the ways, were the years when the Christian traditions about Jesus were moulded and when the Gospels came to be written. The written Gospels came to be in the second half of the first century and they reflect the controversies which originated in the days of Jesus and continued as Jewish Christians sought to win a hearing among those who clung to the faith of their fathers and mothers. But the Gospels record the disputes as they happened toward the end of the first century, not as they were argued in the villages of Galilee in the days of Jesus. To present Jesus in their time and in their place, the Gospels engage in the arguments which preoccupied Christian and Jewish relations in the years when the Gospels were being written. Matters became more black and white, opponents were more clearly defined, positions more acutely determined, lines more clearly drawn. The Gospels teach us as much, if not more, about some early communities of Christianity as they do about the Jesus. They present Jesus as they understood his teaching and works in the world which had moved on from the first days of the preaching of Jesus in Galilee. But, and we cannot over-emphasise this, the Gospels were written in the light of the resurrection of Jesus, written with the clarity of faith which came from that experience. The Twelve and all the intimate associates of Jesus (except the women) fled the scene of crucifixion, having denied and betrayed. It was the resurrection of Jesus that changed everything – and everyone – forever. When we read the Gospels we must be aware that we are reading Jesus through the filter of the resurrection and post-resurrection beliefs, and the controversies those strange beliefs engendered, profoundly colour everything we read in them. The Jesus who *was* is not the Jesus who *is* in our Gospels.

The Fourth Pillar: The Temple

The centrality of the Temple in the life of every Jew at the time of Jesus, whether living in the Holy Land or in the diaspora, calls for some sober reflection. The routine of daily animal sacrifices and prayer was punctuated by the celebration of the great feast days, chief of which was the celebration of the Feast of Passover in the spring. Not only in Jerusalem and Judaea but in Galilee, too, the Temple was the heart-centre of faith. Readers of the Gospels are charmed by the priest Zechariah whose priestly prayers were interrupted by a rather pompous angel called Gabriel *(Gospel of Luke 1:5-24)*. Joseph and Mary, devote Jews that they were, took the infant there and presented him before the Lord. The twelve year old boy, sitting among the teachers, listening and asking them questions, romantically hints at tranquil and gentle times *(Gospel of Luke 2:41-52)*. But the picture of that same boy, now a man, driving from the Temple precincts those who did business there, points to a Temple that was a sign of contradiction *(Gospel of Luke 19:45-46)*. These two faces of the Temple, at once a house of prayer and yet a sign of contradiction, need to be pondered.

Every Jew was passionately devoted to and proud of the Temple. While there were temples to every god under the sun in every city from London to Babylon and beyond, for Jews there was only one place on earth where the one, true God made his dwelling-place and that was in the Temple in Jerusalem. The Temple of Solomon was completed, let us surmise, around 950 BC, destroyed by King Nebuchadnezzar of Babylon in 587 BC, rededicated by Zerubbabel in 516 BC, dramatically restored and expanded during the lifetime of Jesus by Herod the Great, beginning in 20 BC, and finally razed to the ground by the Roman army under a future emperor Titus in 70 AD.

Herod the Great (37-4 BC), a half-Jew whose political astuteness and brutality persuaded Rome to accept him as its main man in Palestine, and whose inclinations were more to cosmopolitan Greco-Roman culture than to Jewish religious sensitivities, greatly enhanced the reputation of Jerusalem among Jews and pagans alike by the magnificence of his building projects in and around the city. He undertook a massive restoration and extension of the Temple and the Temple esplanade on which it stood. He built palaces, streets, an aqueduct, the Fortress Antonia, a hippodrome and an amphitheatre. His building projects provided work for twenty thousand people for many years. The enhancement of the beauty and splendour of the Holy City was not without religious price, for it gave Herod control of the most important institution in Jewish faith, the Temple. Herod established his own line of High Priests and gave confiscated land to his cronies. This meant that there was, at the time Jesus was born, a priestly hierarchy and a Jewish land-owning aristocracy in Jerusalem who were despised by the ordinary people. And these were the very people who controlled the central symbol of Jewish faith. As archaeological discoveries make all too plain, the Jerusalem priestly aristocracy, supported by their Sadducean allies, lived an ostentatiously wealthy life. The tithes paid by an impoverished peasantry for the upkeep of local priests were diverted to support the Jerusalem elite. Jews, both in Judaea, Galilee, and throughout the communities scattered around the Mediterranean world, were immensely devoted to the Temple as God's dwelling-place and the focus of their religious life. But many were critical of the priestly and aristocratic elements whose oversight of the holy Temple was not always shot through with holiness.

Of course, the Temple provided employment. Not only did its rituals of sacrifice and prayer require priests and assistants of various ranks, there was need for incense makers, wood-cutters, purity inspectors, janitors and cleaners, water providers, money-changers, sellers of animals and birds, candle makers, and police. Many of these were looked down upon by their betters and formed an urban poor. The vast income supplied by

Jewry around the world had to be managed and the Temple treasury did so, not without criticism, as the *Gospel of Mark* 12:41-44 pointedly records. Each circumcised Jew was required to pay a half-shekel tax each year for the Temple's upkeep. Pilgrims flocked to the city and sustained a very healthy tourist industry which brought prosperity to those in place to benefit from it. Those who grew wealthy out of the Temple and who used their religious roles to enhance their wealth, the aristocratic priestly families, were those who were supposed to uphold the ideals of sharing, caring, and protecting, enshrined in the words of Israel's conscience, the prophets. That is why the people of Qumran sought life in the desert, away from Jerusalem and its corrupting influences, where they could pray and prepare themselves for a divine cleansing and renewal of the Temple. That is why the Pharisees espoused a simple lifestyle and looked on poverty as a religious ideal and not as a divine judgement on unclean and unholy peasants. There is an ambivalence here. There was deep devotion to the Temple, God's dwelling place. There was immense pride in the beautiful edifice reconstructed by Herod the Great. At the same time, it is not difficult to understand that deep animosity, even hatred, for those who ran Temple affairs and who grew wealthy in the process, can spring from one's love of everything the Temple symbolised. And that is why a Galilean prophet, Jesus of Nazareth, turned his face to Jerusalem and confronted those who shamed God's holy city and God's glorious Temple.

Galilee
A brief word about Galilee, the region which nurtured Jesus, gave him his religious faith, and in which he preached. At the death of King Solomon, the northern part of David's kingdom broke away from the south and from its allegiance to the capital city of Jerusalem. It went its own ways and nourished its own religious aspirations at its own temples and shrines. Galilee does not appear prominently in the biblical saga and, indeed, the Old Testament, as we have it, is a product of the south. After the death of Solomon, David's kingdom disintegrated and the north went its own way with its own kings and religious centres, a rupture clearly evidenced in the *Books of the Kings*.

After three hundred years of separation from Jerusalem and
Solomon's Temple, Galilee met disaster:

The Assyrian came down like the wolf on the fold,
And his cohorts were gleaming in purple and gold:
And the sheen of their spears was like stars on the sea,
When the blue wave rolls nightly on deep Galilee.
Lord Byron: *The Destruction of Sennacherib*

The Assyrian imperial armies totally devastated and depopulated
Galilee (733-22 BC). For centuries it remained a sparsely inhabited
wilderness and was extensively re-colonised by Jews from the
south only at the beginning of the first century BC. It was only
with the Jewish revival which took place under the impetus of
the Maccabees, who ruled the Jews from 165 to 63 BC, that a significant Jewish population from Judaea resettled in Galilee and
brought to the north of the country the racial, cultural, and religious aspirations of the southern Judaism. These immigrants
embedded in Galilee loyalty to Jerusalem and the Jerusalem
Temple and established there what archaeologists regard as
clear evidence of devote religious practice just as in the best religious circles in Jerusalem and Judaea.

Archaeologists have found domestic chalk vessels which indicate a concern for ritual cleanness. They have found plastered
pools and baths which also indicate the importance given to ritual washing. They have found ossuaries, bone-boxes, which
imply secondary burial and a belief in resurrection to the life to
come. And they have not found any pork bones, an indication
that dietary laws were observed. All of this means that, when
the Romans walked into Palestine in 63 BC, the population of
Galilee was devoutly Jewish and looked to Jerusalem and its
Temple as the visible centre of its faith. This is not to say that the
ancient Galilean tradition of producing great prophets like
Elijah, Elisha, and Jonah, had totally vanished from the face of
the earth. Nor does it mean that northern people loved everything that went on in the south (northerners never do!). Nor
does it mean that Galilee was so tied to southern apron-strings
that it was not capable of producing a prophet greater than
Jonah whose criticism of the elite down south voiced legitimate
religious dissatisfaction and a steely determination to put things
to rights *(Gospel of Luke 11:29-32)*.

Perhaps an insight into the the minds of people in the street, as it were, may be gleaned from the words of bystanders to Peter as Jesus was under interrogation by the High Priest: *Surely you are one of them; for you are a Galilean (Gospel of Mark 14:70)*. For Jerusalem folk, close to those of wealth and power, Galileans seem to have been regarded as somewhat quarrelsome, not meticulous in their adherence to the demands of torah, and harping critics of the Holy City and its holy Temple. Equally, one might conclude that, from the Galilean point-of-view, Jerusalem ears were firmly closed to legitimate and, indeed, prophetical criticism.

To sum up ...

The four pillars of Judaism, no matter how they may have been understood, no matter that they may have given rise to varying interpretations, even provoking hostilities that often arise when opinions on matters of great moment differ, firmly supported the edifice of Jewish faith. Each, however, was exposed to re-evaluation by a small but vociferous sect, a band of (initially) Galilean Jews who, in the name of one Jesus of Nazareth, claimed that their novel understanding of each of the four pillars of Judaism was the only understanding which truly reflected God's purpose for the people of Israel and for the world. The very nature of God, covenant, and Torah was questioned by a radical and maverick group who, in time, saw themselves as the new temple of God, a new people replacing old stones. We can see the assertions of the new sect growing in confidence and boldness as we read the pages of the New Testament, and there, too, we can see the arguments grow bitter, the controversies acrid, dissensions turning into parting of the ways, and the whole sorry story descending into the bitterness evident in the *Gospel of John*. The Gospels are not a story of gentle Jesus meek and mild. For all their hope and wonder, they are a sad record of deep failure – on all sides.

CHAPTER TEN

Jesus prays

> It happened when *he was praying* alone and the disciples
> were with him, he asked them 'Who do the crowds say
> that I am?' *Gospel of Luke 9:16-17*

Here's a strange thing. In the *Gospel according to John*, Jesus never
prays. The writings which are misleadingly associated with the
name John (the Gospel, three letters, and the *Book of Revelation*)
do not record a single occurrence of Jesus at prayer, and, indeed,
in only three instances *(Book of Revelation 5:8; 8:3; 8:4)* is prayer
mentioned, in each case the prayers of the saints which rise from
earth to heaven like incense. There is no Agony in the Garden (as
the incident in the other three Gospels is carelessly called) in the
Gospel of John, no prayer from the cross, and no mention of the
Our Father. The Word became flesh and dwelt amongst us, yet
never uttered a single prayer.

Each Gospel presents readers with its understanding of Jesus
of Nazareth. The Jesus of the *Gospel of Mark* is not the Jesus of the
Gospel of John. It is not a question of contradictory portraits;
rather, each presents the person of Jesus in keeping with the
strategy of each gospel-maker and, presumably, in order to meet
the needs of Christians living in different places and in the face
of different challenges to Christian faith. That Jesus does not
utter a prayer in the Fourth Gospel is entirely consistent with its
portrait of Jesus, and serves to highlight how the Jesus who *was*
becomes the Jesus who *is* for those who wrote the *Gospel according to John* and lived the kind of Christianity it espoused.

The *Gospel according to John* emerged toward the end of the
first century, at least seventy years after the death of Jesus. It is a
story bruised and scarred with conflict, a record of bitter and depressing antipathy between, on the one hand, some Jewish people who had come to believe that Jesus is the Messiah, the Son of

God and, through that believing, have life in his name *(Gospel of John 20:31)* and, on the other hand, some Jewish opponents who regarded such believers as deluded and subversive elements within the body of Jewish faith. In the aftermath of the Jewish War (66 AD-73 AD), which saw the Romans devastate Palestine and its people, which left Jerusalem and the Temple with not a stone standing on a stone, religious leaders sought to rebuild the nation. Religion, always a cohesive but contentious force within the Jewish family, was in disarray because the Temple had been destroyed, the system of sacrifice ended, and the prayers once wafted to God on the incense of Temple ritual were at an end. Pharisees and others (those who came to be called rabbis) instituted a reform which readjusted faith to new and dangerous times. This rehabilitation of Jewish faith, and of the identity which went with adherence to God's covenant with Israel, demanded a theological rigidity which could ill afford to accommodate maverick messianic hybrids such as Christianity appeared to be. Relations between those Jews who had become Christians and those who were engaged in re-building the nation and its covenant faith were inevitably fractured beyond repair. Out of different theologies grew hostility, out of hostility grew enmity, and out of enmity grew detestation. And, out of all this, grew the *Gospel according to John.*

Coming, as it does, at the end of the century, John's Gospel reflects the turmoil of the times. But it has the advantage of seventy years of Christian experience and reflection and, not least, the time to hone its own vision of Jesus for its time and its place. The New Testament presents its readers with Paul's portrait of Jesus, the extraordinary portrait of the *Letter to the Hebrews*, the portraits of Mark, Matthew, Luke and John. Each presents Jesus in different light and shade but in each we recognise Jesus the Messiah, the Son of God, who was crucified and raised by God from amongst the dead. We are familiar with the Jesus of Mark, Matthew, and Luke, the Jesus who casts out demons, the Jesus who tells parables, the Jesus who talks with people about the kingdom of God. None of these recognisable features are to be found in John's painting, or, if found, are but marginal strokes of the Johannine brush. John's bold strokes depict the Word of God, the Word who exists eternally in the mind of God and, in the fulness of time, mysteriously is sent into our world, trailing clouds of divine glory as he comes. This Jesus comes to us divinely confident of his mission, divinely certain that he and the Father are one and that to see him is to see the Father. Every word that he speaks, every deed that he does, every instruction he imparts, are signs of the glory of God who has come to dwell amongst us. This is the one who talks with God as Son to Father. He does not pray; his intimacy goes beyond prayer.

It is attention to detail that reveals the hidden depths of any portrait. The detail of prayer is a key to reading Luke's portrait of Jesus, just as the absence of it in John speaks volumes. The whole of the *Gospel according to Luke* is decked with praying people. It opens with Zechariah praying with and for the people in the Temple. It ends with the specially chosen Eleven and all those who were with them, including the two who had run back from Emmaus, leaving the Mount of Olives where they had witnessed the ascension of Jesus and returning to Jerusalem with great joy to spend their days continually in the Temple praising God *(Gospel of Luke 24:50-53)*. Praying is the colour which gives defining light and shade to Luke's portrait of Jesus.

Beginnings and Endings

Luke's story begins with people praying. It is evening. The priest Zechariah is in the inner court of the Temple, enkindling the incense on which wafted the prayers of the whole congregation of the people to their God, the precise moment of prayer in which the angel Gabriel appeared to the prophet Daniel as he, too, was praying *(Prophecy of Daniel 9:21)*. To Zechariah, the man too old to hope, Gabriel comes again and announces a much prayed-for child. The meeting of mothers, a meeting which discloses the identity of Mary's child, bursts into prayer, into a song of praise which has never palled:

> My soul glorifies the Lord
> and my spirit rejoices in God, my Saviour!

The birth of John (the *Benedictus*), the birth of Jesus (the *Gloria*), his presentation in the Temple (the *Nunc Dimittis*), all are garlanded in prayers. When Jesus is baptised and the work of welcoming and healing is about to begin, instantly he turns to prayer and, in that praying, the heavens open, the Holy Spirit descends and God tells who it is that is anointed to preach good news in a broken world: *You are my beloved Son; in you have I taken delight*. Beginnings are cradled in prayer.

The ending of Luke's Gospel is, in broad outline, the same as the endings of the other Gospels. The trials, death and resurrection of Jesus are presented by all four gospel-makers, each with individual emphasis, to be sure, but the same story may be traced in each. It is in the detail that differences abound and, in Luke's case, one detail, among his many peculiarities, catches the attention of the careful reader. According to Luke, the ending of the life of Jesus is shrouded in prayer.

After the Last Supper with his apostles, Jesus, followed by disciples, went, as was his custom, to the Mount of Olives. Having warned his followers to pray lest they be brought by God to a test of fidelity that they will surely fail, he withdrew from them and prayed:

> Then he himself withdrew from them about a stone's throw, and falling on his knees, he prayed, saying, 'Father, if it is your will, take this cup from me; yet not my will but yours be done'. *Gospel of Luke 22:40-41*

Some ancient traditions add that an angel appeared to comfort him and that his sweat fell like drops of blood as he prayed the more fervently. While such may not be the case, the agony of his prayer is plain. When he rose from his prayer and returned to find his disciples asleep, yet again he warned them to pray. Lacking prayer, they will be brought to the test and will fail. Jesus will not fail; sustained by prayer, he will face what must be faced.

Brought to the Place of the Skull and crucified, there are two last prayers, death prayers, entirely in keeping with the life lived. For those who brought him to the place of crucifixion: *Father, forgive them; they do not know what they are doing*. And for himself, a final prayer, at the evening of life, an offering: *Father, into your hands I commit my spirit*. A prayer by one sent to seek and to save the lost, a prayer that the seeking and the saving have not been in vain. And a prayer that the Spirit given at the baptism to a beloved Son and, in this man, accomplished the

Father's will, having been handed back to his Father, will be out-poured on all flesh on Pentecost Day. A prayer, therefore, that all will be well, all manner of thing will be well.

In between

The beginnings are swaddled in prayer. The endings are shrouded in prayer. In between there is a whole manual of praying which is a guide for those who would make the Jesus who *was* a Jesus who *is* in our time and place. First, there is Jesus, the man who prays. Luke tells that he was accustomed to retreat to the desert or to the mountain to pray. Before hard choices are made, pray-ing is imperative:

> In those days, he went out on to the mountain to pray, and he passed the whole night in the prayer of God. When it was day, he called his disciples to him and, choosing twelve from among them, he named them apostles: Simon, whom he called Peter, and his brother Andrew, James and John ... and Judas who turned out to be a traitor. *Gospel of Luke 6:12-16*

In the prayer of God! A phrase so awkward that some ancient manuscripts omit it and modern translators tidy it up. But Luke is seldom clumsy and his very awkwardness is our gain. In the *Acts of the Apostles*, Luke insists that the apostles were chosen through the Holy Spirit *(1:2)*. The prayer of Jesus is an empow-ered prayer, a prayer with all the strength of God's Spirit. St Paul, who knew a thing or two about praying, tells that *When we cry, Abba! Father!, it is the very Spirit witnessing in our spirit that we are God's children (Letter to the Romans 8:15-16)*. The prayer of God's Son is empowered by the same Spirit which empowers our praying. A prayer of Jesus, a prayer made as he rejoiced in the power of the Spirit in him, is a template for our praying:

> At that same hour,
> Jesus rejoiced in the Holy Spirit.
> and he said,
>
> 'Father,
> Lord of heaven and earth,
> I thank you,
> because you have concealed these things
> from the wise and the intelligent,

and revealed them to tiny children.
Yes, Father,
for so it was well pleasing to you.
All things have been placed in my hands
by my Father.
No one knows who the Son is
except the Father,
and no one knows who the Father is,
except the Son,
and those whom the Son
wishes to enlighten.'
Gospel of Luke 10:21-22

The point of this window into the prayer of Jesus is to see that otherwise insignificant people, who are tiny acorns at the business of praying, become mighty praying oaks because their praying is in the same Spirit that gives strength to the praying of Jesus. The welcoming Jesus welcomes people into his praying and all praying is thus a praying-with, part of the intimate chatting which makes the coming of Jesus into our world so loving, so vulnerable, and so re-assuring.

Consider Luke's account of Jesus giving the Lord's Prayer to his disciples. Again Jesus is praying:

And it happened in his praying, as he came to an end, one of his disciples said to him, 'Lord, teach us to pray, just as John taught his disciples'. He said to them:
'Whenever you pray, say,
"Father,
may your name be hallowed.
May your kingdom come.
Give us each day bread to sustain us.
And forgive us our sins,
even as we forgive all who wrong us.
And do not bring us to a testing".'
Gospel of Luke 11:1-4

St Matthew's version of the Lord's Prayer is by way of an example of prayer. But the context in which Luke places the giving of the prayer, and the way he tells of its giving, Luke seems to be insisting that the prayer is a prototype of all prayer, the mother of all praying (whenever you pray…). How can this one prayer give content and shape to all prayers?

First, look at Martha, a woman who welcomes the Lord into her home. She is not a woman who mutters into her apron. While she is distracted from giving her full attention to Jesus by her rush to get a meal on the table, Mary is sitting at the feet of Jesus, listening to his every word. Martha is spitting nails (you know the feeling) and has her say. It is Martha (not Mary) who gets (for us) a word from Jesus which raises the domestic squabble into the divine order of things. Remember the woman who called out to Jesus, *Blessed is the womb that carried you, and the breasts that suckled you.* And the reply of Jesus? *Blessed rather are those who hear the word of God and keep it (Gospel of Luke 11:27-28).* A lesson for all disciples. Listen to the Lord first, then do what you hear. Would-be disciples are transformed, indeed, as we shall see, they are transfigured by listening. What makes the mother of Jesus blessed among women is not that she bore a son. It is that she first listened to God and then bore God's Son. Listening is all. At the Eucharist, listening to the word of the Lord gives meaning to bread and wine, hearts burning at the words soon recognise the voice *(Gospel of Luke 24:13-35).*

Father! The first word is Father. When you pray, first attend to God. While Luke's version of the Lord's Prayer may be nearer the original than Matthew's, Matthew is more helpful at this point: it is Our Father, that is to say, the one who is Father to Jesus is Father to all of us. When Mary Magdalen seeks to hug the risen Jesus, he says to her:

I am ascending to
MY FATHER and to YOUR FATHER,
to MY GOD and to YOUR GOD.
Gospel of John 20:17

His Father becomes *Our* Father. *His* God becomes *Our* God. The death of Jesus confirms our place as sons and daughters in the family of God. All prayer must begin with a recognition of the creative presence of God. All prayer, says Luke, must begin with a recognition of our being God's children, a recognition that God brought us into being and is responsible for us. The reality we have to keep in mind is the father we discover in the story of the Prodigal Son *(Gospel of Luke 15:11-32)*. It is the story of the father who is looking out for us, who is every moment expecting to glimpse wandering sons and daughters. It is the story of a father whose is determined to seek and to save that which is lost, to restore life to those who are dead. Prayer begins with knowing and acknowledging our fathering/mothering God.

And the newness of it! There is nothing in the Jewish way of prayer in the Palestine in which Jesus grew up that would permit, much less encourage, anyone to address God as *Abba*, Father. Twice we have heard Jesus pray to God with all the intimacy expressed by *Abba (10:21-22)*. How intimate, even more than the beautiful but ornate daily prayer found on the lips of every devout Jew:

Lord God of Abraham,
God of Isaac,
God of Jacob!
God most High,
Creator of heaven and earth!
Our shield!
The shield of our fathers!

Beautiful, indeed. But Jesus invites us into the intimacy of his prayer where there is no need for phrases; he shares his *Abba* with us and *Abba* is enough. Always in our prayer, Jesus reminds us, God is near. God listens and understands as a good parent hears and understands.

May your name be hallowed. Making holy God's name, making the world aware of God's presence as its creator, nurturer and saviour, is itself a work only God can do. Long ago and far away, in Iraq, in the city of Babylon, the prophet Ezekiel spoke to fellow Jewish exiles and gave it as his opinion that their misfortunes were self-inflicted. He reasoned that when they lived in God's land, the land of Israel, they were given to idolatry, to worshipping the false gods of wealth, violence, and to injustices of every kind. They defiled the very land with their unholy ways. The catastrophe of exile was God's punishment and they were scattered among the nations. Ezekiel, however, made a quantum leap at this point. If God's good name in the world depends on God's people mirroring God's holiness, then we are in

cloud cuckoo land. The old assurance, *You shall be holy because I
am holy (Book of Leviticus 11:45)* was more frequently breached
than honoured. Certainly, Ezekiel believed that unholy people
who defiled their holy God were bound to suffer from an outpouring of God's anger. But he believed that punishment was
not an end it itself and that God would come up with an alternative strategy. If the people did not safeguard God's reputation
before the nations of the world, then God would do it for them.
Ezekiel's message is emphatic:

Thus says the Lord God:
'It is not for your sake,
O house of Israel,
that I am about to act,
but for the sake of my holy name,
which you have profaned
among the nations to which you came.
I WILL MAKE HOLY MY GREAT NAME,
which has been profaned among the nations,
and which you have profaned among them;
and the nations will know that
I AM THE LORD,
says the Lord God,
when through you
I display my holiness before their eyes.
Book of Ezekiel 36:22-23

But how can this come to pass? How can God's name be hallowed on earth as it is in heaven? Ezekiel supplies a startling explanation:

I will take you from the nations,
and gather you from all the countries,
and bring you into your own land.
I will sprinkle clean water upon you,
and you shall be clean
from all your uncleanness,
and from all your idols
I will cleanse you.
A new heart I will give you,
and a new spirit I will put within you;

and I will remove from your body
the heart of stone
and give you a heart of flesh.
I will put my spirit within you,
and make you follow my statutes
and be careful to observe my ordinances.
Then you shall live in the land
that I gave to your ancestors;
and you shall be my people,
and I will be your God.
Book of Ezekiel 36:24-28

Ezekiel was a great poet, and his imagination runs riot at the thought of what it will be like when the great day dawns and people are transfigured into a mirror-image of God's holiness. It will, he says, be like the Garden of Eden! Of course, Eden, no more than Rome, can't be built in a day.

Cleansing water, empowering spirit, and a call to faithful adherence to God's will. It hardly needs a poet's insight to see the creative power of God at work. What *May your name be hallowed* underlines is that the Christian at prayer is forever reminded that the power of the Holy Spirit, the waters of baptism, and the call to follow, effect Ezekiel's heart transplant. Christian disciples are constituted by God to be in their time and place the praying presence of Jesus of Nazareth.

May your kingdom come. We are between times. The church, in Luke's perspective, is both the patient and the surgeon. It is the patient in that it is forever undergoing surgery on its stone heart in order that it may be replaced by a heart of flesh, to use Ezekiel's startlingly modern image. The church, too, is a surgeon to the world. The surgical procedures of Jesus – welcoming, chatting, feeding, and healing – are the procedures by which the church does what Jesus did. These are the life-saving operations by which the church goes about doing good. Unheralded, unnoticed and unsung, the church serves God's kingdom building, that is to say, the church, by its service to the peoples of the world, witnesses that God is responsible for creation and that we are all safe in God's hands. Lost children will be found, dead sons and daughters restored to life. Praying is about entering

into God's excitement that all will be well, all manner of thing
will be well.

Praying, then, must always be an act of faith, an act of trust, a
journeying with God into the future that belongs only to God.
What Jesus did in his day, can be done in ours. Slowly, but surely,
serving the world will effect the heart change and stone will be
turned into flesh. In his version of the Lord's Prayer, Matthew
spells out what the kingdom of God will be. It will be the will of
God done on earth as it is in heaven. That is the new Jerusalem
to be buildéd here among our dark satanic mills and which will,
in God's good time, if Ezekiel and Jesus (and Blake) are to be believed, create a new green and pleasant land.

Give us each day bread to sustain us. Prayer moves from recognition to need. Christian prayer is not a private thing. It begins
with a recognition that followers of Jesus form a community
with Jesus and, consequently, with each other. The One who is
Father to Jesus is Father to all who would be disciples. There is a
solidarity in praying which expresses the unity of Jesus with all
God's children. And there is a communal recognition that the re-
creation of a holy world where God's will is done can only come
to be when those who have ears hear, those who have eyes see,
and those who have hearts burn with the instinctive joy of tiny
children. There needs to be a community of peasants and poets,
of romantics and visionaries, of sturdy realists and pragmatists,
a community of hope whose common prayer subverts the
powers which chain humanity and has the courage to imagine
an alternative future.

A community on the hazardous journey to discover the kingdom of God needs food for the journey. The sustenance which
Jesus provided those who welcomed him and were welcomed
by him was bread and fish. But what Jesus did on that day in the
desert must be viewed in the light of testing with which he set
out on his kingdom journey. Forty days without bread provided
the devil with a window of opportunity. Attacks are launched
on three fronts and each is repulsed by an assertion of a godly
alternative. Each counter-attack is rooted in kingdom values,
God's values. Humanity can survive on bread alone but one
would hardly call it living – there is more to life than cakes and
ale: *One does not live on bread only (Gospel of Luke 4:3).* Power with-

out accountability, glory without substance, sooner or later come to judgement: *You shall worship the Lord you God, and him only shall you adore (Gospel of Luke 4:8)*. Service, not celebrity, is the key to the kingdom.

The testing of Jesus *(Gospel of Luke 4:1-13)* is a psycho-drama which those who would be followers must watch and about which they must pray. The Jesus who was tested is the disciple who, in our time and place, is similarly brought to the test. And, as Jesus was not without sustenance in his testing, so those who would follow him are not left alone to hunger in the desert. When the Lord's Prayer turns from reverencing God, it looks to human need. To make the journey to God's good land requires provisions. Over the centuries, Christians have reflected on bread that must be prayed for. Our prayer for bread which will sustain us each step of the way (each day) asks for more than loaves and fishes.

First, of course, we pray for bread. Most people in our world do not have enough bread. Although we produce enough food to feed all of us here many times over, each day thousands die of starvation. That is to say, God has answered our prayer for bread which will sustain all peoples but there are distribution problems (recall: he gave the loaves and fishes to the disciples to give to the people). Millions believe and know that human beings do not live on bread alone but a full belly is a good start and, without it, it is hard to start living at all. So we pray for loaves and fishes – to start with. For many that is a blasphemous prayer for the freezer is full and shopping is therapy. Prayer is thus turned into greed and what we rich fools pray for is bigger barns *(Gospel of Luke 12:13-21)*. Consider:

Is there any father among you who, when the son asks for a fish, instead of a fish, hands him a snake? Or, if he asks for an egg, hands him a scorpion? *Gospel of Luke 11:11-12*

Well, yes, actually.

That is why, secondly, we need to feed on every word that comes from the mouth of the Lord *(Book of Deuteronomy 8:3*, on which Jesus relied in his testing time). Our prayer must be for that word which sets our hearts on fire, which quickens our steps on the way to kingdom living. The word of the Lord is food and drink to those who have ears to hear. But the word is also a word of warning, a reminder that God will not be gainsaid and that human selfishness will not ultimately prevail. There will be a reckoning. Without listening we end up with hardened arteries and hardened hearts and, should we fail to heed the implications of the parable about the rich man and the poor man at his gate, we may cry out in vain for one drop of water to cool a burning tongue *(Gospel of Luke 16:19-34)*. Whereas, as we shall shortly learn, we are transfigured by listening. Listening and feeding on the word of God gives strength to the weary, transforms merely existing into true living. Those who wait in prayer for the daily sustenance of God's word will fly like eagles:

Even the young will grow faint and weary,
and youth itself fall exhausted;
but those who wait for the Lord
shall restore their strength,
they shall mount up with eagles' wings,
they shall run and not grow weary,
they shall walk and never tire.
Book of Isaiah 40:29-31

The Lord's Prayer, the model of all our praying, bids us pray to feed on the food of God's word, today and everyday.

And, thirdly, that is why we have bread and wine. We pray for food for our bodies. We beg for words that will give sustenance to our minds and hearts.

And we need food for our spirit. When Jesus wished to impress the stamp of his love on all who would seek to remember him, he broke a piece of bread, filled a cup with wine, and shared them with a command: *Do this in remembrance of me*. To understand what to expect when we pray for this daily bread, we need to do no more than take a Sunday afternoon walk – to Emmaus.

On the Sunday after the death of Jesus, as the day was dawning, Mary Magdalen, Joanna, Mary the mother of James, and other women of their company, went to the tomb wherein Jesus was laid to anoint the body. They found an empty tomb and two men, dressed in dazzling clothing remarkably like the clothes of Jesus on the mountain of Transfiguration, who reminded them of the words of Jesus while he was still in Galilee. Even in those days of excitement and public acclaim, Jesus had plainly explained that he would be betrayed into the hands of sinners and crucified, and on the third day he would be raised from among the dead. The women remembered the words and, one gathers, believed what the two men had to say. They hastened to tell all to the Eleven (that is, the Twelve minus Judas Iscariot) and to all the others with them. But, as emphatically as the women kept repeating the story, equally persistently the men disbelieved them and, dismissively, put it down as a bit of nonsense.

Later in the day, two of them, a man named Cleophas and (possibly) his wife, set off for home, in despair that all the hopes they had placed in Jesus of Nazareth had died on a cross. The risen Jesus drew near but their eyes were stopped (by God) and they could not recognise him. The stranger inquired what they were discussing and the two of them halted in their tracks, utterly astounded that anyone could be ignorant of what had happened in the city: Are you the only stranger in Jerusalem? Don't you know about the things that have happened there these past days? Of course, the irony is that only Jesus, of all the population of Jerusalem, knew exactly what happened there. And he goes on to spell it out:

> 'And he said to them, 'Oh how lacking in understanding you are! How slow of heart to believe all the things of which the prophets spoke! Was it not necessary for the Messiah to suffer these things and enter into his glory?' And beginning from Moses and all the prophets he explained to them the things about himself in all the scriptures.
> *Gospel of Luke 24:25-27*

Notice that Jesus starts with the holy bread of God's words, with the scriptures. On the word and authority of God laid out in the holy books he finds for his bewildered friends an explanation of all that had taken place. He moved them from their human perspective to a God's-eye view of all that had happened these past days. So, remember, Jesus opens his heart and himself in words: what has happened is according to the word of the Lord.

Invited to stay, Jesus sat down to eat with them (nothing new in that). The details recall the feeding of all the people (*9:12-17*):

in both, the day was drawing to a close; they reclined at table as the crowd reclined on the ground; Jesus took bread, broke it and gave it to them, as he did in the desert. At the Last Supper, Jesus took bread, gave thanks, broke the bread, and gave it to those at table with him. There is a oneness here. All point to the Eucharist, to the Communion Table, to the Mass, to altars in our place and our time where Christians gather to hear the word and break the bread. *Were not our hearts burning within us as he was talking with us along the way as he opened the scriptures for us?* And was not Jesus made known to them in the breaking of the bread?

When we pray for bread to sustain us each day, we pray for that which will nourish our bodies. But the western world already has this kind of bread in abundance. What the western world needs is the bread of God's holy words, the bread which brings Jesus into our hearts and souls and feeds us with his life. If our prayer for holy words and for Jesus in our hearts were heard in the worlds of power and wealth, if Christian hearts burned at the word of God, if Christian faith recognised the welcoming, chatting, healing, feeding Jesus who comes to them along the way to the kingdom, there would be no need to pray for more flour.

The Our Father is a community prayer. Our longing for the realisation of God's holy name among us, a longing for God's reign to be established in our midst, is followed by begging that the we may be fitted for the presence of God in our midst. The community must request *Abba*, Father, to provide each day for whatever food is needed for the journey to the kingdom where God reigns in our hearts and in our spirit. Together we entreat divine forgiveness for our refusal to welcome, to heal, and to share. With one voice, we beg not be confronted with testing of our faith too severe to bear. The 'us' of the prayer is a weighty reminder that no one enters the kingdom alone. Union with God is always communion. As the Jesus who *was* becomes the Jesus who *is* in our midst, Christians must realise that the Lord's Supper is where we sit together at table and share together the bread of heaven.

And forgive us our sins, even as we forgive all who wrong us. Because we do not look to heaven, give thanks, break bread and give it to those who sit at life's table with us, we need forgiveness.

Because we do not hear the words of God, ponder them in our hearts, and obey them on the streets, we need forgiveness. Because we carry whatever goodness lies within us in vessels of clay, we need forgiveness.

Forgiveness is the most difficult demand made on the human heart. Significantly, it is the longest petition in the Lord's Prayer and the only one which is hedged about with what may be a condition ('if you don't forgive, God won't forgive you') or may be a warning. The very ambiguity in the prayer reflects the human tendency to tread around forgiveness as if walking on eggshells.

To err is human, to forgive divine. Christian disciples know too well that they sin and are sinned against. The capacity of the human family to sin is everywhere in evidence but the need for forgiveness is not everywhere acknowledged. All too many believe that you can get away with murder – or any fast-buck philosophy which walks on the faces of the poor, the weak, and the powerless. Private ambition, selfish demand, public indifference, a thirst for power, all of these beget misery and fly in the face of God. Our sins cry to heaven for forgiveness. Let us return to the Pharisee who invited Jesus to dine with him, the Pharisee who could not grasp that the business of forgiveness is far distant from getting what one deserves:

And, take note,

a woman in the city, a sinner, having found out that he was reclining at table in the house of a Pharisee, brought an alabaster jar of perfume, and, standing behind at his feet, weeping the while, she began to bathe his feet and to dry them with her hair. And she was all the time kissing his feet and anointing them with the perfume.

Gospel of Luke 7:36-38

Embarrassing, or what?

But to the Pharisee the unsavoury incident clearly showed that this Jesus of Nazareth, the same man who a few sentences earlier was marked down as a glutton and a drunkard, a friend of tax collectors, an intimate of sinners, did not know the ways of God:

Now the Pharisee who had invited him, when he saw what

was happening, said to himself, 'If this man were a prophet, he would have known who this woman is and what kind of woman she is – a sinner.' *Gospel of Luke 7:39*

Again, a few lines ago, a large crowd had shouted out glorias to God and declared, *A great prophet has arisen in our midst! God has looked kindly on his people!* But Simon knew better; not being one of the crowd which shouts in the streets and is easily taken in, he reckoned he could spot a phoney a mile off. So Jesus asked if he might have a word, and condescendingly, Simon said, 'Teacher, speak away'. And he did:

'A money-lender had two debtors. One owed him five thousand denarii, the other owed fifty. Neither were in a position to pay up. So he cancelled the debt of both of them. Now which of them will love him the more?'
Gospel of Luke 7:41-42

And this is where the nasty insult happens. Simon may not think much of the reputation of Jesus as a prophet but there is no need to regard him as a fool. His answer is deeply offensive: *I suppose the one whom the greater debt had been cancelled.* It is the *I suppose* that is scurrilous. There is no supposing about it; it's as clear as the nose on your face. And that is why Jesus went for him with an anger and a disgust that are rare in the pages of our Gospels:

'You're right.'

And turning to the woman, he said to Simon:

'Do you see this woman? I came into this house of yours. You gave me no water for my feet. She, on the other hand, has not ceased to bathe my feet with her tears and to dry them with her hair. You did not greet me with a kiss. But she, from the minute I came in, hasn't stopped kissing my feet. You didn't anoint my head with oil. She has anointed my feet with perfume.' *Gospel of Luke 7:43-46*

Simon knows all about sin and sinners and what they deserve. The know-it-all who hasn't even got manners, the host who 'forgot' to see to the customary demands of hospitality, knows all about God, can judge other people, put them in boxes, and rest content in his own self-righteousness. But Simon knows no courtesy; he is unlikely to fathom forgiveness:

'And so, I'm telling you, her sins,
her many sins,
have been forgiven her.
And that being the case,
she has shown great love.
After all, the one who is forgiven only little,
loves only a little.' (Ouch!)

Then he said to her,
'Your sins are forgiven.'

And those who recline at the table
began to say among themselves,
'WHO IS THIS MAN
who forgives sins?'

But he said to the woman,
'Your faith has saved you.
Go in peace!'
Gospel of Luke 7:47-50

Forgive and forget. Not a divine policy. One of the great words in the Bible is *remember*. God remembers our pain. But God also remembers our sins. God's remembering is, however, not as ours. The human heart, God reckons, inclines to evil and there is little to be gained by sending one flood after another *(Book of Genesis 8:21)*. God's forgiveness is, therefore, commensurate with God's remembering. The sins of humanity cry out for judgement but they cry out, too, for understanding and for help. Merely to forget is not a divine option. To pretend that all is well, that sin does not matter, is to abandon responsibility and ignore what Mark Antony understood, that the evil which men do lives after them. What we pray for is that God can cope with sin. People can't. The onus is on God to remember our sins and the heartache and the thousand natural shocks that flesh is heir to.

Forgiveness is not forgetting. *Forget about it!* we might say to one who has hurt us. But true forgiveness is not forgetting about it. Forgiveness given and forgiveness received is about remembering. While God must remember human sin and try to cope, men and women must not forget that judgement belongs to God. What awaits the sinful heart in this world and the next is not so clearly outlined that we can claim to have a ringside seat on eternity. We cannot know the mind of God and must not claim the right to decide the eternal destiny of any of God's children. God's stewardship of the human family is not ours to measure and the wind blows where it wills.

Forgiveness demands forgiveness. God's forgiveness is unconditional but that does not mean that it is cheap. Few who have ever needed forgiveness and experienced it will underestimate its cost. One who forgives and one who is forgiven agree to share the pain that has been caused, to carry the burden of hurt together. Forgiveness is a covenant to carry together what cannot be endured alone; it is a covenant of together remembering hurt so that hurt may not be repeated. There is always a firm purpose of amendment in forgiveness. Sharing the pain carries a promise to watch and pray that what cannot be undone will not be done again.

The cross of Jesus is shared pain, as all forgiveness shares the burden of hurt. Unforgiving hearts are hearts which refuse to carry the burden of other people's sins and God's is not an unforgiving heart. In the Christian vision of things, the cross of Jesus is God's bearing the hurt of the sin of the world. The cross of Jesus defines a pattern. If we cannot forgive, we will never understand the great burden which is laid on the shoulders of those who are forgiven. We will never understand the burden which God places on those whose sins are forgiven. We will never understand why God's carrying of our sins leads Jesus to crucifixion. And we will never understand why the cross takes away the sin of the world. *A contrite and humble heart create for me, O Lord. And do not break a bruised reed.*

The rule of God, at the end of the day, is where forgiveness is the rule. God's glory, God's will, is always expressed in forgiveness. God's power is always the power to forgive. There may very well be a Seat of Judgement, before which human hearts will be called to account. But God's favourite seat and the more comfortable chair is the Seat of Mercy. It is said to be the worse for wear.

And do not bring us to a testing. This is not a prayer to ward off casual temptations. It is best understood by attending to the testings by which Luke warns those who would follow Jesus to

Jerusalem and beyond. The stories of testings, so carefully constructed and so strategically placed in Luke's writings (there are
severe testings in the *Acts of the Apostles*), dramatically illustrate
how the Jesus who *was* becomes the Jesus who *is*. We have seen
Jesus brought to the test and what is to be learned from the battle
of wills between the Son of God and the devil. We see, too, the
testing of the privileged Twelve. We learn how Christians in our
time and place must face testing and the danger of falling away
and, in the certain knowledge that we carry God's gifts in vessels of clay, we know that praying that we are not put to the test
is the safer policy. To pray that God spare us from testing is to
recognise that we are not the stuff of martyrs.

The first testing of the Twelve is a cautionary tale for all disciples in every time and place. For his testing, Jesus trusted in the
strength of God's holy Spirit. His time of testing found him fasting and praying. Not so Simon Peter and the rest. At the table of
the Last Supper, far from grasping the meaning of the food
which had been given them, they broke into acrimonious dispute about which one of them was to be the greatest. Though
Jesus warned that true greatness is to be found in service and
that he himself was among them as a servant, not a master, they
failed to grasp that true glory means enduring the trials which
Jesus endured in his work among them and, indeed, enduring
unto death. If the Twelve were to win through to the kingdom,
they must learn to stand with Jesus in his testing. There must be
a solidarity among the followers of Jesus which extends to laying down one's life for brothers and sisters. The warning to
Simon Peter is spoken to all:

> Simon, Simon, look out! Satan has claimed the right to sift all
> of you like wheat. But I have interceded for you that your
> faith may not fail and, when you have come to your senses
> again, you may strengthen your brothers [and sisters]. And
> he said to him, 'Lord, I am prepared to go with you to prison
> and to death.' But he said, 'I say to you, Peter, the cock will
> not crow this day, before you have denied three times that
> you know me.' *Gospel of Luke 22:31-34*

The warning went unheeded. When they reached the Mount of
Olives, the warning was repeated: *Pray that you do not come to a*

testing (Gospel of Luke 22:40). When Jesus withdrew from them to pray that the Father would remove the cup of suffering from his life, the disciples slept. When his prayer had been made, Jesus found them asleep and a third warning was issued: *Why are you sleeping? Get up and pray lest you come into a time of testing (Gospel of Luke 22:46)*. There was no praying. The test came in the form of a mob with Judas, one of the Twelve, leading them. Only Peter ventured to follow from afar and, in the face of the taunts of a servant-girl and a couple of fellows standing around, Simon Peter denied and denied and denied.

By contrast, Jesus went to his death, bravely defending his mission and his true identity, and the strength and courage which came to him from his praying issued in death. But Good Friday gave way to Easter Sunday. All of which means that the prayer not to be brought to the test is a prayer for fidelity. It is a prayer for endurance in faith in the teeth of whatever entices us to infidelity. In the Lord's Prayer, we do not pray to be delivered from the daily personal temptations to selfishness. The prayer is a community prayer that the Christian churches do not abandon fidelity to the way of Jesus. We pray to be saved from the communal loss of nerve in the face of the attractions of the world and from the communal betrayal of the values for which the martyrs died. It is a prayer likely to afflict the comfortable.

Perhaps the last word on prayer should come from a serious sinner who knew how to pray:

[Jesus] spoke a parable to some people who were cocksure of their own righteousness and regarded other people with contempt:

'Two men went up to the Temple to pray. One was a Pharisee, the other a tax collector. The Pharisee stood up boldly and prayed thus: "I give thanks to you, O God, that I am not like the rest of humanity, rapacious, unjust, adulterers, nor, indeed, like this tax collector. I fast twice a week, I pay tithes on everything I acquire!"

But the tax collector, standing afar off, and reluctant even to raise his eyes to heaven, struck his breast and said, "O God, be merciful to me, a sinner."

I tell you this man went home right before God unlike the

other fellow. For people who exalt themselves will be humbled; people who humble themselves will be exalted.'
Gospel of Luke 18:9-14

Another last word on the Jesus who prays and, from his experience, tells us how to pray. If you ask why did Jesus pray, the answer is quite simple. He needed to.

CHAPTER ELEVEN

You are the Messiah (I)

It happened when he was praying alone and the disciples were with him, he asked them, 'Who do the crowds say that I am?' Answering him, they said, 'John the Baptist; others Elijah; still others a prophet of old who has risen.' But he said to them, 'But you, who do you say that I am?' Answering, Peter said, *'You are the Messiah of God.'* But Jesus gave them strict orders not to say this to anyone, saying that it was necessary for the Son of Man to suffer many things, be rejected by the elders, by the chief priests, and by the scribes, be put to death, and be raised on the third day. *Gospel of Luke 9:18-22*

Here is an account of a coronation. It is a very ancient account and the ritual of the ceremony was old when this coronation occurred. King David (possibly, b.1040; d.970 BC), as he lay on his deathbed, named his son Solomon as his successor (though he was not the eldest son) and ordered the priest Zadok to proceed with the coronation service:

So Zadok the priest, Nathan the prophet, and Benaiah, son of Jehoiada, and the Cherethites and the Pelethites, went down and caused Solomon to ride on King David's mule and brought him to Gihon. There Zadok the priest took the horn of oil from the tent and anointed Solomon. Then they sounded the *shofar*, and all the people said, 'Long live King Solomon!' And all the people went up following him, playing on pipes and rejoicing with great joy, so that the earth was shaken with their noise. *First Book of the Kings 1:38-40*

King David named his son as the one who would be responsible for carrying out the royal duties imposed on him when God appointed him to shepherd the people in place of King Saul. Zadok the priest had the young prince placed on the royal mule,

the State Coach of its day, and all the courtiers led the procession
to Gihon which lies at the foot of the Mount of Olives. The oil
used in the coronation was very special, very expensive perfumed oil:

The Lord spoke to Moses:

'Take the finest spices: five hundred shekels weight of liquid
myrrh, half that amount, that is two hundred and fifty
shekels of fragrant cinnamon; two hundred and fifty shekels
of fragrant cane; five hundred shekels of cassia – all according to the standard weight of the sanctuary shekel – together
with a hin of olive oil [about ten pints]. Blend them together
like a perfumer into sacred anointing-oil; it shall be a holy
anointing-oil. With this you shall anoint the tent of meeting,
the Ark of the Covenant, the table and its vessels, the lamp-
stand and its accoutrements, and the altar of incense, the
altar of burnt sacrifices with its accoutrements, and the basin
with its stand. You shall set them apart [consecrate], so that
they may be most holy. Whatever touches them will become
holy. *Book of the Exodus 30:22-29*

This expensive perfumed oil was not to be used as an attractive
cosmetic; it was not for adorning the body beautiful, as Moses is
commanded by God to spell out to the people:

As sacred anointing-oil this shall belong to me throughout
your generations. It shall not be used for any ordinary
anointing of the body, and you shall not make any other oil
of similar ingredients. It is holy, and you shall treat it as sacred.
Anyone who who makes such perfume, or puts it on an un-
designated person, shall be expelled from the people.
Book of the Exodus 30:31-33

Such precious oil was to be used publicly to designate that one
was to exercise priesthood:

Then you shall bring out Aaron and his sons to the entrance
to the Tent of Meeting, and there you shall wash them with
water. Clothe Aaron with the sacred vestments, anoint him
and consecrate him, so that he shall serve me as a priest.
Bring out his sons as well, and clothe them with tunics.
Anoint them, as you have anointed their father, that they

may serve me as priests. By anointing they shall be designated priests forever throughout all generations to come.
Book of the Exodus 40:12-15

What is obvious is that Aaron and the generations of priests which came after him were ceremonially anointed (smeared) with oil in order to indicate to people that a special task had been assigned. The anointing marked off the priest as the one designated to ensure that the people's prayer and sacrifices were offered to God. The priest was set apart to make sure that the commandment to worship the Lord God was carried out. One might say that the priest was there to look to heaven on behalf of the people.

The king was there to look after the people on behalf of heaven. So kings, too, had to be anointed into the job in a public ceremony which highlighted the task which was being imposed by God and accepted by the anointed one. The Lord revealed to the prophet Samuel that he must anoint Saul as king for the people of Israel and the task to be undertaken is spelled out:

This time tomorrow I will send you a man from the land of Benjamin, and you shall anoint him to be ruler over my people Israel. He shall save my people from the hand of the Philistines; for I have seen the suffering of my people, and their cry for help has come to me. *First Book of Samuel 9:16*

Royal actions are determined by heavenly policy. The coronation was duly carried out:

Samuel took a phial of oil and poured it on [Saul's] head, and kissed him, and he said, 'The Lord anoints you ruler over his people Israel. You shall reign over the people of the Lord and you shall save them from the clutches of their enemies all around.' *First Book of Samuel 10:1*

The king was, therefore, God's representative; the king was to be the human face of God before the people. The authority of the king was God's authority for the ultimate King of Israel and of all creation is God:

The Lord is king,
robed in majesty;
the Lord is robed,

girded with strength.
He has set the world in place,
and it shall not be moved.

O Lord,
your throne stands firm
from of old!
You are from everlasting!
Psalm 93:1-2

The earth's people do not belong to the kings of this world:
Come, let us sing to the Lord!
Let us cry out joyfully to the rock of our salvation!
Let us greet him with thanksgiving hymns.
Let us come into his presence with songs of praise.
For the LORD is a great God,
and the Great King above all gods …

Come!
Let us worship and bow low,
let us kneel before the Lord, our Creator!
For he is our God,
we are the people of his pasture,
the sheep of a well-tended flock!
Psalm 95:1-7

God's reign is not that of the tyrant. God rules according to divine, not human, standards. The Lord is the Good Shepherd of his flock:
O Lord,
You are the Most High
over all the earth,
exalted far above all other gods.

The Lord loves those who hate evil;
he guards the lives of his faithful people,
he rescues them
from the hand of the wicked.

Light dawns for righteous people,
joy for those of upright heart.

Righteous people,
rejoice in the Lord!
Give thanks to his holy name!
Psalm 97:9-12

Of course, with some few but notable exceptions, the kings never lived up to their high calling. To an overwhelming extent, the *Books of the Kings* are a catalogue of kings who were no better than their pagan counterparts. The prophet Ezekiel angrily pronounced God's judgement upon a failed procession of kings:

Thus the word of the Lord came to me:
'Son of man, prophesy against the shepherds of Israel, prophesy, and say to the shepherds of Israel, say to them, Thus says the Lord God:
"Woe to you, shepherds of Israel! You have been feeding yourselves! Should not shepherds feed the sheep? You have drunk their milk, you have worn their wool, you have slaughtered their fat lambs, but you have not fed the sheep. You have not strengthened the weak, you have not healed the sick, you have not bandaged the injured, you have not brought back the strayed, you have not sought those who were lost. Instead, you have lorded over them with harshness and brutality. So they were scattered like sheep who had no shepherd, and thus scattered, they became a prey to wild beasts. My sheep were scattered over the face of all the earth, with no one to search for them, no one to look out for them."
Book of Ezekiel 34:1-6

The story of these venal shepherds is, in humanity's sorry history, depressingly familiar.

Royal History: The Enemy Within
There were two enemies: the royal enemy within and the coercive, exploitative, imperial powers without. First, the failure of the kings, the shepherds of Israel. The obituary notes on the kings in the *Second Book of the Kings* again and again, almost as a refrain, carry the sad comment, *He did what was evil in the sight of the Lord*. The complaints of the prophet Amos may stand for the protests of all against the exploitation by kings and their cronies:

They have rejected the law of the Lord, and have not obeyed
his statutes, but they have been led astray by the same lies
which their ancestors lived by. *Book of Amos 2:4*

Their crimes are the usual list nailed to the doors of petty
tyrants:
They sell [into slavery]
the just man for silver,
the poor man for a pair of sandals.
They trample the heads of poor people
into the dust of the earth,
and push the weak to one side.
Father and son sleep with the same woman,
so that my holy name is besmirched.
They recline before altars
on garments taken as a down-payment;
in the house of their God
they drink wine extracted as fines.
Book of Amos 2:6-7

God's charge against the persistent exploitation of the people is
angry and precise:
'What do you mean by crushing my people, by grinding the
faces of the poor?', says the Lord God of hosts.
Book of Isaiah 3:15

The second enemy, and, in the long run the more destructive,
was the enemy without.

Imperial History: The Enemy at the Gate
The Jewish people never had peaceful occupation of the land
flowing with milk and honey. Even if one discounts the exagger-
ated triumphalism of the blitzkrieg described in the *Book of
Joshua* as no more than propaganda, it is clear that their hold on
the land was always precarious. There were constant threats
from the people they displaced in the land and there were endless battles with neighbouring petty kings and princes. But it
was the imperial powers who wrought the most havoc.

The land of Palestine/Israel is not in itself much of a place. It
has few natural resources, apart from water which, of course, is
more precious than oil. Not much to attract the attention of

marauding world powers, one would suppose. But unfortunately this little land is at the crossroads of Asia, Africa, and Europe. That is what brought the armies in. The Egyptian Pharaoh Thutmosis III defeated a mighty coalition of Asian kings in the north of Israel in 1468 BC. The British fought the Ottoman Turks in the same place in the Great War (1914-1918 AD). Almost anyone who's anybody, from Mark Antony to Napoleon, had armies crisscrossing the narrow strip of earth on the Mediterranean coast which many call the Holy Land.

The Assyrians came down like a wolf on the fold, as Lord Byron dramatically describes. Tiglath-pileser (reigned 747-727 BC) pushed Assyrian power from northern Iraq as far as the Gaza Strip. His successor, Shalmaneser V (reigned 736-722 BC) defeated the Egyptians (the real enemy) and consolidated control of most of Palestine. The northern part of the land was devastated and its people deported to Assyria, to be replaced by peoples brought in from hither and yon and planted in the devastated land. The biblical understanding of the sorry tale is told in the *Second Book of the Kings*, chapter fifteen to the end of chapter seventeen. For the moment, Jerusalem and the land around remained safely tucked into the hills.

The Assyrian ascendancy came to an end when the Babylonians and the Medes destroyed their capital of Nineveh in 612 BC, an event which inspired the prophet Nahum to write his nasty little revenge text *(Book of Nahum)*. The great King Nebuchadnezzar (reigned 605-562 BC), once more pushing eastern imperial power against the might of Egypt, turned on Jerusalem and reduced the city and the Temple of Solomon to rubble. That was in March, 597 BC and it marks the beginning of the exile on the banks of the waters of Babylon where despair put an end to singing the songs of Zion (Jerusalem):

By the rivers of Babylon,
we sat down and wept
when we remembered Zion,
We hung up our harps on the willow trees.
Our captors asked for our songs,
our tormentors wanted a lively tune!
But how could we sing the Lord's song
in a foreign land? *Psalm 137:1-4*

The whole *Book of Jeremiah* is taken up with the tragedy. Of course, not every single Jew was exiled but the back of the people was broken and the exile in Babylon is the great watershed in the story of God's people from the time of Moses to the time of Jesus and even to our own day. When St Matthew was dividing his people's history into great epochs, the exile is one of the defining, turning points *(Gospel of Matthew 1:17)*.

By now most of the Israelite peoples and the other strands of peoples who made up the population of Palestine were scattered, their lands planted by foreigners. But the next wave of unrest in the Middle East saw the Medes and the Persians overcome the Babylonians. These are the people who so tormented the Greeks, whose armies campaigned as far west as the River Danube and the Ionian islands in the Mediterranean Sea. Their empire ranged from the Indus and Jaxartes rivers in the east to Egypt and the Aegean in the west, and from the Persian Gulf in the south to the Caspian Sea and Black Sea in the north. The great battlefields of the time still echo in European and Asian memory: Thermopylae, Salamis, Miletus, Platea, Mycale, and, of course, Marathon in 490 BC.

An imperial policy change helped God's people once more to gain a tiny foothold in their native land. The Persians allowed displaced peoples to return home. Some Jews, a trickle, returned to Jerusalem. In 520 BC, in the second year of King Darius (reigned 522-486 BC), building a new Temple was earnestly pursued. The *Book of Ezra*, our biblical source, tells that the leader of the returned people was Zerubbabel (a descendant of David), the high priest was a man named Yeshua (= Joshua = Jesus), and two prophets, Haggai and Zechariah; all were influential in helping to encourage the daunting task of rebuilding a Jewish presence in Jerusalem. What is of supreme importance is that the monarchy had now been replaced in this postexilic period by a dominant priesthood centred on the Second Temple. Kings had given way to priests and the more well-to-do priestly families. From this time to the day the Temple was razed to the ground by the Romans (70 AD) the high priest will be a major player in the story of the Jewish people, dominating its religious life and central to its political fortunes.

The great world went on. We know little of what happened

to the returned exiles for the next hundred years or so. We know that they had difficulties with the people who were planted in Palestine and emerge in history as the Samaritans. We know that the community in Jerusalem and its environs kept in touch with what we may now begin to call the Diaspora, that is, communities of Jews scattered throughout the Middle East and Mediterranean world. The communities in Iraq (especially, Babylon) and Persia helped to support the Jews at home and the growing numbers who had fled to Egypt to avoid deportation (see the *Book of Jeremiah*) would, in time, become a powerful and influential force within the religious and cultural life of Judaism. And we know something of their romantic and unrealistic hopes and aspirations as we find them in the fictional *Book of Esther*, and the bizarre outpourings of the *Book of Daniel*.

The Persian imperial might came to an end with the first serious European incursion into Asia, that of the Macedonians under Alexander the Great. Having defeated the Persians at Issus (near Antioch) in 333 BC, he turned south capturing Syria, Palestine, and Egypt with some stubborn but futile resistance. Striking at the heartland of Darius III, he defeated him at Gaugamela on the Tigris in 330 BC. He pushed on through Persia and Afghanistan to India, returning to Babylon where he died in 323 BC. He was thirty-three. The young man led his soldiers eastwards for eight and a half years, covering 11,000 miles. On his death, his army commanders sought to divide the spoils and their warring with one another for the next two hundred and fifty years created turbulent times. The Macedonians brought Greek culture, the Greek language, and Greek power into the Middle East and these forces were both widespread and dominant. The new cultural and political realities deeply impinged on both Jewish and Christian history and thought for centuries and, indeed, to our own time. The Age of the Greeks, the Hellenistic Age, as historians call it, lasted until 63 BC and its cultural influence continued when the new barbarians, otherwise known as the Romans, turned up in Jerusalem in 63 BC.

As far as the Jewish people were concerned, the Hellenistic Period (332-63 BC) was characterised by the often brutal attempts to impose Greek culture on Jewish life but also by Jewish assimilation and acceptance of exciting foreign ways. Many

Jews went to Alexandria and prospered there. It was there that the Jewish holy scriptures were translated into Greek by seventy-two scholars from the homeland who were dispatched to the great library of the city by Jerusalem's high priest for the purpose (so the story goes). The Septuagint translation would have profound influence on early Christianity and on the writings which it produced, most prominently on those which make up the New Testament. The impact of all this cultural imperialism may be judged (not entirely superficially) by noting that a religion, Christianity, which originated with a Galilean Jew, was pioneered exclusively by Jews who remain its honoured founding fathers and mothers, and whose earliest adherents, prophets, preachers and writers were almost exclusively Jewish, has for sacred texts a collection of books written in the language of the Greeks. Although Rome ruled the world, it was the cultural legacy of Greece, its art, architecture and its literature, which held sway. While Latin was the predominant language in western regions of the Empire, Greek was the *lingua franca* in Italy and all points east. The poet Juvenal sarcastically complained that Italian girls spoke poor Latin and made love in Greek (*Satires* 6.191 – early second century AD). St Paul wrote his *Letter to the Romans* in Greek, not Latin. With some bitterness, Horace wrote 'Greece, the captive, made her savage victor captive' (*Epistles* 2.1.156).

Two of the successors of Alexander the Great, Ptolemy and Seleucus, gave their names to ruling families, the former establishing itself in Egypt (Cleopatra was one of these) and its dependencies, the latter controlling some of Asia Minor, Syria and the lands to the east. At first, the Ptolomies gained control of Palestine and the tiny enclave of Jews in Jerusalem and its hinterland. The usual see-saw between Asian powers and African (Egyptian) ambitions ensured constant warring between the two families for decades. The Seleucid faction won a decisive battle at Panion, near what came to be known as Caesarea Philippi (modern Banias), in 200 BC, and captured Jerusalem two years later. These Macedonian Greeks imposed their will over the tiny city state of Jerusalem for the next hundred years or more. In 190 BC the Seleucids were defeated in a battle at Magnesia in Asia Minor (Turkey). The victors imposed huge war indemnities which seriously strained the Seleucid finances and marked the arrival of a new force in the eastern Mediterranean: Rome.

The Seleucid treatment of subject peoples involved the implantation of Greek culture (as well as learning from the scientific, artistic and philosophical riches of the East). Allowances were made for those who stubbornly stuck to old ways in religion and the Jews and Jerusalem benefitted from an initially tolerant policy which went back to the days of the Persians. But when the Seleucid monarch, Antiochus IV (reigned 175-164 BC) came to power, as far as the Jews were concerned, all that changed. As with any conquered people, there were always Jews who bought the cultural package on offer and embraced the new ways as modern, sophisticated, and, above all, financially rewarding.

Whatever efforts were made to keep the integrity of Jewish culture and faith intact, the accession of the Seleucid Antiochus IV was marked by an aggressive policy of forced assimilation to Greek ways:

> When Seleucus died and Antiochus, known as Epiphanes, succeeded to his kingdom, Jason, the brother of Onias [the high priest], obtained the high priesthood by means of corruption. In a petition to the king, he promised three hundred and sixty talents of silver, and from another source of income a further eighty talents. In addition, he agreed to pay a further one hundred and fifty talents, if he were authorised to establish a gymnasium and to enlist a corp of youth to use it, and to enroll the populace of Jerusalem as [if they were] citizens of Antioch. When the king agreed and Jason took up the office [of high priest], he immediately imposed the Greek way of life on his fellow countrymen.
>
> *Second Book of the Maccabees 4:7-10*

The upshot of an alliance of foreign power and local collaboration imposing Greek culture on the people of Jerusalem and Judaea was to create the seeds of rebellion. One can sense the approaching storm when, in 167 BC, Antiochus IV issued a policy statement:

> Then the king wrote to his whole kingdom that all should be one people, and that everyone should abandon local cus-

toms. And all the Gentiles adhered to the word of the king. Even from Israel many endorsed his religion and sacrificed to idols and polluted the Sabbath. And the king sent letters by personal messenger to Jerusalem and to the cities of Judah ordering them to adopt customs alien to the land, prohibiting holocausts, sacrifices and [holy] libations in the sanctuary, to profane sabbaths and feast days, to defile the sanctuary and the priests, to build altars, sacred groves and shrines for idols, to sacrifice pigs and unclean animals, and to desist from the circumcision of their sons. They were to defile themselves with every kind of impurity and profanity, so that they would forget the Law and change all godly observances. And he wrote, 'Whosoever does not adhere to the king's word shall die.'

According to all these words he wrote to all his kingdom and he appointed people to oversee all the people and he commanded the cities of Judah, one after another, to offer sacrifices. Many of the people, those who forsook the Law, conformed and did evil things in the land. They drove Israel [that is, faithful Jews] into hiding, into every refuge hole that could be found. *First Book of the Maccabees 1:41-53*

The Temple in Jerusalem was rededicated to Zeus, cultic prostitution was introduced, and the people were forced to eat unclean animals used in sacrificial ritual. Holy scriptures were burnt; anyone caught in possession was executed. What happened was entirely predictable:

But many in Israel [= Jerusalem and its hinterland only] stood firm and were firmly resolved not to eat unclean food. They welcomed death rather than to be defiled by food or to profane the holy covenant. And die they did. A very great anger came upon Israel. *First Book of the Maccabees 1:64*

The upshot was that a rebellion broke out in 167 BC and, *mirabile dictu*, the Hasmonean (the family name) or Maccabean (a nickname meaning 'the Hammers') priestly clan managed to establish home-rule which extended eventually to all the land from Mount Hermon in the north to Beer-sheba in the south. A free land for a free people! Jews spread from the Jerusalem and Judah heartlands to re-populate Galilee in the north, to control

Samaria in the middle, and to extend control southward into the desert. The Hasmonean brothers transformed a tiny hole-in-the-wall state, not much bigger than Luxembourg, into an independent nation. They controlled the army, the economy, the politics, and, tellingly, cornered the office of high priest.

A significant and prominent feature of the Bible is its proclivity for re-writing history or, at least, re-interpreting the past in the light of current vicissitudes. The *Book of Numbers* suggests that the priesthood, and especially the high priesthood, may be traced in an unbroken chain back to Aaron and the days of the Exodus. But the *Book of Ezekiel*, coming out of the experience of exile in Babylon, when it describes the new Temple to be built in place of that of Solomon which had been destroyed, lays down the regulations on which the office of high priest must be based as a new departure. The new order that God would establish bears little continuity with the past. The kingship and its rights to perform priestly functions in the Temple are consigned to history (in this regard, it is interesting to see how the later *Books of the Chronicles* re-tell the *Books of Samuel* and the *Books of the Kings* and remove any suggestion that kings exercised priestly functions). The kingship had failed; it is now the turn of the priests. For the returned exiles, Yeshua, a descendant of Zadok, David's priest, was the new man. And thereafter the high priest came from his direct descendants. Henceforth, the high priest, who was supposed to rule for life, was the supreme authority in Judaism, the sole inheritor of the prestige and dignity that had formerly belonged to the king. And the office of high priest frequently became the plaything of power politics down to 70 AD.

The concentration of power and the mingling of the political with the religious, were causes of constant internal divisions for the Hasmoneans who, though a priestly family, were not descended from Aaron and their marriages diluted any claims they had to hold the office of high priest. There was constant internal mayhem within the ruling family and a tendency to seek the aid of outsiders to support one faction against another. One new power appeared on the horizon and became a broker between local claimants. Unfortunately, the new power was Rome and its dominance in the Middle East changed Jewish history forever.

Pompey arrived in Jerusalem in 63 BC and, either indirectly through local clients such as Herod the Great (37-4 BC) or by means of direct rule through prefects and procurators, Rome's coercive, avaricious rule held sway in the Holy Land until its empire collapsed. The devastation caused by attempts to throw off the yoke of Rome, in 66 AD and again in 135 AD, more or less condemned most Jews to exile from their homeland until the United Nations intervened in 1948.

What has all this history got to do with Jewish faith, Jesus, Christianity and the Jesus who is? Almost everything. Without the Romans there would have been no crucifixion and the story would have been very different – if, that is, there would have been any story worth the telling. The claims that Jesus is the Messiah of God, made in the quotation at the head of this chapter, are directly related to the sad history we have outlined. It is time to return to Luke's story though, in truth, we haven't left it.

CHAPTER TWELVE

You are the Messiah (II)

It happened when he was praying alone and the disciples were with him, he asked them, 'Who do the crowds say that I am?' Answering him, they said, 'John the Baptist; others Elijah; still others a prophet of old who has risen.' But he said to them, 'But you, who do you say that I am?' Answering, Peter said, *'You are the Messiah of God.'* But Jesus gave them strict orders not to say this to anyone, saying that it was necessary for the *Son of Man* to suffer many things, be rejected by the elders, by the chief priests, and by the scribes, be put to death, and be raised on the third day. *Gospel of Luke 9:18-22*

Prophets are odd bods. They have, if they are good eggs, an insatiable thirst for justice and, for the most part, are what we might call realistic optimists. They are not the Mr Micawbers of this world, forever hoping that something will turn up. For optimism is of little use if it is not founded on the likelihood of something being in the offing. In any case, prophets were not primarily concerned with the future. Biblical prophets were preoccupied, in the first instance, with contemporary social, political, and religious realities, rather than with prediction. Their efforts, fired by their intense personal experience of God, were expended in laying ethical and spiritual foundations which, in God's good time, would bear the weight of a glorious future. It was their especial talent to analyse what was happening around them and to subject their time and their place to divine scrutiny. It was highly irritating for the powers-that-be to have people who claimed to see the world through the eyes of God and who went about proclaiming that everyone else was short-sighted. That is why prophets were the awkward squad. Their job was to be a pain in the neck of the body politic. And yet they had the good of the body politic at heart and their mission in life was to root out and to pull down so that a great beauty could be born. What the prophets did was to put service at the heart of the human enterprise. That is why prophets were incorrigible realists and the enemies of kings.

The sad history of the people of Israel, as we have seen, is a history of exploitation, exploitation from within and without. The prophets were the voices which cried to high heaven against all who created a desert and called it peace. To understand how prophets managed to be disturbers of complacent indifference, we may do no more than look at how they went about their work.

Weeping

Why are prophets always weeping? They go about crying in the streets, tears of sadness and recrimination wetting their cheeks. The spectacle of someone crying in a loud voice at the city gates is, to say the least, disconcerting. But the first duty of the prophet is to articulate the pain of the people. Public lamentation challenges those who exploit the poor and batten on the weak because it gives a voice to the downtrodden and warns the guilty that their crimes do not pass unnoticed. Weeping in the streets opens the pain to public scrutiny and brings into the market-place the plight of the poor. Weeping is a prophetic weapon because it gives the lie to the cliché that it is no use crying over spilt milk. Amos knew well the power of sitting on the ground and weeping:

> In every city square there shall be weeping,
> and in every street they shall cry out,
> 'Alas! Alas!'
> *Book of Amos 5:16*

If the very ground will not cry out, the prophet will:

> They sell [into slavery]
> the just man for silver,
> the poor man for a pair of sandals.
> They trample the heads of poor people
> into the dust of the earth,
> and push the weak to one side!
> *Book of Amos 2:6-7*

The wives of the wealthy who want more, more, are, as ever, fat cows:

> You cows of Bashan
> on mountains of Samaria,
> who oppress the poor,
> and crush the needy,
> who badger your husbands,
> 'More drink, more drink!'
> *Book of Amos 4:1*

To weep for the wrongs done to the poor was the first duty of prophets. Weeping creates solidarity. Blessed are those who mourn.

Anger

Weeping, however, is not enough. Weeping leads to anger and the cry to heaven becomes a cry for vengeance. If weeping articulates the pain of the people by pointing to their impoverishment, hot anger points to the guilty. Weeping without anger is merely wallowing in this vale of tears and becomes another tool of oppression. Anger is creative precisely because it points the finger, lays the blame, afflicts the comfortable:

> Elders and princes of the people:
> You are the ones!
> You have devoured the vineyard;
> the spoils wrested from the poor are in your houses!
> What do you mean by crushing my people,
> by grinding down the faces of the poor?
> *Book of Isaiah 3:14*

Anger enters prayer and God is called upon to vent divine wrath:

> O Lord,
> God of vengeance,
> shine forth!
> Rise up,
> O judge of the earth.
> Give the haughty their comeuppance!
> O Lord,
> how long shall the wicked,

how long shall the godless
have the glory?
Psalm 94:1-3

Anger points the finger at those who trample on the heads of the poor, who create economic systems that impoverish and enslave people, who build summer houses and winter houses, who line walls with ivory, who turn justice to wormwood and bring the righteous to the ground (all in the *Book of Amos*). Anger identifies the cesspool of injustice. The angry voice names names.

Imagining a Future

Weeping and anger always come up against the voice of experience. Everyone will tell you that nothing around here ever changes, that it's always been the same, and that you've got to grin and bear it. There are people who go about telling you that suffering is good for you, that we'll soon be out of it, that death is but a sleep, and that heaven awaits. And, unfortunately, there are mugs who believe this nonsense. Not prophets.

Weeping and anger are but the tactics of prophets. It is the prophetic imagination that defines the strategy. What the prophet does is to imagine an alternative future. That is why the prophet is dangerous and that is why so many get killed. The lackey who tells you that it will all be the same in a hundred years is the enemy who has just castrated you. The prophet who imagines an alternative future is the one who empowers you.

And that is what the ancient Jewish prophets did. Once the horrors of the times, the internal and external coercive and exploitative powers were exposed by persistent weeping and burning anger, a future is imagined. Once the prophets have articulated the pain of the people, once they have poured the smouldering anger of the oppressed on to the streets, a new future can begin to empower change in the here and now. It is a future birthed in a keen realisation of the transforming power of God. Prophets are not manipulating fortune-tellers. Because they know God, know in deep intimacy the character of God, they can anticipate that God's steadfast love will characterise the future as in the past. The ancient faith, *I will be your God and you will be my people,* newly embraced, is the cornerstone of the new heaven and the new earth:

I will have pity on the household of Judah,
I will save them,
as only the Lord their God saves.
Not by bow, nor by sword!
Not by war, not by horses, not by horsemen!
Book of Hosea 1:7

The imagined future, the future which belongs to God and not to kings and princes, will be a time of plenty, when the earth is so fruitful that the reaper trips up the sower:

The days are surely coming,
says the Lord,
when one who ploughs
shall overtake the reaper,
the one who treads the grapes
overtakes the one who sows the seed.
The mountains will drip with wine
and it will run down the hills.
I will restore the fortunes of my people Israel;
they shall rebuild their ruined cities
and they shall live in them.
They shall plant vineyards and drink wine;
they shall set out gardens and eat their fruit.
I will plant them in their own land
and they shall never again be rooted out
of the land that I have given them,
says the Lord.
Book of Amos 9:13-15

The imagined future will be a time of peace, peace at home and peace abroad:

Out of Zion will come Torah,
out of Jerusalem God's word.
God will judge between many peoples,
and impose terms on strong nations far away.
They will beat their swords into ploughshares,
and their spears into pruning forks.
Nation shall not raise sword against nation,
neither shall they learn war any more.
But they shall all sit down,

everyone under their own vines,
and under their own fig trees,
and no one shall be afraid,
for the mouth of the Lord has spoken.
Book of Micah 4:2-4

The imagined future will be a time for a new heart in humanity, a new spirit, a new gentleness, an ingathering of people exiled from God and from homeland:

Thus says the Lord God:
I will gather you from among the nations,
and assemble you from among the peoples
where you have been scattered,
and I will give you the land of Israel ...
I will give them a new heart;
I will put a new spirit in them;
I will take out the heart of stone from their bodies
and give them a heart of flesh,
so that they will follow my ways,
and keep my statutes and obey them.
Then they shall be my people,
and I will be their God.
Book of Ezekiel 11:17-20

But how? How shall peace come dropping slow? How shall nations speak peace unto nation? How shall the hungry be fed, the land flow with milk and honey? How shall hearts of stone be transfigured into hearts of flesh?

It is the imagination of the prophets which sketch in rich profusion the joys of things to come. But who will realise the vision? The answer on all prophetic lips was the same: God. The question on the lips of the hungry sheep who look up and are not fed is ever the same: How? How will it come about? How will God realise the dream? The future constructs are probably as many as there are prophets to imagine them. But in Israel's prophetic imagination we can identify how God might fashion a new future. The foundation stone of all future imaginings is a return to faith in the eternal truth. To live justice now is to embrace the future now.

Looking Back to the Future

The Bible-honoured way of imagining the future is to look to the past. This is no more than looking at what God has done in olden days and extrapolating from that what will be done on earth in the future. Of course, when persecuted, downtrodden people look to the past in order to imagine a future, they romanticise the good old days and iron out the creases. The prophets of Israel are not different, in this respect, from other visionaries and poets. But they are constrained to keep within a demarcation line: they must be faithful to the understandings of God which permeate the ancient stories. It is, however, by selecting the ancient stories which best resonate with and speak to popular religious faith that they communicate what they imagine will come to be in God's good time. Three familiar stories stand out: Paradise, Exodus, David and Solomon.

Paradise

Perhaps what God will do is re-open the Garden of Eden. Isaiah encourages right-living people who seek the Lord to look to the rock from which they were hewn and the quarry from which they were chiselled:

Look to your father, to Abraham,
look to Sarah, the mother who bore you.
For he was but one man when I called him,
but I blessed him and made of him many people.
Book of Isaiah 51:1-2

Armed with faith as strong as Abraham's, people with faith in their bones will realise God's potential. God will overcome present disaster and coercion and provide a future, not only for beleaguered Israel but for all peoples who seek justice and pursue peace. And the how of it? Simple! God will turn the desert of their lives into a Garden of Eden. Isaiah paints a new creation in bold and familiar strokes:

Eden Joy
For I am about to create new heavens and a new earth;
the former things shall not be remembered
or come to mind.

But be glad and rejoice forever
in what I am creating;
for I am about to create Jerusalem as a joy,
and its people as a delight.
I will rejoice in Jerusalem,
and delight in my people;
no more shall the sound of weeping be heard in it,
or the cry of distress.

Eden long-life
No more shall there be in it
an infant that lives but a few days,
or an old person who does not live out a lifetime;
for one who dies at a hundred years
will be considered a youth,
and one who falls short of a hundred years
will be considered accursed.

Tilling the Garden in Peace
They shall build houses and inhabit them;
they shall plant vineyards and eat their fruit.
They shall not build and another inhabit;
they shall not plant and another eat;
for like the days of a tree
shall the days of my people be,
and my chosen shall long enjoy
the work of their hands.

Fruitful and Multiply
They shall not labour in vain,
or bear children in calamity;
for they shall be offspring blessed by the Lord –
and their descendants as well.

Every Need Anticipated
Before they call I will answer,
while they are yet speaking I will hear.

Perfect Peace – No Serpent
The wolf and the lamb shall feed together,
the lion shall eat straw like an ox;
but the serpent –

its food shall be dust!
They shall not hurt or destroy
on all my holy mountain,
says the Lord.
Book of Isaiah 65:17-25

The old story of the Garden of Eden furnishes the prophetic imagination with the window dressings of the new world order. But it is not the trappings that are of the essence here. It is the firm belief that the future belongs to God and God will make all things well. It places the responsibility for downtrodden people firmly where it belongs: on God's shoulders. Again, Isaiah:

For the Lord will comfort Zion,
and show pity to her ruined places.
he will turn her desert into Eden,
her wilderness into the Garden of the Lord.
Joy and gladness will be found in her,
thanksgiving and an outbreak of song.

My people, listen to me.
O my people, give ear to me.
For torah will issue from my presence,
and my righteousness as a light to the peoples.
I will speedily bring near my deliverance;
my salvation will go forth,
and my strength will prevail over the nations.
Coastlands shall live in hope;
in my strength they shall hope.
Book of Isaiah 51:4-5

The *Book of Zechariah* (14:8) includes the great rivers of Eden in its vision of the Lord's future victory, and, indeed, the *Book of Revelation* (22:1-2) does the same, adding the tree of life which will produce fruit for the healing of all the peoples of the earth to its phantasmagoric dreams. Anyone who remains firm in the face of persecution will, says one of Revelation's angels, have permission to eat from the tree of life in the Paradise of God (2:7). There is an arcane reference to Paradise in St Paul's *Second Letter to the Corinthians* 2:2-4 and everyone is familiar with the thief who managed to pinch Paradise while dying on a cross

(Gospel of Luke 23:43). That is about as far as Paradise gets in the New Testament imagination. One might add that the idea had still some mileage in it as a work such as the *Second Book of Esdras* (2nd century AD) testifies. Interestingly, in the holy book of Islam, the Koran, Paradise appears as a beautiful garden where righteous men, in the company of beautiful women, drink a heavenly potion which will produce neither drunkenness nor madness *(Sura 18:32)*.

Exodus

Prophetic imagination is fired even more profoundly by the Exodus and all the events surrounding this archetypal act of deliverance from slavery. The Exodus from Egypt and the journey into the promised land of milk and honey is the resurrection story of the Old Testament. What Jesus is to Christians, Moses is to the people of Israel. What the resurrection is to the New Testament, the Exodus is to the Old. Each is seen as the embodiment of hope and the template of hope's fulfilment.

Each year Jewish people celebrate the Feast of Passover which ends with a joyous shout, *Next Year in Jerusalem!* This is not simply a desire to celebrate the feast in the Holy City but a hope that the New Jerusalem will, in Blake's phrase, be buildéd here, as it is in heaven. What is at the centre of things is the longing for freedom, for well-being, for righteousness, for justice, for everything that is embraced by the word *shalôm*, peace. God, acting through his servant Moses, led the people from the oppression of slavery, through the discipline of the desert experience when the covenant was sealed and the torah proclaimed, to the joyous experience of God's presence leading the people into the land flowing with milk and honey. The story in the Pentateuch [= the *Books of Genesis, Exodus, Leviticus, Numbers* and *Deuteronomy*] provides the template for the future. To leave security and journey, as Abraham did, is to come, in God's good time, through the Sea of Reeds to the River Jordan and to cross into the promised land of milk and honey. To inherit the earth, today's wanderers must be turned into tomorrow's pilgrims, a people who know with whom they are travelling, a people who know where they are going, a people who have faith that a promise made is a promise kept.

The most influential conceptual framework for the future of humanity, then, is the Exodus event, God's deliverance of his enslaved people from the tyranny of Egypt. Each generation recalls the glorious past, not to wallow in the good old days, as a futile exercise in romanticism. Rather, the past empowers people by instilling confidence that what once was will be again:

My father [=ancestor] was a wandering Aramaean who went down into Egypt, a small people, and lived there as an immigrant. There he became a great nation, mighty and numerous. When the Egyptians treated us with harshness and oppression, imposing hard labour upon us, we cried out to the Lord, the God of our ancestors. The Lord heard our prayer and saw our torment, our toil and oppression. The Lord brought us out of Egypt with a mighty hand and an outstretched arm, with awesome power, with signs and wonders. He brought us into this country. He gave us this land, a land flowing with milk and honey.

Book of Deuteronomy 26:5-9

The God whose steadfast love moulded world events to shape Israel's freedom in the past, that very God will do so again. The work of liberation from slavery is a paradigm for the future. The past not only defines God's responsibility for humanity, it charters the exercise of that responsibility into future stormy waters. That vision of a responsible God is the stuff of songs:

O give thanks to the Lord for he is good.

for his steadfast love endures for ever.

O give thanks to the Lord,

... who struck Egypt through their firstborn,

for his steadfast love endures forever;

... and brought Israel out from among them.

with a strong hand and an outstretched arm,

... who divided the Red Sea in two,

... and made Israel pass through the midst of it,

... but overthrew Pharaoh and his army in the red Sea,

... who led his people through the wilderness,

... who struck down great kings,

... and killed famous kings,

... and gave their land as a heritage

... to his servant Israel ...

> It is he who remembered us in our low estate,
> ... and rescued us from our foes,
> ... who gives food to all flesh,
> for his steadfast love endures forever!
> *Psalm 136 passim*

As we well know, the phrase, *His steadfast love endures forever*, occurs twenty-six times in Psalm 136. It is the chorus to the song; everyone joins in to be reminded that what happened in the past is not past tense because the love which saved a people in the past is the love which endures forever, a love which is now and ever shall be. Remember: a psalm for slow learners.

The dynamics of the Exodus recalled in festive celebration, in song, in saga, may be encapsulated in three words: Saviour, Revealer, Emmanuel. God saves people from slavery; God reveals to people a way to live in peace; God determines to be with and for people come hell or high water.

David the King

But how can this be? Moses was God's right-hand-man in the past. Who will be God's champion in the future? When some Jewish people looked to the past for a model leader, there was really no contest. David, the man from Bethlehem, the swashbuckling hero, the slayer of mighty Goliath, the Hollywood lover, the doting father, the snappy dancer, the hit song-writer, the all-too-human tragic figure, the shepherd-king, the only one in the whole Bible to be called a man after God's own heart – there's only one King David!

The Bible devotes more space to David than to any other character, including even Moses and Jesus, if we include the *Book of Psalms*. The time of David and Solomon saw a brief interlude in the ascendancy of mighty empires in the Middle East and the relatively tiny kingdom of Israel and Judah, with hegemony over some neighbouring peoples, flourished in the vacuum. An all-to-brief interlude from marauding super powers allowed the temporary development of a kingdom which was secure, prosperous, relatively peaceful and, above all, ruled by its own kings beholden to no one. The rise of Assyrian power, c.850 BC, put an end to the brief independence enjoyed for a hundred years or so by little peoples. It is hardly surprising, therefore, that the reigns of David and of the son of David, Solomon, became a magic time, a time of freedom and prosperity, a time of independence and peace. The little kingdom of King David and King Solomon was romanticised into a vision of a blissful future. David became the once and future king.

There is an old piece of doggerel which may contain one or two elements of truth:

King David and King Solomon
led very merry lives,
with very many concubines,
and very many wives.
But when they both grew older,
and they were full of qualms,
King Solomon built the Temple,
and King David wrote the Psalms.

To be sure, David did write some poetry but hardly the ninety-seven psalms which are, one way or another, associated with his name in the *Book of Psalms*. Solomon built a temple, no bigger, perhaps, than an average country chapel. But, like all good stories, nothing is lost in the telling. The fact that the reigns of David and the son of David were relatively prosperous and trouble free was enough to ensure that the two kings became legendary heroes. From being reasonably successful leaders, they were elevated to the status of icons. Would that the righteousness of King David and the wisdom of King Solomon might come again to champion the downtrodden as in the days of old!

An Ideal King
The prophets, of course, blame tyrants for the pain of the people. But they also blame the people as a whole. Infidelity, idolatry – sinfulness of every kind – fly in the face of the God who brought slaves to freedom. The price of freedom is constant vigilance and Israel did not keep watch. It did not remember to worship the Lord with integrity of heart. Isaiah castigates the Temple and the Monarchy power complex (the king, remember, ran the Temple) for those who had the responsibility of leadership in the religious and political life of the nation did not walk in the

ways of the Lord. Jeremiah castigates the people for abandoning torah, the very foundational document which outlines how freedom is to be lived. Ezekiel, all his life an exile among (as he sees it) unholy people, far from the Temple and far from the holy land, decries the loss of personal holiness, of the duty of God's people to be holy as God is holy. But where there is condemnation for failure, there is hope for the future. All the major prophetical voices are strong on condemnation but they are even stronger on hope. The future belongs to God, not to tyrants.

To long for the good old days of David and Solomon was not an exercise in nostalgia. During the misery of Assyrian domination, and in the several centuries of subsequent oppression, the *Book of Isaiah* came into being, its original inspiration going back to the prophet Isaiah (?742-689 BC) but its final form providing a meditation on many years of hardship and woe. While Jerusalem and its hierarchies are subjected to harsh judgement, there is an ever-present promise that God would redress both self-inflicted hurt and imperial coercion. One way in which a new future is imagined is to envisage hope incarnated in a new king on the throne of David. There is light at the end of the tunnel of darkness:

Darkness to Light
The people who walked in darkness
have seen a great light;
those who lived in a land of deep darkness –
on them light has shined.

Sadness to Joy
You [= the Lord] have multiplied the nation,
you have increased its joy;
they rejoice before you
as with joy at the harvest,
as people rejoice when dividing plunder.

Oppression to Freedom
For the yoke of their burden,
and the bar across their shoulders,
the rod of their oppressor,

you have broken
– as on the day of Midian.
For all the boots of the trampling warriors
and all the garments rolled in blood
shall be burned as fuel for the fire.

A New King
For a child has been born for us,
a son given to us;
authority rests on his shoulders;
and he is named
Wonderful Counsellor!
Mighty God!
Everlasting Father!
Prince of Peace!

A New Peace
His authority shall grow continually,
and there shall be endless peace
for the throne of David and his kingdom.

A New Justice
He will establish and uphold it
with justice and with righteousness
from this time onwards,
and for evermore.

A Sure Promise
The zeal of the Lord of hosts
will do this.
Book of Isaiah 9:2-7

An ancient prayer, probably from a coronation liturgy, is projected into the future to describe the reign of God and his good servant the king in the new heaven and the new earth:

Justice for the people
O God,
give the king your justice,
and your righteousness to a king's son.
May he judge your people with righteousness,
and your poor with justice.

Defender of the Poor
May the mountains yield prosperity
for the people,
and the hills yield righteousness.
May he defend the cause of the poor of the people,
give deliverance to the needy,
and crush the oppressor.

Everlasting Peacemaker
May he live while the sun endures,
as long as the moon,
throughout all generations.
May he be like rain that falls
on the mown grass,
like showers that water the earth.
In his days may righteousness flourish
and peace abound
until the moon is no more.

Valiant for Justice
For he delivers the needy when they call,
the poor and those who have no helper.
He has pity on the weak and the needy,
and saves the lives of the needy.
From the oppression and violence
he redeems their life,
and precious is their blood in his sight.

From Sea to Sea
May he have dominion from sea to sea,
and from the River [Euphrates]
to the ends of the earth.
May his foes bow down before him,
and his enemies lick the dust ...
may all kings fall down before him,
all nations give him service

God's Will on Earth
Blessed be the Lord,
the God of Israel,
who alone does wondrous things.

Blessed be his glorious name for ever;
may his glory fill the whole earth.
Amen and Amen!
Psalm 72

The future, then, is in God's hands. The future may be realised
on earth in the person of a goodly king, a new David, a new
Solomon, son of David. The future king is but the instrument of
well-being for the whole earth. The real power behind the imaginary throne is God. The day of God's championing the poor
and the needy is not dependent on the king; the royal appearance is only the wrapping in which justice, righteousness, and
peace are delivered from God's good hand. What is of the
essence here is that harsh judgement on a people who have
abandoned torah, is not the final word. The final word is that
God saves the people from their sins.

A Recap

To recap. The tragedies which beset the people of Israel were, for
the most part, inflicted by foreign powers. The greatest tragedy
of all, and the one which indelibly marked the Jewish people,
was the exile of 587 BC. It was that deportation to the waters of
Babylon which confronted God's supposedly holy people with
the terrifying realisation that they had not lost merely the land.
Perhaps they had lost their God as well. When the stragglers
were allowed to return to Jerusalem in 537 BC, everything had to
be rebuilt, not least, faith in God. The struggle to foster and sustain faith in the midst of external and internal calamities marks
Jewish experience from the days of Exile to our own day. Over
five hundred years after the rebuilding of the Second Temple,
Jesus was born. He was brought up with the burden of his people's history and the extravagancy of their hopes. Expectations of
how and when God would undo the hurts of history and fulfil
hopes for the future were many and varied. For Christians, Jesus
was the one to undo the pain and fulfil the hopes of every heart.
The many ways in which a new future was imagined (and we
have looked at only a few) provided a palette of colours from
which Christians painted their portraits of the man from
Nazareth. To some of these portraits we now turn.

Anointing the Future

The portraits of Jesus painted in the texts of the New Testament are many and varied. They are all, however, painted with the colours and textures inherited from Israel's faith. There is no predominant colour. Jesus is an amazing dream-coat of many colours, a patchwork of old and new. All the expectations of a suffering people, all the prophetic configurations of the future, all the traditional expressions of Israel's understandings of God, all, that is, of centuries of faith, hope, and love come to rest on the shoulders of the man from Nazareth. The century into which Jesus was born into the Jewish people was a time of familiar coercive and exploitative suffering and consequent bewilderment of faith. Suffering engendered commensurate expectations. A cacophony of voices filled the air. A variety of imagined futures, founded on the prophetical visions and hopes we have seen, and on a host of other strands of expectation. Israel's longing for freedom, for justice, for peace, were not placed in one basket. Not everyone looked to a Messiah, a single outcrop from the root of Jesse, a new King David; not everyone looked for a new Moses to lead a people to a new promised land of plenty; not everyone looked to a fiery Elijah to slaughter the false prophets of an evil world; not everyone looked to an inrush of divine power to sweep away the horrors of the times and create a new heaven and a new earth. Not everyone looked for a truly holy High Priest who would inspire that holiness of life which would transform pain into peace. Some looked to meet steel with steel and called for ploughshares to be turned into swords. What everyone looked to was an anointed future.

An anointed future. However God may create a new beginning, however poets and prophets imagined a promised land, everyone hoped that there would be such a future and knew that God alone would be its creator. What Christians proclaimed was that every hope, every heart's longing, was fulfilled in Jesus. Jesus is, they declared, the anointed future. To him is given every name.

An Advent of Sundays

In the time of Advent, Christians paint their portraits of Jesus, the one who has died, risen, and will come again. Trawling

through the Sunday readings which form Christian meditation
during these days, a stranger in our midst might identify the
colours with which a Christmas portrait is painted. You may
even enjoy chasing up the quotations for yourselves:

He will wield authority over the nations
and impose his terms on the peoples:
they shall beat their swords into ploughshares.

A righteous Branch shall spring from David,
a branch which will do justice,
and practise righteousness in the land.

A shoot springs from the stock of jesse,
a branch from his old roots;
and on him shall rest the Lord's spirit:
a spirit of wisdom and understanding,
a spirit of counsel and might,
a spirit of knowledge and reverence for the Lord.

Look!
Your God is coming!

The eyes of the blind shall be opened,
the ears of the deaf unsealed,
the lame shall leap like a deer,
and the tongue of the mute sing for joy,

The spirit of the Lord God is upon me,
for the Lord has anointed me.
He has sent me to gospel the poor.

Behold!
A young woman is pregnant
and shall bear a son.
She will name him Emmanuel.

He shall stand and feed his flock
in the strength of the Lord,
in the majesty of the name
of the Lord his God,

The people who walked in darkness
have seen a great light.

Behold, your Saviour comes to you!

How beautiful on the mountains
are the feet of the one who gospels peace,
who gospels good things,
who makes salvation heard,
who tells Zion:
'Your God reigns!'

Blessed is the King
who comes in the name of the Lord!
Peace in heaven,
and glory in the highest heaven!

Your King comes to you,
humble, riding on a donkey!

Every expectation that ever was is seen to come to be in the coming of the child. Every hope that was ever hoped is fulfilled in his birth. Every name with which the future has been baptised is given unto him. God's work of justice and righteous in the earth is exclusively laid on his shoulders and there is no other name to honour and only one name in heaven and on earth to be acclaimed Christ the Lord (*Letter to the Philippians 2:11*). It is, therefore, misleading to trawl through the Old Testament looking for sentences which predict the life and work of Jesus of Nazareth. The process of understanding was quite the reverse. First came the experience, the transformative personal presence of the man. Then came the search for the words to describe who it was who had come into the world. The great storehouse of Israel's words, its Bible, became the Christian quarry. Now we will explore what Christians made of what they found there.

Saviour

An angel of the Lord came by night to the shepherds' fields gospelling the frightened men with a great joy for all the people:

Do not be afraid! Behold! I am gospelling you with a great joy which shall be for all the people. Today in the city of David is born a Saviour, who is the Messiah, the Lord.
Gospel of Luke 2:10-11

The angel confers three titles on the swaddled child. Other designations and titles will come to light as Luke's story unfolds and we shall concern ourselves with them. But we shall begin here with the angel's word.

First, then, *Saviour*. Surprisingly, Jesus is called Saviour only once in Luke's Gospel and only once in John's Gospel (4:42). There are twenty-one occurrences elsewhere in the New Testament. Just as Luke seldom uses the noun gospel (never in his gospel, only twice in his *Acts of the Apostles*) and everywhere prefers a verb *gospelling*, so he names Jesus Saviour only once but everywhere speaks of Jesus saving people. However, the very first time we find the word Saviour in his Gospel provides the careful reader with the key to unravelling the mystery of who this man is:

> My soul magnifies the Lord,
> and my spirit rejoices in
> God my Saviour.
> *Gospel of Luke 1:46-47*

The Lord God is, as Mary sings, the Saviour and what the Lord God dispenses is salvation, as Zechariah says three times in his Benedictus hymn. The angel proclaims to the shepherds that Jesus is Saviour. What Luke does is to show the saving work of God through the saving activity of the Son of the Most High. At the end of the journey from Galilee to Jerusalem and when so many things had been done, Jesus tells that salvation has entered into the home of the little man Zacchaeus, for his purpose was to seek out and to save that which is lost *(Gospel of Luke 19:10)*. To list those who have been found and saved is to list again the mixum-gatherum of the welcomed, the healed and the fed:

A Man with a Withered Right Hand (6:6-11)
I ask you, is it permissible to do good or to do harm on the Sabbath, to save life or to destroy it?

A Woman of the Town (7:36-50)
He said to her, Your faith has saved you. Go in peace!

Explaining a Parable (8:4-15)

The seed on the path are those who have heard; then the devil comes and takes away the word from their hearts, so that they may not believe and be *saved*.

The Gerasene Demoniac (8:26-39)

Those who had seen it told them how the one who had been possessed by the demons had been *saved*.

A Touching Woman (8:42-48)

He said to her, *Daughter, you faith has saved you. Go in peace!*

A Dead Child (8:40-56)

Do not be afraid. Only believe, and she will be saved.

A Saving Prescription (9:24)

Those who wish to save their life will lose it, and those who lose their life for my sake will save it.

A Narrow Door (13:22-30)

Someone asked him, 'Lord, will only a few be *saved*?' But he said to them, *Strive to enter through the narrow door.*

One Leper in Ten (17:11-19)

He said to him, *Get up and go! Your faith has saved you!*

Saving God (18:26)

Those who heard it said, 'Then who can be saved?' He answered, *What is impossible for human beings is possible for God.*

A Blind Beggar (18:42)

Jesus said to him, *Receive your sight; your faith has saved you.*

A Final Mission Statement (19:10)

The Son of Man came to seek and to save that which is lost.

Lost Leaders (23:35)

And the people stood by, watching; but the leaders mocked him, saying, 'He *saved* others; let him *save* himself, if he is God's Messiah, his Chosen One!' Even the soldiers were mocking him, coming up and offering him sour wine, and saying, 'If you are the King of the Jews, *save* yourself!'

An Unlucky Thief (23:39)
One of the criminals who were hanged there kept mocking him and saying, 'Are you the Messiah? *Save* yourself and us!'

What is first to be noted in all this is that the saving programme of Jesus is precisely that which meets the Old Testament long-ings for God to be a Saviour for the people. The very being of God is to be a saving God:

For I am the Lord your God,
the Holy One of Israel,
your Saviour.
Book of Isaiah 43:3

I, I am the Lord,
and besides me there is no Saviour.
Book of Isaiah 43:11

O Hope of Israel!
Its Saviour in time of trouble!
Book of Jeremiah 14:8

Yet I have been the Lord your God
ever since the land of Egypt;
you know no God but me,
and besides me there is no Saviour.
Book of Hosea 13:4

The yearning, so long and so often expressed, is answered in the welcoming, healing, saving work of Jesus. Thus is scripture ful-filled. Who is this Jesus of Nazareth who, in the perception of gospellers like Luke, comes to our world bearing God's salva-tion?

And here's another thing. The title Saviour must be seen in its political environment. Emperors, kings, and statesmen were called saviours. In the famous Rosetta Stone, one of the Ptolemy kings is called 'saviour and god'. Julius Caesar was hailed as 'god manifest and common saviour of human life'. Augustus, the emperor, as Luke pointedly reminds us, when Jesus was born, was, as we have seen, dubbed 'the saviour of the world'. The saving which Jesus undertakes is not to be seen in an anæmic way. If the kingdom of God is to come to be in our world, it will be at the expense of the powers of this world. The

Peace of Augustus is not God's peace, not the Peace of Christ conferred on desolate people. The Saviour in the manger at Bethlehem, a great joy to all the people, is a very subversive baby, indeed.

The Messiah of God
In the *First Letter of Peter* 4:16 the followers of Jesus are called Christians and owning up to the name is, so we are told, likely to bring suffering. In the writer's estimation, this is a cause for rejoicing insofar as it means sharing Christ's sufferings. But Luke is the first New Testament writer to designate the followers of the man from Galilee as Christians:

> It was at Antioch that the disciples were first called 'Christians'.
> *(Luke's home city? Local pride?)*
> Acts of the Apostles 11:26
> See also 26:28

One must conclude from this that all who glory in the name are Messiahs, and, indeed, potentially at least, Suffering Messiahs. This is not so off the wall as it seems.

In the days after the Exile (587 BC), and at least from the beginning of the second century BC, the old romantic view of the ideal King David and the ideal time of the Davidic kingdom of justice, righteousness, and peace, began to work their way into Jewish imagination as a paradigm for the future. A newly anointed David for a restored kingdom of David became for some people the shape of the future in which the reign of God would come to earth. The Hebrew verb for 'anoint' is *msh* and the Greek verb is *chriein*, from which we get 'Messiah' or 'Christ' in English. And from 'Christ' we acquire the name Christian for those who are anointed with oil at baptism. The very first disciples of Jesus appropriated the title Messiah and applied it exclusively to Jesus. Not only that, but all Jewish expectations, no matter what shape such expectations took in the imagination of poets, prophets, and people, were seen to be realised in the life and ministry of Jesus.

A New Creation
For we are [God's] creation, created in Christ Jesus for good works, which God prepared beforehand in order that we should walk in them.
Letter to the Ephesians 2:10

A New Moses
When Jesus saw the crowds, he went up the mountain. He sat down and his disciples came to him. Then he opened his mouth and was teaching them, saying …
Gospel of Matthew 5:1-2

'Listen to him.'
Gospel of Luke 9:35

A New Law in New Hearts
For Christ is the fulfilment of Torah in order that there be righteousness for all who believe. Moses writes about right-eousness which comes from Torah: the person who adheres to these things will live in them. But righteousness out of *faith* says this: 'Do not say in your heart, "Who will go up into heaven?" (that is, to bring Christ down), or, "Who will go down into the abyss?" (that is, to bring Christ up from amongst the dead).' But what does it [scripture] say?:

The word is near you,
on your lips and in your heart !

(that is, the word of *faith* which we proclaim). For if you ac-knowledge with your lips that *Jesus is Lord*, and believe in your heart that God raised him from among the dead, you will be saved.
Letter to the Romans 10:4-9

A New Temple
The Jews therefore answered him and said to him, 'What sign are you showing us for doing these things?' Jesus an-swered and said to them, 'Destroy this temple and in three days I will raise it.' So the Jews said, 'This Temple has been forty-six years in the building! And you will raise it up in three days!' But he was speaking of the temple of his body. After he was raised from among the dead, his disciples re-

membered that this is what he had said; and they believed the scripture and the word that Jesus had spoken.
Gospel of John 2:18-22

By the time Luke was writing his Gospel Messiah/Christ was the title most frequently employed to describe the rôle of Jesus in God's dispensation and by which was expressed all the hopes and expectations of a downtrodden people. The understanding that Jesus was the Lord's Anointed One issued further in two designations of particular importance: Son of David and King. We can see this borne out in Luke's story.

Consider what we learn at the beginning of Luke's story and at its ending. The angel Gabriel tells Mary:

Mary,
do not be afraid.
You have found favour with God.
Behold,
you will conceive and bear a son,
and you will call his name Jesus.
He will be great and will be called
Son of the Most High,
and the Lord God will give to him
the throne of David his father,
and he will be king over the house of Jacob forever,
and his kingship will have no end.
Gospel of Luke 1:30-33

The child then is born to be king. He will sit on the throne of his ancestor King David and will reign forever. At the end, his fate decided by Pontius Pilate, we read:

Then the whole gathering of them got up and brought him to Pilate. They began to accuse him, saying, 'We have found this man subverting our nation, opposing the payment of tax to Caesar, and saying that he is Christ, a king.' Then Pilate asked him, saying, 'Are you the King of the Jews?' But, in answer, he replied, 'That's what you say.' *Gospel of Luke 23:1-3*

The soldiers also mocked him, coming up and offering him sour wine. They said, 'If you are the King of the Jews, save yourself!' And there was an epigraph over him: THIS MAN IS THE KING OF THE JEWS. *Gospel of Luke 23:36*

It isn't simply that all the longings for freedom and justice which were encapsulated in the hope for a new David and a new kingdom of peace are seen to have come to fruition in the life and person of Jesus. It is that. But more, much more. Recall that the true King of Israel is God. Remember that the Lord is King and no other. Then try to appreciate the profundity of the irony that has Jewish leaders, the Roman prefect, Pontius Pilate, and pagan soldiers, all declaring that this man on the cross is the King.

A Suffering Messiah

This man on the cross. That is the totally unexpected, the never imagined vision of the future. Nothing in Israel's Bible, nothing in the centuries of longing, anticipated that God's future would be nailed to a cross. The revelation that Jesus was a suffering Messiah is almost entirely St Luke's. The idea is found nowhere in the Old Testament nor in any Jewish literature prior to or contemporaneous with the writing of the New Testament. Indeed, no other New Testament writer, not even Paul, speaks of Jesus as the suffering Messiah, though, of course, there are intimations and nudges aplenty. Luke, however, is crystal clear:

> And he said to them, 'Oh how lacking in understanding you are! How slow of heart to believe all the things of which the prophets spoke! Was it not necessary *for the Messiah to suffer* these things and enter into his glory?' And beginning from Moses and all the prophets he explained to them the things about himself in all the scriptures.
>
> *Gospel of Luke 24:25-27*

Not that there is a single sentence in the Bible of the Jewish people which foretells that God's holy Messiah would suffer and come to an ignominious death. Rather, it is the character of God revealed in every page of Israel's holy books which leads, inevitably, to the Place of the Skull. Recall Luke's Lord's Prayer and what it has to teach about forgiveness. Forgiveness is about remembering, about sharing the hurt which has been done, about healing which comes only when hurt is borne by the forgiving and the forgiven. To take away the sin of the world, God must enter into the world's pain and bear humanity's indifference. In the deepest sense, sin is unbearable unless it is borne by God, even unto death, death on a cross *(Letter to the Philippians 2:8)*.

Son of Man

The elusive title, Son of Man, which Jesus gives to himself, and by which no one ever addresses him, points inexorably to Golgotha. The phase is used in Jewish tradition to refer – albeit in a rather deferential way – to a human being, as may be seen in the *Book of Ezekiel* and elsewhere. It occurs in the *Book of Daniel* 7:13-14, there to refer to one who seems to assume the outer garb of a man yet is but 'like a human being'. This figure, in the phantasmagoria of that strange book, is given dominion over all creation for ever and a day. Whether this is has some bearing on the use of Son of Man in the Gospels generally, and in Luke in particular, we shall explore in our next chapter.

Raised from among the dead
On the third day be raised. Does anybody out there know what this means?

CHAPTER THIRTEEN

Jesus: The Glory of the Father
The Son of Man

He was saying to them all, 'If anyone wishes to follow after me, let him deny himself and take up his cross every day and follow me. For anyone who wishes to save his life will lose it, and anyone who loses his life for my sake will save it. What does it profit a man to gain the whole world but lose or forfeit his very self? Those who are ashamed of me and of my words, of these the *Son of Man* will be ashamed when *he comes in his glory and the glory of the Father* and of the holy angels. Truly I say to you, there are some standing here who will not taste death before they see the kingdom of God. *Gospel of Luke 9:26-27*

When we move from the foot of the cross to the edge of the empty tomb, we have, perhaps unbeknownst to ourselves, made a huge step in history and a mighty leap of faith. To stand at the entrance to the rock-hewn tomb, in which, according to the *Gospel of Luke* 23:53, Joseph of Arimathea buried Jesus, is no small matter. For Jesus of Nazareth was crucified and crucified criminals didn't get buried. There is a real question for Christians here which ought to compel them to pay more attention to history than they habitually do. St Paul's great sentence, *If Christ has not been raised, then our preaching has been in vain and your faith has been in vain (First Letter to the Corinthians 15:14)*, would appear very silly (but not totally silly!) if it turned out that Jesus had not been buried in the first place. Serious stuff, then.

The first three Gospels, Mark, Matthew and Luke, state simply that the body of Jesus was quickly disposed of, with no keening and none of the customary burial rites (John's Gospel is significantly different). An honourable Jewish burial, such as we know from somewhat later than the first century, would have involved washing the corpse, anointing it with oil, laying it out, binding up the chin, closing the eyes, trimming the hair, covering the head with a veil, clothing the body with a (linen) shroud, and binding the hands and feet.

Concerning incidents leading to the Jewish War (66-73 AD), one reporter who fought in that war, a Jerusalem priest called Josephus (and a very famous historian, indeed), condemns Idumaeans for failing to bury Jews they had slaughtered: *they proceeded to that degree of impiety, as to cast away their dead bodies without burial, although the Jews used to take so much care of the burial of men that they took down even those who had been condemned and crucified, and buried them before the going down of the sun (Jewish War, 4.5.2.317).* The *Book of Deuteronomy* 21:22-23 clearly states: 'If a man has committed a crime punishable by death and he is put to death, and you hang him on a tree [= crucifixion], his body shall not remain all night on the tree, but you shall bury him the same day, for a hanged man is accursed by God.' But Josephus interprets these words of torah as follows: *He that blasphemes God, let him be stoned, and let him hang upon a tree all that day, and then let him be buried in an ignominious and obscure manner (Antiquities, 4.8.6.202).* Burial, yes. Dignity, no.

Yet the Roman practice was to deprive executed criminals of all burial rites and to leave them to rot and be scavenged by carrion birds and wild dogs. Was the body of Jesus abandoned to scavengers or was it buried? And, if it was buried, was it the hurried burial of a crucified criminal or an honourable interment?

From a Jewish point of view, there are two indications that Jesus may have been buried. First, condemned by priestly authority as a blasphemer, Jesus died as the Feast of Passover was to be celebrated (whether on the eve of the feast or on the first day of the feast is much debated) and as the Sabbath (Saturday) approached. Jewish sensitivity would demand that neither the Passover nor the Sabbath would be profaned by a naked crucified corpse remaining in public view. Secondly, the demands of torah, explicitly expressed in the *Book of Deuteronomy*, required immediate burial, if not an honourable one.

From the Roman point of view – and that was what counted – Jesus was condemned to death by Pilate, the prefect who, in the exercise of his duty, sent Jesus to death as one claiming to be or alleged to be King of the Jews. Is it likely, knowing what we know of Pilate, knowing what we know of his boss, the emperor Tiberius (see *Gospel of John* 19:12 for the real politique), and the almost total absence of any archaeological remains of the hundreds of thousands of crucifixion's victims, that Jesus was an exception to what was everywhere else the rule? Crucified criminals don't get buried. Why was Jesus buried? Was Jesus buried?

Yehohanan

In June, 1968, Vassilios Tzaferis, of the Israel Antiquities Authority, was excavating several burial caves in the northern Jerusalem suburb of Givat Hamivtar. In one rock-hewn tomb he found eight ossuaries (bone boxes), one of which contained the skeletal remains of two men and a young child. One of the men and the child were named Yehohanan. The man had been crucified.

Yehohanan was 5 feet 5 inches tall and about twenty-five years old. His right heel bone had been pierced by a four-and-a-half inch nail at the head of which was still attached a small olive-wood washer. The man's legs seem to have straddled the upright of his cross (an old stripped olive tree?), so that his feet were nailed to either side, not to the front. Each nail was hammered first through the wooden washer, then through the heel bone, and so into the cross or tree. The washer prevented the crucified victim from pulling his feet free of the nail. Because the nail in his right ankle bent when it was hammered home and could not be easily extracted, the ankle, the nail and washer remained together when the body was taken down from the cross and buried. Sometime later the bones of the victim were deposited in an ossuary (itself a sign of wealth), with the heel, the nail and the washer. The arms of the victim were tied, not nailed, to the crossbeam, as the wrist bones and hand bones were undamaged. The leg bones appear to have been broken when the bones were deposited in the ossuary and not deliberately broken when Yehohanan was dying on the cross.

The remains of Yehohanan, who met his death within a few years of the crucifixion of Jesus, shed much light on how Jesus died. Jesus would have carried the crossbeam and, on arrival at

Golgotha, he would have been hoisted on to a vertical post or tree. He may have been nailed to the crossbeam or roped to it, as in the case of Yehohanan. His legs would have been straddled around the upright and nailed to it through his ankles. There might have been a *suppedaneum*, a footrest or similar support, not as an act of mercy but to enable the victim to breathe by lifting himself. In this way, suffering would last longer but breaking the legs would curtail the agony if, for whatever reason, the execution detail decided to end matters.

Thousands upon thousands of people were crucified in the ancient world. Of them there is no archaeological trace except the bones of the young man from Jerusalem. Victims of crucifixion were not given back to their families for burial. That was part, a devastating part, of the humiliation and punishment. Bodies were left on the cross to rot, with no public mourning, no burial, no lying with one's ancestors in the family grave. As the poet Horace observes, those who hang on the cross feed the crows (Horace, *Epistle* 1.16.48). So why was there an exception made in the case of Yehohanan? And why in the case of the man from Galilee?

The discovery of the bones of the crucified Yehohanan provided scholars with two pieces of evidence that are supportive of the claim in the Gospels that Pilate handed over the body of Jesus to Joseph of Arimathea. First, there is the fact that we now know of an exception to the almost universal rule that corpses of the crucified were deliberately withheld from family and friends and left to rot as a public warning to others. Secondly, Yehohanan was buried in a complex burial area in a rock-hewn tomb and the family used ossuary boxes. In other words, his family had money and money talks.

Joseph of Arimathea was a member of the Jewish council and, as an influential member of the Jerusalem élite, would have been able to gain access to Pilate. His reluctance to participate in the condemnation of Jesus by the assembly of the elders of the people, both chief priests and scribes, indeed, the whole council, would suggest that he was kindly disposed toward Jesus, if not an active disciple. He 'took courage', so St Marks tells us, indicating that his request was entirely beyond what was normally the case and was, in point of fact, against state policy. He was able to provide a tomb which had been hewn out of a rock and it was sealed with a stone, a tomb, that is, of a wealthy family. It is possible that Joseph was able to secure for Jesus what the family of Yehohanan had secured for that unfortunate young man. It is noticeable that the family and friends of Jesus, Galilean strangers to the Jerusalem power blocs, perhaps, not well-off, and cowed by the swift brutality that had descended upon them, were not involved in securing or burying the body of Jesus. Further, all the Gospels are at pains to emphasise that Jesus was buried. From an historical perspective, that may not prove much. But those who campaigned against Christian claims in the early days and centuries of the church frequently questioned the veracity of Christian witness to the resurrection of Jesus. They never questioned his burial.

The Jesus who was

Why this canter into history? We are about to consider the resurrection of Jesus, his exaltation, and his return *in his glory and the glory of the Father and of the holy angels (Gospel of Luke 9:26)*. Before we enter into discussions which will take us beyond anything within an historian's competence, it is well to remind ourselves that we cannot lightly jump, with an unconscionable degree of cockiness, from that with which history must wrestle to establish, into what only faith can affirm, thus leaving those of us who struggle in our faith gasping, not at serene, unruffled faith, but at arrant foolhardiness. If we are to move from the Jesus who walked in Galilee, to the Jesus embraced by the earliest disciples at Pentecost, to the Jesus of the first Christian communities, to the portraits of Jesus differently offered in our Gospels, to the Jesus who comes to us out of the traditions of our churches, to the Jesus who is (or can be) in our time and place, we must walk with intelligent and perspicacious tread, before we come to that fulness of faith which is the truth that sets us free *(Gospel of John 8:32)*.

Bible Resurrection

What do we mean by resurrection? What would the friends and neighbours of Jesus in Nazareth have understood resurrection to be? Did they hope in a life to come, a life immediately beyond the grave? Did they believe that only good people were brought to this promised land? What, in their view, was to be the fate of the wicked? A short excursion through Jewish thoughts will prove instructive.

The faith which is reflected in the pages of Israel's sacred literature concerns itself with living life in the world. For most of Israel's journey in faith, as reflected in its holy books and its sacred feasts and festivals, there is no expectation that one's life in this world was, in some manner, a preparation for being with God in a world to come. Dead people were consigned to the abode of the dead, to a condition called *Sheol*. The verb from which the Hebrew word *Sheol* derives means 'to be extinguished', 'to have misfortune'. The Greek version of the Old Testament translates the word as *Hades*, the Latin as *inferum* or *inferi*. Sheol is sometimes described as a place of punishment, as in Psalm 31:17 but the destiny of every human being, good or bad, was conceived to be the shadowy, non-existence of Sheol:

Man cannot abide in his pomp;
he is like the beasts that perish.
This is the fate of those who have foolish confidence,
the end of those who are pleased with their lot.
Like sheep they are appointed for Sheol.
Death shall be their shepherd;
straight to the grave they descend,
and their form shall pass away.
Sheol shall be their dwelling.
But God will ransom my soul from Sheol,
for he will receive me.
Psalm 49:12-15

The hope expressed in the last lines of the psalm is a prayerful longing, but is it any more than that? Psalm 16:8-11 and the upbeat ending to Psalm 22 seem to hold out hope but are more concerned with the possibility of deliverance from an ignominious death than an eternity of bliss. The steadfast love which endures forever does not endure for humanity beyond the portals of death and a cry for deliverance from death's finality falls on God's deaf ears:

O Lord, my God,
I call for help by day,
in the night I cry out before you.
let my prayer come before you,
bend your ear to my call!

My soul is filled with troubles
as my life draws near to Sheol.
I am numbered among those who go down to the Pit;
I am feeble and without strength,
like the forsaken among the dead,
like the slain that lie in the grave,
like everyone you remember no more,
all who are cut off from your hand.
You have plunged me into a bottomless Pit,
into regions dark and deep.
Your anger lies heavy upon me,
your waves of anger overwhelm me …

O Lord,
every day I call upon you,
I spread out my hands before you.
Do you work wonders for dead?
Do shadows rise up and praise you?
Is your steadfast love proclaimed in the grave?
Psalm 88:1-8 and *10-12*

To try to come to grips with a very complex matter, we will enter, as it were, into three dimensions of time: the past of the Old Testament, the present of Jesus, and the future of God's resurrecting love.

Old Testament Worries
The writings of the Old Testament do not have a doctrine of the after-life (apart from dismal Sheol, which was no life at all). But there are worries about God and the future. Bible thinking about the fate of humanity after death has nothing to do with our immortality and everything to do with God's credibility. If the catch-phrase of faith, *I will be your God and you shall be my people,* means anything, then how are we to explain the constant disas-

ters inflicted on God's people by pagan powers forever overrunning God's chosen people, forever inflicting rape and pillage, death and destruction, on people who trusted in God's saving power? As a matter of biblical record, God overcame Pharaoh and brought his people triumphantly to the land flowing with milk and honey. But to any ancient Jew keeping the score, God does not appear to have laid a glove on anyone since. Even if, as some maintain, it is the sins of the people which bring divine punishment, what about those who strive for holiness, who live torah, and who pray the prayers? Why are the saints bundled with the sinners? And what of those valiant warriors who openly resisted foreign and homegrown tyranny in order to stand up for God and who died doing so? What of the martyrs? Is God so impotent? Is the Almighty, when the chips are down, a pushover for every bully on the block? And, if God is your average six stone weakling, why bother? What Israel hoped for, strongly and constantly, was for the security and freedom to enjoy the gift of the land, to increase and multiply from generation unto generation. What everyone prayed for was that their children would be safe and have a prosperous future. But when these are denied, what is there left to hope for?

Intimations of Immortality

The reputation of God is now on trial. The witnesses for the prosecution are the devastated people of God, living and dead. The witnesses for the defence are few, but they are bold, imaginative, and utterly convinced that steadfast love does, indeed, endure forever.

The most confident, as befits an optimist who is but lately delivered from a fiery furnace and a lions' den, is Daniel, whose name means 'God has judged' (remember *The Merchant of Venice*?). There are, in fact, two Daniels. There is the one we meet in the first six chapters of the Book of Daniel. He is the great figure of learning, wisdom, and piety, the one of daring exploits and canny insight during the days when Nebuchadnezzar was the king of Babylon and the enemy of God and of God's faithful people. Nebuchadnezzar is the one who destroyed Jerusalem and its First Temple and who deported the inhabitants to faraway Iraq. Daniel is the one who stands up for Shadrach,

Meshach, and Abednego who were cast into the fiery furnace, the one who unravelled the mysteries of MENE, MENE, TEKEL, and PARSIN, the one whom God delivered from the den of lions. That is to say, the first Daniel is a fictional hero of the sixth century BC whose exploits map out a path along which Jews must walk, if they are to survive the dangerous world of exile in Babylon. The street-wise will embrace daring and cunning, wisdom and watchfulness, in order to hold on to their faith in the God of Israel who is a sure guide in times of trouble. What this first Daniel affirms is total faith in that steadfast love which will endure as long as Israel's people. He is also the one who speaks of a God who is a revealer of mysteries. And this revealer of mysteries is the One who speaks to the second Daniel.

The second Daniel is placed in a different time and a different place. We must fast-forward to the crisis of 167-164 BC, to the days when Antiochus Epiphanes of the Seleucids of Syria made a direct onslaught on Jews and Judaism. We have seen his determination to eradicate Jewish faith, his cultural imperialism, and the cruelty with which he enforced his policies. We have noted the Maccabean revolt and its success. The *Book of Daniel*, in chapters 7-12, offers an altogether different reaction to dangerous times. What we are presented with is a series of visions (destined to have a most profound effect on early Christian thinking) naming and shaming the great ones of the earth. The empires of the world, for all their posturing, are ephemeral and will pass away before the mighty power of God. The God of Israel presides over heaven and earth and will be seen to do so. What the second Daniel recommends is not resistance but faith. The future belongs to God.

God will appoint one like a Son of Man to have everlasting dominion (*Book of Daniel 7:13-14*), a dominion shared by the saints of the Most High, that is, the remnant who remain faithful; only such as these will receive the kingdom and possess it for ever and ever (*7:18*). The strutting Antiochus (contemptuously called 'a little horn') will receive his comeuppance but the awesome vision (*8:1-14*) requires explanation. Who better to explain visions and dreams than the angel Gabriel? Gabriel reveals that the vision is for the time of the end (*8:17*). Daniel turns to prayer for all his people, for those in Jerusalem, those in the countryside of Judah, and those in exile, beseeching mercy for a repentant people. His prayer is beautiful and precisely identifies the dilemma: when will God redress the balance in an evil world in favour of a repentant, God-fearing people? First, there is repentance with fasting, and sackcloth and ashes:

Then I turned my face to the Lord God, seeking him by prayer and supplication with fasting, and sackcloth and ashes. I prayed to the Lord my God, and made confession, saying:
O Lord,
the great and awesome God,
you who keep covenant and steadfast love
with those who love him
and keep his commandments:
we have sinned!
We have done wrong,
acted wickedly and rebelled,
turning away
from your commandments and ordinances.
We have not listened to your servants the prophets
who spoke in your name
to our kings, our princes, our fathers,
to all the people of the land.
Book of Daniel 9:3-6

Then comes the cry for help, the cry that mercy may rise before punishment stirs, that steadfast love endure beyond present suffering:

Now, therefore,
O our God,
listen to the prayer of your servant!
Listen to his supplications,
and for your own sake,
O my God,
give ear and listen.
Open you eyes:
look on our ruins,
the city which is called by your name.
We do not make our prayers to you

on the strength of our righteousness,
but on the ground of your great mercy.
O Lord, listen!
O Lord, forgive!
O Lord, pay attention!
For your own sake,
do not delay,
O my God,
because your city and your people
are called by your name!
Book of Daniel 9:17-19

If there is to be a future, it rests exclusively in the hands of God and is founded on God's steadfast love, not on human piety. Gabriel again provides an insight into the divine mind: God will be faithful even if the time of the end remains hidden from mortal calculation.

So far we have hope that the steadfast love of the Most High will endure beyond time and that there will be an end to human degradation and suffering: there will be an everlasting kingdom where God's will (and only God's) will be done *(Book of Daniel 7:27)*. But here is where God, the revealer of mysteries, moves beyond the despair of Sheol, beyond the impotent God who appears to lie prostrate before the world's tyrants. The future is not to be, as 7:27 might suggest, an earthly existence where peace reigns from one generation to the next. We are transported to life beyond death.

Recall the main theme of the whole of the *Book of Daniel*. Again and again, in all its parts, it tells of pagan rulers attacking God's people, trying to make them conform to pagan ways, belittling the God of the wise and faithful Jews who stand up for the faith of their fathers and mothers. Particularly, it speaks for the martyrs who laid down their lives during the crisis inflicted by Antiochus IV Epiphanes (which, as in the Feast of Epiphany, means a manifestation of the gods – what hubris!) and who, like the Maccabees, stood against political, economic, cultural and religious imperialism. This is the context within which the word of resurrection comes. It is a true epiphany. The guardian angel of Israel, the great prince who has charge of God's people,

Michael, whose name means *the one who is like God*, is the true re-vealer of the final secret:

> At that time Michael will arise, the great prince, the guardian of your people. And there shall be a time of trouble, such as never has been before since nations began until that [new] time. And at that [new] time, your people shall be delivered, every one whose name shall be found written in the book. And many of those who sleep in the dust of the earth shall awake, some to everlasting life, and some to shame and ever-lasting disgrace. But the wise shall shine brightly like the splendour of the firmament. And those who lead the many to righteousness shall be like the stars forever and ever.
> *Book of Daniel 12:1-3*

At last! After all the doubt and misgivings, after all the accus-ations that God was powerless, vindictive or merely indifferent, after all the centuries of worry at the fragility of God's love, there is a break in the clouds and a new vision is revealed. Or at least hinted at.

However ...

From the days in which the *Book of Daniel* saw the light of day (probably 164 BC) to the days of Jesus, there was much specul-ation of what these words might mean. But most strands of Jewish faith (but by no means all) began to look beyond this world, began to see that steadfast love does not end with death, and that beyond the culmination of history lay God's victory on behalf of the righteous in a world populated by the saints in glory and by their enemies in contemptuous disarray.

However, let's be clear on what is on offer and not on offer here:

1. Only the martyrs and teachers who guided Jewish people to fidelity will awake to everlasting life. Not all Jews, and not humanity in general.

2. Wicked pagans who have oppressed Jews will be con-signed to an ignominious but unspecified fate. Again, not all humanity.

3. The future in store for the martyrs and the wise is not at the moment of death. These people will die like everyone else,

but, unlike everyone else, they will be delivered from death, from the state of being dead. They will sleep in death and be awakened from this state of death. There is no question here of instant resurrection at the moment of death. At some future 'time', some dead people will be awakened from being dead to eternal life, and some to everlasting contempt. The great majority of human beings don't come into this vision of the future beyond death.

4. What is proposed is bodily resurrection. There is no question here of select souls passing into some eternal state at the moment of death and, at a later 'time', acquiring a body. What is envisaged is that some dead people will be raised up from among the whole universe of dead bodies with new bodies constructed on the old. Resurrection means, in this context, resurrection of the bodies (persons) who have been dead to a new bodily existence which will gloriously endure forever. Resurrection is something that happens to some dead people long after they are dead.

5. Those who are resurrected to eternal life are resurrected not because they are good but because God is great.

It is imperative that we come to the time of Jesus, and to the pages of the Gospels, with a clear understanding that we are not talking about the immortality of the soul when we discuss what Jesus and his contemporaries understood by resurrection. And we are not talking about the immortality of the soul when we try to understand what Christians, then and now, understand by resurrection.

The constant factor throughout our journey to Luke's understanding of the resurrection and glorious return of Jesus is the nature of God. The Old Testament (and much Jewish writings besides) is a journey of struggle, a struggle with the God who created the world, who made covenant with Israel, and who gave the land to a people of no account. The journey is a struggle because, on every side, God is hailed as the one whose steadfast love endures forever, but, on every side, God's people suffer from every kind of calamity. It is fine to sing the praises of God when all is well, quite another when you are sitting on a dungheap. In its struggle to fathom God, most Jews came to believe that the covenant with the God whose love endures forever could only be unbreakable if it perdured beyond death. God had to vindicate God's good name by vindicating martyrs and saints. And, by such swings and roundabouts, they came to believe in resurrection from the dead.

Enter into his glory
Each Gospel presents the resurrection of Jesus in accordance with its understanding of three interdependent factors. First, there is the individual portrait of Jesus in each Gospel. Secondly, there is the portrait of the disciples as each gospel-maker sees them. Thirdly, there is the circumstance of the Christian community to which each Gospel was addressed and whose task it was to be disciples in their time and their place. Our task is to identify the 'place' of resurrection in Luke's portrait of Jesus, its place in the mission given by Jesus to those who walked the way with him, and to infer from these the place of resurrection in the church of disciples in our time and place.

Thus far in Luke's portrait of Jesus we have discovered that:
Jesus welcomes people.
Jesus chats/talks about the kingdom of God.
Jesus heals where healing is needed.
Jesus feeds the hungry.
Jesus prays.
Jesus is the Messiah of God.

This is resurrection. This is the glory. When Jesus walked and talked with the two friends on the way to Emmaus, he pointed out that to enter into his glory the journey to Calvary was necessary. *Glory* is Luke's way of speaking of Jesus being with his Father; glory is his origin, his way to Jerusalem, and his destiny. To try to understand all this is hard work, mainly because when Christians talk about resurrection they are talking about something new under the sun.

When the shepherds gather around the manger were the baby was laid, the heavenly army proclaims God's praise:
Glory to God in the highest heaven,
and
Peace on earth, goodwill to all people. *Gospel of Luke 2:14*

Glory, so it seems, is the word used to describe 'where' God is and the 'atmoshpere' in which those who are 'with' God (like the heavenly army) 'live'. *Glory in highest heaven* translates into *peace on earth*. Insofar as there is peace on earth, then God's will is being done and God's glory is on earth as it is in heaven. Goodwill is in people when peace is in people. God's glory transforms people when they are transformed into peace. The coming of Jesus into the world is the culmination of the process we have seen in the ancient scriptures of Israel, a process which brings to earth God's steadfast love which endures forever. It is, as it were, a process of bedding down God's love in our world. To watch the process is to observe the career of Jesus from Bethelehem to the Place of the Skull, to Emmaus, and beyond. If we follow the word 'peace' through Luke's story, we will begin to understand how glory comes into and transforms our world, and thus we will come to begin to understand what 'resurrection' means. I would have you understand that I am mucking about here, as much in the dark as everyone else. To understand God is to be God.

Peace
The words of Zechariah might serve as a summary of the whole divine enterprise. In his Benedictus prayer *(Gospel of Luke 1:67-79)*, the old man takes us through a potted history of the Lord God of Israel's romance with his people, leading to the final, definitive outpouring of love. His child, our John the Baptist, is destined to go on ahead to prepare the way for the coming of the Lord. In that preparation and in the coming of the Lord Jesus, a host of blessings rain upon us:

salvation to his people,
forgiveness for their sins,
the tender mercy of our God.

All of this is 'the dawn from on high' breaking in upon us – I take this to mean that the glory of God is breaking into our world. Glory on earth is salvation, forgiveness, mercy. It is,

light to those who sit in darkness
light to those who sit in the shadow of death.

The shadow of death? Isn't this precisely what God's people

hoped would be removed by steadfast love? Yet notice to what safe haven our feet are brought as we are led from the shadow of death:

To guide our feet in the way of PEACE!

To be on the way to glory is to be on the path of peace. Look what happens to Simeon when he takes the child in his arms:

Lord,
now you are letting your servant go in PEACE,
according to your promise;
for my eyes have seen your SALVATION,
made ready by you in the sight of all peoples,
a LIGHT for enlightening pagan people,
and for revealing GLORY to your people Israel.
Gospel of Luke 2:29-32

Read it again! Peace = salvation = forgiveness = tender mercy = enlightening = glory.

The coming of the woman to wash feet with her tears and dry them with her hair is the coming of someone carrying the burden of her sins. But look at the going of her:

Your sins are forgiven!
Your faith has made you whole!
Go in peace! *Gospel of Luke 7:48-50*

The woman who suffered from debilitating haemorrhages for twelve years, a woman unclean to God and neighbour, simply touches his coat and away she goes, made whole, and at peace with God and the world *(Gospel of Luke 8:48)*. The finger of God, writing the life of Jesus, places the strong man at the gates of our earthly castle and we are safe and at peace *(Gospel of Luke 11:20-21)*. The fight for peace will be hard won – it will take a cross to do it – and if peace is to come, it comes, as Yeats said, dropping slow. But it comes, as surely as a cloud appearing in the west means rain is on the way (read *Gospel of Luke 12:49-56* – but carefully). And look at who and what comes in procession over the Mount of Olives:

Blessed is the King
who comes in the name of the Lord!
Peace in heaven!
Glory in the highest heaven. *Gospel of Luke 19:38*

If only the city of Jerusalem (then and now) could recognise that on that day, in that coming over the mountain, were and are the things which make for peace and glory *(Gospel of Luke 19:41)*. And the final gift to his disciples, before the ascension: *Peace be with you! (Gospel of Luke 24:36)*.

The journey of Jesus, a journey of welcoming, talking, healing, and feeding, a journey of anointing our world with God's humanity, is a journey through our world to God. All that we have seen, everyone we have met, all those ne'er-do-wells, those has-beens and never-weres, all those lost people, are visited with God's glory, welcomed, healed, fed, made whole and resurrected into peace. The resurrection of Jesus is at once the end and the beginning of a journey, a journey on the way to God. What we have got to grasp is that the way of Jesus to glory is the way to glory for all peoples. We can see this in the second concern of Luke: what must disciples do?

Disciples
Be Jesus:
> If anyone wishes to come after me, let him deny himself, take up his cross each and every day, and follow me. For if anyone wishes to save his life, he will lose it; whoever loses his life for my sake will save it.
> *Gospel of Luke 9:23-24*

To do what Jesus did, to walk his way, to follow in his footsteps, to be in our time and in our place, what he was in his, that is discipleship. Two manuals of instruction are provided. The first:
> Calling the twelve together, he gave them power and authority over all demons and to heal diseases. And he sent them to herald the kingdom of God and to heal. He said to them,
>
> 'Take nothing along the way, no staff, no bag, no bread, no money – not so much as an extra shirt. Whatever house you enter, stay there and go from there. Those who do not welcome you, on leaving that city shake the dust off your feet as a witness against them.'
>
> And going out, they went through one village after another, gospelling and healing everywhere.
> *Gospel of Luke 9:1-6*

And the second manual follows on an account of would-be disciples who approach Jesus at the precise moment he sets his face to go to Jerusalem, there to be 'taken up'. A pregnant moment, and it is, too, a moment along the way:

Along the way, as they journeyed, someone said to him, 'I will follow you wherever you go.' And Jesus said to to him, 'Foxes have holes, birds of the sky have nests. But the Son of Man has nowhere to lay his head.' Jesus said to another man, 'Follow me.' But he said, 'Let me first go to bury my father.' He said to him, 'Let the dead bury their own dead; as for you, go and proclaim the kingdom of God.' Yet another man said, 'Lord, I will follow you; but allow me first to take leave of my people at home.' Jesus said to him, 'No one who puts a hand to the plough and is forever looking back is fit for the kingdom of God.' *Gospel of Luke 9:57-62*

Then comes the second instruction for would-be disciples:

After these things, the Lord appointed seventy-two others and sent them ahead of him two-by-two to every city and place where he himself intended to go. He was saying to them,

'The harvest is plentiful, the workers few; pray, therefore, to the Lord of the harvest to send out workers into his harvest. Go! Behold, I am sending you out like lambs among wolves. Carry no purse, no bag, no sandals; and greet no one along the way. Whatever house you enter, first say, "Peace be upon this house!", and if there is a man of peace there, your peace will rest upon him. If not, it will return to you. Remain in that house, eating and drinking what is set before you, for the worker deserves his pay. Do not go from house to house. Whenever you enter a city and they welcome you, eat what is set before you. Heal the sick in that place, and say to them, "The kingdom of God is near to you!" But when you enter a city and they do not welcome you, go into their streets and say, "We shake off the dust of your city sticking to our feet against you. But know this: the kingdom of God is near!"' *Gospel of Luke 10:1-11*

It's important to pick up details in these long quotations. Notice that the phrase *along the way* occurs in all three. Of course, this simply means 'on the road'. But nothing in Luke is quite so simple. In his *Acts of the Apostles*, Luke talks of the Christian community as people 'belonging to the Way' *(Acts of the Apostles 9:2)*; people are instructed 'in the Way' which is called 'the Way of God' *(Acts of the Apostles 18:26-27)*; St Paul admits that he persecuted 'the Way' *(Acts of the Apostles 22:4)*; even officials are well informed about 'the Way' *(Acts of the Apostles 24:22)*. When Luke tells us in his Gospel that Jesus speaks to his disciples 'along the way', we will not take his words at face value and think of roads and highways. We will think of the Baptist who prepares the way of the Lord *(Gospel of Luke 1:76* and *3:4)*; we will ponder on the way of peace which Jesus creates as he makes his way to Jerusalem and to his death; we will think of all who walk the way with Jesus. We will think of the church, where it is, what it is for.

Notice, too, that the disciples are instructed to do what Jesus does: to welcome, to gospel people with God's word, to heal those who need healing, to break bread wherever they go. All of this is called taking up the cross and carrying it everyday. For those who follow Jesus to glory must pass the Place of the Skull, the inevitable stop along the way. As Luke broadly hints, be Jesus.

Son of Man

Trailing clouds of glory, Jesus comes into our world. As we have seen, every 'must' in Luke's Gospel is a station along the way, a work that must be done. Key milestones are signalled by use of the title Son of Man, a title briefly sketched in the last chapter and which now requires more detailed attention.

Nobody ever prays to the Son of Man. In our long tradition of Christian praying and hymn singing, there is no prayer, no hymn, no praise nor intercession which calls upon the Son of Man. Yet it is the name which Jesus consistently uses of himself in all our Gospels, sparingly in that of John, everywhere in Matthew, Mark, and Luke. And a further surprise: nobody ever addresses Jesus as Son of Man. There is one exception in the *Acts of the Apostles* 7:56 but even there St Stephen is quoting words of Jesus. It is as if Christian tradition, from the earliest days, acknowledged that here was a title intensely personal to Jesus and respectfully allowed the Son of Man to speak for himself. Of course, reluctance to intrude means that we do not know with any precision what Jesus meant by calling himself Son of Man and speculation is endless. Does it come from the *Book of Daniel* ('one like a son of man')? Does it come from the traditions, found, for example, in the *Book of Ezekiel*, which use the phrase to refer in a very formal way to a human being, especially to a human being who is privy to God's thoughts and plans and authorised to reveal to humanity what has been learned in the very heart of God? Lord only knows.

What meaning Jesus gave to the title and why he adopted it as his own may be obscure. But the contexts in which he used Son of Man are clear enough. First, the occasions when Jesus describes his mission to our world:

Knowing their contentious thoughts, in answer Jesus said to them, 'Why do you argue in your hearts? Which is easier? To say, "Your sins are forgiven you", or to say, "Arise and walk"? But in order that you may know that the Son of Man has authority on earth to forgive sin', – here he spoke to the paralysed man – 'I say to you, arise, take up your bed and go home.' Immediately, rising up before them, he took up what he had been lying on, and went to his own home, glorifying God. Amazement seized everyone and they glorified God, and they were filled with fear, saying, 'We have seen strange things today.' *Gospel of Luke 5:22-26*

He said to them, 'The Son of Man is lord of the Sabbath'. *Gospel of Luke 6:5*

'The Son of Man has come eating and drinking, and you say, "Look, a glutton and a drunkard, a friend of tax collectors and sinners!"' *Gospel of Luke 7:34*

'Foxes have holes, and birds of the air have nests; but the Son of Man has nowhere to lay his head.' *Gospel of Luke 9:58*

'For the Son of Man came to seek and to save that which is lost.' *Gospel of Luke 19:10*

The work begins with the exercise of God-given authority to forgive sin, an authority which takes precedence over hallowed Sabbath observance, even to the extent of eating and drinking with the unclean and the unholy, for it is precisely the lost who are being gathered in by God. But notice how this gathering in by the Son of Man leads to amazement, awe, and glory.

The second context within which Jesus speaks of himself as the Son of Man is the intense teaching which he gives to his disciples (and only to them) about his death and resurrection. The first instruction comes in response to Herod's question concerning the identity of Jesus and Peter's declaration that Jesus is none other than 'The Messiah of God'. Both Herod's question and Peter's affirmation must be removed from, on the one hand, the expectation that Jesus came to perform tricks (see *Gospel of Luke* 23:6-12) and, on the other, from the hope that the Messiah would prove to be a warrior determined to turn ploughshares into swords. The new thing on the face of the earth is that God's Messiah, as distinct from every expectation that ever was, is a Suffering Messiah. Yet not a Messiah abandoned by God: the cross is not the end of the story:

'But who do you say that I am?'

In answer, Peter said,

'The Messiah of God.'

He strictly admonished and commanded them not to tell anyone, saying,

'The Son of Man must suffer many things, be rejected by the elders, chief priests and scribes, and be killed, and on the third day be raised.' *Gospel of Luke* 9:20-22

'Let these words penetrate your ears: The Son of Man is going to be betrayed into the hands of men.' But they did not understand this saying; the meaning of it was hid from them, so that they could not comprehend it.
Gospel of Luke 9:44

Taking the twelve to one side, he said to them, 'Behold, we are going up to Jerusalem, and everything that is written about the Son of Man by the prophets will come to pass. For he will be handed over to the Gentiles; and he will be mocked and derided and spat upon. Having flogged him, they will

kill him, and on the third day he will rise again.' But they understood nothing of these things.
Gospel of Luke 18:31-34

Tellingly, this teaching of Jesus is confirmed by the heavenly witness of the two men in dazzling dress at the empty tomb:

'Why do you seek the living among the dead? Remember how he told you, while he was still in Galilee, that the Son of Man must be handed over into the hands of sinners, and be crucified, and on the third day rise.'
Gospel of Luke 24:5-6

The revelation that the Son of Man will suffer, die, and be raised from death is for the ears of intimate disciples only. And they did not understand what was being told them because God had stopped their ears and blinded their eyes. Unless and until they could grasp that God's Messiah stands before the world as a Suffering Messiah, they would not be able to grasp that resurrection comes through suffering. That is what must be. And that is what remains a mystery in our time and in our place, be we ever so good at explanation.

The third setting in which Jesus speaks of the Son of Man concerns the future. What is intriguing is that the future of disciples is wrapped up in the future of Jesus. Consider this:

He was saying to them all, 'If anyone wishes to follow after me, let him deny himself and take up his cross every day and follow me. For anyone who wishes to save his life will lose it, and anyone who loses his life for my sake will save it. What does it profit a man to gain the whole world but lose or forfeit his very self? Those who are ashamed of me and of my words, of these the Son of Man will be ashamed when he comes in his glory and the glory of the Father and of the holy angels. Truly I say to you, there are some standing here who will not taste death before they see the kingdom of God.'
Gospel of Luke 9:26-27

Following Jesus means every day sharing the fate that lies ahead in Jerusalem and continuing to live after the death of Jesus under the burden of the cross. The way that Jesus must go becomes the way that the disciple must follow. The cross is not merely a sign, a badge of Christian commitment; it is a determination to love the unloved and the unlovely, to love into life that which is lost in oneself and in the rest of the walking dead. Those who pray not to be brought to the test, those who pray that the cup might pass, know what cross-carrying is about. But they know, too, with seriousness of heart, that you have to lose your life to make it worth the living.

Such a way of discipleship means the kind of disregard for oneself which is subsumed into love. A whole world gained cannot compare with the world that awaits anyone who takes Jesus at his word and walks the way. To outface Jesus in our time and place is to be outfaced by Jesus in the world of glory. The disciples who thus heard the words of Jesus had yet to stand at the entrance to the empty tomb. It is only when they have done that they will enter fully into an understanding of the kingdom of God. We shall have to stand there, too.

The same point is made in Luke's version of what in St Matthew's Gospel we call the Sermon on the Mount. Look at how the worst of human misery is transformed:

Then Jesus looked on his disciples and said:

> 'Bless are you who are poor,
>   for yours is the kingdom of God.
> Blessed are you who are hungry now,
>   for you will be satisfied.
> Blessed are you who weep now,
>   for you shall laugh.
> Blessed are you when people hate you,
>   cast you aside,
>   denounce you,
>   defame you,
>   reject you as evil,
> on account of the Son of Man.
>
> Rejoice on that day,
> leap for joy!
> for surely your reward will be great in heaven!
> *Gospel of Luke 6:20-23*

God will shower blessings on those who bear the pain of the world now. Rejoicing and jumping for joy will be the reward in heaven. Another word to the same effect:

'I say to you, all who acknowledge me before men, the Son of Man will acknowledge before the angels of God; but whoever denies me before men will be denied before the angels of God.' *Gospel of Luke 12:8-9*

What we have in these three contexts which are characterised by sayings of Jesus which speak of him as the Son of Man is a seamless garment. The glory which surrounded the baby in Bethlehem, the glory manifested in the words and works of the Son of Man is the glory which is restored to him after death. The Son of Man is the Messiah of God's glory, the true epiphany to the world of God's love for all who are lost. And it is that same glory which imbues and enervates the faith and work of the disciples who work in Jesus' name, that is, who walk with him in our time and our place. Glory to God is still on earth as it is in heaven in those who take up the cross every day and follow and for those who are an anxiety to the God who seeks to find lost people. That is the meaning of resurrection, the meaning we can see if we journey from the place of the Skull to the village of Emmaus.

On the Way to Emmaus
We have been here before. But one sentence uttered on that journey into the future of people of the Way needs some clarification:

And he said to them, 'Oh how lacking in understanding you are! How slow of heart to believe all the things of which the prophets spoke! Was it not necessary for the Messiah to suffer these things and enter into his glory?' And beginning from Moses and all the prophets, he explained to them the things about himself in all the scriptures.
Gospel of Luke 24:25-27

The Gospels do not explain the resurrection of Jesus. They do not tell us what happened. They do not give an account of the stone being rolled back or of the emergence of the tomb's occupant. Gospel-makers were not concerned to prove that Jesus had been raised from the dead but to proclaim the significance of that event for those who formed the first Christian communities. No document of the New Testament was written to explain or defend Christian beliefs to outsiders nor even to win outsiders to faith. They do not provide historical evidence for the sceptical nor evangelical outreach to the interested bystander. They are in-house writings, faith speaking unto faith, and they take Christian beliefs as the basis for fostering *your work of love, your labour of love and your steadfastness of hope in our Lord Jesus Christ (First Letter to the Thessalonians 1:3)*. Consequently, gospel-makers are concerned, each in his own way, to spell out the meaning of the resurrection of Jesus for continuing discipleship. That is to say, they are attempting to explain what the resurrection means in their time and in their place. They are preaching to the converted.

To start with, the resurrection of Jesus is something entirely new. It is not a realisation of Jewish hopes in the sense that it fulfils any of the expectations expressed in the Old Testament and other Jewish writings of the time. For the resurrection of Jesus is not something that happens to Jesus alone, as if it were a personal reward or a personal vindication of a life lived in total obedience to God. What makes the resurrection of Jesus unique is that it changes the world.

That is what Christians claim and that is what gospel-makers proclaim. While the speculations we have examined help to clarify our thoughts, they do not prepare us for the surprise that comes to those who stand at the empty tomb and confess Jesus as Lord. The very earliest Christians saw themselves intimately bound up with what happened on that first Easter Day. For those first followers were convinced that their lives were changed by what happened to Jesus, that their destiny and the destiny of all humanity were intimately and inextricably bound up with the raising of Jesus from among the dead.

We can follow the trajectory of Christian thinking by attending yet again to the two erstwhile disciples of Jesus making their way to the village of Emmaus *(Gospel of Luke 24:13-35)*. It is, after all, the story of the church kaleidoscoped into an afternoon. Two disillusioned ex-disciples are walking away from it all, making their way away from Jerusalem, away from what had happened there. The implication is that they have decided to leave Jesus in the idle tale told by the women. Their hopes that Jesus the Nazarene would have delivered the people of Israel from

Roman domination and whatever other ills beset them were dashed in the most cruel way. Optimism that in Jesus they had found the hope of Israel, its saviour in time of trouble *(Book of Jeremiah 14:8)* is misplaced when resting on the shoulders of a crucified criminal. At this point, the stranger walking the way with them, gives them the true word of what had really happened at the Place of the Skull.

Note that first there are words. The first insight is in words, in the listening to words, to grasping the meaning of words. The first revelation of the mystery is an unravelling of words, of things written down, of scriptures. The first insight into what has truly happened *these last days* is to be found in listening: we are transfigured by listening.

The stranger in their midst is revealed in words. If followers of Jesus are to grasp the meaning of things, then they must attend to words:

And beginning from Moses and all the prophets he explained to them the things about himself in all the scriptures. *Gospel of Luke 24:27*

We must not forget that, in order to assure Theophilus of the truth concerning these things, Luke wrote down words *(Gospel of Luke 1:1-4)*. This is not an idle remark but is pivotal in our understanding of what Luke wishes to teach people in his time and place about what the resurrection means for everyday following of Jesus. At first Jesus is hidden from the two on the way to Emmaus where, in God's good time, recognition will happen. The first disclosure is in the word of Jesus directing them to the holy words of the scriptures. For Luke – and for us – that is where to begin. Luke does not tell us what sentences to look at. What is revealed is in *all the scriptures*. To break all the words is the work of a lifetime. Since there is no single sentence in *Moses and all the prophets* pointing to a Suffering Messiah, what we are guided to is the nature of God to be found in the Bible's pages, the God whose steadfast, merciful love is everywhere there displayed, never more dramatically, never more personally, never so totally, than in the work of the criminal who hung on the cross.

Did not our heart (singular!) *burn within us while he talked with*

*us on the way, as he was opening to us the scriptures? (Gospel of Luke
24:32)*. The risen Lord reaches into human hearts by revealing
the purpose of God. *This is the word of the Lord* becomes *This is the
word for our hearts*. The resurrection of Jesus enables Jesus to lift
up our hearts, to raise them up to the Lord. The resurrection of
Jesus embraces all who hear the word and keep it so that hearers
and doers are drawn into the presence of God and there live,
and move and have their being.

When the three drew near to the village, the two companions
pressed the stranger *to stay with them*. But how? How could the
one raised from the dead stay on earth with the living? Yet *he
went in to stay with them*:

> While reclining at table with them, taking the bread, he
> blessed [God] and breaking [it], was giving [it] to them.
> *Gospel of Luke 24:30*

They ran to tell what had happened on the way, and how he was
known to them in the breaking of the bread.

For Luke, the word of God and the breaking of the bread
make present in his time and in his place the very presence of
God-with-us, the glory of God which shone round about the
manger in Bethlehem. *And so enter his glory* is not only the fulfilment of *Father, into your hands I commit my spirit*, that last utter-
ing on the cross. Being with the Father is a bringing of all disciples, of all the lost, into the glory of the Father. Luke's second
book, the *Acts of the Apostles*, records the outpouring of the Holy
Spirit on all flesh, on all God's children, and through word and
bread-breaking, the welcome, the talking with, the healing, and
the feeding go on. Thus it is that the resurrection of Jesus, in
being a return to the Father, is, in the same moment, an extension of God's outreach in Jesus beyond the hills of Galilee to the
four corners of the earth.

The Second Coming?

Today is a big word in Luke. By implication, tomorrow is not.
Luke's Gospel emphasises the here-and-now, more than the future
coming again of the Son of Man. Consider:

> '*Today* [in Nazareth] this scripture has been fulfilled in your
> hearing.' *Gospel of Luke 4:21*

... they glorified God, and were filled with awe, saying, 'We have seen strange things *today*'. *Gospel of Luke 5:26*

'*Today* salvation has come to this house ... '
Gospel of Luke 19:9

As he drew near and saw the city, he wept over it, saying, 'If you, even you, had only recognised *today* the things that make for your peace!' *Gospel of Luke 19:41-42*

What the so-called Second Coming will be, when it will be, where it will be, what fate awaits humanity 'when' it 'happens', are not disclosed. There is much speculation, some of it mistaken, in the pages of the New Testament which, across the centuries, has generated more heat than light. On two matters, Christians have been adamant. First, the future, whatever it holds, belongs to God. Secondly, whenever you are having difficulties trying to say something sensible about God, it is wise to tell a story:

There was a certain man and he was rich. Forever clothed in purple and fine linen, he feasted sumptuously every day. A man named Lazarus, a poor man, a man covered in sores, lay at his gate, hoping to be filled with whatever fell from the rich man's table. Not only that, but the dogs came and licked his sores.

The poor man died and was carried by the angels to Abraham's bosom. The rich man died and he was entombed. Being in Hades, in torment, he lifted up his eyes, and saw Abraham afar off and Lazarus at rest in his bosom. And, crying out, he said, 'Father Abraham, have mercy on me and send Lazarus to dip the tip of his finger in water and cool my tongue, for I am tormented in this flame.' But Abraham said, 'Child, remember that in your lifetime you received good things and Lazarus, by the same token, bad things. But he is comforted here, and you are tormented. Besides all this, between us and you a great chasm has been put in place, in order that those who would pass from this side to you may not do so; and none may pass from there to us.'

And he said, 'Then I beg you, Father, to send to my father's house, for I have five brothers, so that he may warn them, in case they also come to this place of torment.'

But Abraham says, 'They have Moses and the prophets;

let them listen to them.' But the man said, 'No, Father Abraham! But if anyone were to come to them from amongst the dead, they would repent.'

Abraham said to him, 'If they do not heed Moses and the prophets, they will not be persuaded even if someone were to rise from the dead.' *Gospel of Luke 16:19-31*

That's the gospel truth.

CHAPTER FOURTEEN

Jesus is God's Son,
The Chosen One

It happened that about eight days after these words, taking Peter, John, and James, he went up the mountain to pray. And it happened that while he was praying, the appearance of his face became different, and his clothing white and dazzling. And, behold, two men were talking with him, Moses and Elijah, who appeared in glory, and they were speaking of his exodus which he was to fulfil in Jerusalem. But Peter and those with him were overcome with sleep. Waking up, they saw his glory and the two men who stood beside him. As they were departing from him, Peter said to Jesus, 'Master, it is good for us to be here, and let us make three tents, one for you, one for Moses, and one for Elijah', not knowing what he was saying. While he was saying this, a cloud came and overshadowed them; as they passed into the cloud, they became afraid. Then a voice came from the cloud, *'This is my Son, my Chosen One; listen to him!'* In the happening of the voice, only Jesus was to be found. And they kept silent, telling no one in those days of anything they had seen.

We began with a baby. In fact, two babies. To be more precise, we began with an expectant father and mother and an expectant mother. In the case of the expectant mother, the age old question hangs heavily in the gossipy air: *who's the father?*

In the case of John the Baptist, both parents are present and correct. There are strange things in their story. There's the age factor. There's the angel, there's old Zechariah getting struck dumb, there's the carfuffle about choosing a name. Above all there are the predictions prompted by the Holy Spirit and there are the thoughts of friends and neighbours. Gabriel, the same revealer of mysteries we found in the *Book of Daniel*, gets his tuppence worth in first:

'Zechariah, do not be afraid. Your prayer has been heard. Your wife will bear you a son, and you will call his name John. And for you there will be joy and gladness, and many people will rejoice at his birth, for he will be great in the sight of the Lord.' *Gospel of Luke 1:13-15*

The old man himself, no less than the son, was filled with the Holy Spirit and, as we have seen, in a speech at the circumcision celebrations, spoke proudly of his child. His tongue untied, he began to speak, praising God for what his son would become. The words tumble out: remembering, promises, holy covenant, mercy, saving, rescuing, holiness, justice. His only son will be herald of an explosion of steadfast love: a prophet, a preparer, a teacher, an announcer of sins forgiven, a herald of the dawning of a new day.

Then there are the women, the calm, steely Elizabeth, and the other woman, bearing the other child, the child with no father. They are less flamboyant, more private and direct in their words. Mary is straight and to the point:

'How can this be since I do not know a man?'

Gospel of Luke 1:34

The angel Gabriel, too, is less flamboyant, more direct in his words to Mary than to the old man:

'Holy Spirit will come upon you, and the power of the Most High will overshadow you. Therefore, the child to be born will be holy; he will be called Son of God.'

Gospel of Luke 1:35

Straightforward Mary again:

'Behold, I am the Lord's servant. Be it done to me according to your word.' *Gospel of Luke 1:38*

Elizabeth, the baby kicking inside her, puts her finger on the pulse of God with unerring faith:

'How is it with me that the mother of my Lord should come to me?' *Gospel of Luke 1:43*

And look at what happens to the two mothers-to-be. The mother of John:

'This is what the Lord has done for me when he looked favourably upon me and took away the disgrace I endured among people.' *Gospel of Luke 1:25*

And Mary:

'A sword will pierce your soul.'
Gospel of Luke 2:35

Who is Jesus?

Transfiguring Words

Talking about God is always ambiguous. We have to use human language to attempt to come to say what we want to say. The words which are addressed to us in the Bible, God's words to us, are equally human and equally ambiguous. To try to put God into words is impossible, for fallible, mortal words cannot come to the heart of the matter. St Paul asks, *Who has known the mind of God? (First Letter to the Corinthians 2:16)*. The answer is, of course, no one. When we read phrases such as Son of God, we must be very careful. A son is a male child begotten by the sexual union of a man and a woman. When we call Jesus Son of God, we do not mean that there is a Mr God and a Mrs God, anymore than when we call God our Father we mean that our Mother is out there somewhere. We mean that God is like a good, caring, providing, loving, directing, responsible, always-there parent (parent? – there we go again!). It is a question of trying to unravel the infinity of God with finite human words. Our words, like our hearts, must be transfigured.

The beginning

Throughout his Gospel, Luke grapples on every page with the identity of Jesus. *Who is this man?* is his perennial question. His efforts to reveal to us the identity of Jesus in answer to the question of Herod Antipas is but a part of his wider design. If we return yet again to the beginning of his story, we can amass a whole host of titles and designations showered upon Jesus in order to clarify who he is. We can draw up an impressive list and in every case we have to ask ourselves what exactly is being said. We have to go scurrying around hither and yon to try to tie down what it is Luke is saying. For he is writing for his time and his place and for a people whose thought patterns and language are not ours. Now that we are coming to the end, I want to go back to the beginning in order to re-gather our thoughts. In the story of the Transfiguration, Luke invites us up the mountain to pray and to listen. We need to be sure that we are equipped for the climb.

Luke's cascade of titles, designations, and descriptions begins with Gabriel's annunciation to Mary *(Gospel of Luke 1:26-35)* and we will return there to tease out what he is about, taking each phrase into account, beginning with,

He will be great
Gabriel, the *revealer of mysteries*, discloses to Zechariah that his child *will be great before the Lord*. He tells Mary that she will conceive and bear a son and that she must name him Jesus for, as he says, *He will be great*. So both children *will be great*. Does this mean that John the Baptist and Jesus are equally great? No. John is great before God because of what he is appointed to do, the life he is empowered by God to live, and the witness the Holy Spirit impels him to bear before the people. He will be like Elijah of old and fulfil the vocation outlined for the old prophet in the last sentence of the *Book of Malachi* 4:5-6. But the greatness of Jesus is an altogether different matter.

The opening words of Psalm 48 are *The Lord is great!* The same shout is echoed in the Koran: *Allah Akbar! God is great!* God, and only God, is truly great *(Psalm 86:10)*. The reason is spelled out clearly in another hymn:

For I know that the Lord is great,
and that our Lord is greater than all gods.
Psalm 135:5

Unlike John, Jesus is great, not on account of the vocation he is given. He is great because of who he is.

And he will be called...
Called by whom? Here we have an example of an old friend, the divine passive. *Called by God* is what is meant. Mary must name the child Jesus but God does not call the child by that name. God declares, through Gabriel and before the world, the precise

nature of the child who is to come into the world. We call him Jesus; God names him Son.

Son of the Most High

We can trace the phrase *Most High* (one word in Greek) as a designation for God in ancient Jewish writings, especially in the Greek version of the Old Testament, but elsewhere in Jewish literature as well and, as we have seen, in one famous fragment among the documents found at Qumran. In that fragment we read, *He shall be hailed Son of God, and they shall call him Son of the Most High*, in reference, so it would seem, to a king who is destined to live forever and bring peace to the earth. There are some who see this sentence as a mocking reference to some hated king among the many tyrants who terrorised the people of God. Some scholars speculate that it might refer to a future messiah/ king of Israel. What we can say is that the phrase existed before Luke used it. Wherever he found it, he employs it to refer to Jesus whom he will shortly designate as Son of God and as the one who will sit on the throne of David. Luke speaks of God as the Most High far more than anyone else in the New Testament: John the Baptist *will be called* (passive voice, a divine passive, and note that it is not son of...) *the prophet of the Most High (Gospel of Luke 1:76)*; those who love their enemies thereby become sons of the Most High *(Gospel of Luke 6:35)*; the demon in the unfortunate man from Gerasa screams at Jesus, 'What have you to do with me, Jesus, Son of the Most High God?' *(Gospel of Luke 8:28)*. There are two occurrences of the phrase in the *Acts of the Apostles* and only two more in the whole of the New Testament. What is clear is that, according to Luke, speaking through the angel Gabriel, God declares that the child of Mary is God's Son and, as such, partakes of that greatness which belongs only to God, the Most High.

And the Lord God will give to him the throne of his father David

The matter of kingship over God's people has concerned us extensively. The Bible emphatically declares that God gave kings to Israel in order that they might exercise God's good care, as a good shepherd is expected to look after his sheep. The throne of Israel is, therefore, a free gift from God and what God gives God can take away. Longings for a return of the halcyon days of David the King were in everyone's hearts, even in the heart of God who now places his own Son on the throne as a true Good Shepherd, indeed! A parable which we have not mentioned before fits readily into place here:

A man planted a vineyard and leased it out to farmers. He himself went abroad for a long time. At an appropriate time, he sent a servant to the farmers so that they should give him some of the profits of the vineyard. But the farmers beat him up, and sent him away with nothing!

So he sent another servant. They beat him and treated him scandalously, and sent him away with nothing! Then he sent a third and they severely injured him and threw him out!

The owner [in Greek, the word used here is *kyrios*, as in *Kyrie, eleison*] of the vineyard said, 'What shall I do? I will send my beloved son; perhaps they will respect him.'

But the farmers reasoned among themselves, 'This is the heir; let us kill him, that the inheritance may be ours.' And, throwing him out of the vineyard, they killed him.

What will the owner of the vineyard do to them? He will come and destroy those farmers and give the vineyard to other people. *Gospel of Luke 20:9-16*

Who is this owner, the father of a beloved son, and who is the beloved son, the one chosen to be sent, who is taken out and killed?

Reign over the house of Jacob

A king, then, who will reign over the descendants of the great patriarch Jacob, whose wrestling with God won him the name Israel *(Book of Genesis 32:22-32)*. But where will be his throne?

Of his kingdom there will be no end

The final, definitive work of God is in the beloved Son who will be driven outside the city gates and killed. But that is precisely how God's will is done on earth as it is in heaven. That is how the kingdom comes.

Its coming begins with Mary. When she protests that what Gabriel demands cannot come to be because she has not known a man, the all-knowing revealer of God's secrets tells her that *Holy Spirit will come upon her*, that is, as Gabriel explains, she will be enveloped by the power of the Most High, and that, as a consequence, her child will

Be called 'holy', 'Son of God'

That divine passive again: called by God. And holiness is a quality that uniquely belongs to God. To be sure, human beings must strive to be holy as God is holy. The *Book of Leviticus* 11:44 commands the whole people: *Be holy, for I am holy*. Holiness is an attribute of God which may be imitated by people, may and must be aspired to by those who would be perfect. But it never belongs to people. It is always a gift. Whereas, says Gabriel of Jesus, like Father, like Son.

What the title Son of God means for Luke and his readers is all that we have seen in the stories of Zechariah and Elizabeth and in the stories about Mary and the baby in the manger.

The End

If we fast-forward to the end of the story, we find another cluster of titles, designations, and descriptions, this time in another conversation *(Gospel of Luke 22:66-71)*. Not Mary and Gabriel. Rather the leaders of the people place Jesus on trial for his life:

> And when it was day, the assembly of the elders of the people, chief priests and scribes, came together. And they led him away to their council chamber, and they said,
> *If you are the Messiah, tell us.*

What we have here is not a court record, with speedy stenographers transcribing every word uttered. What we have is an artificial Christian construction in which the identity of the prisoner is the crucial issue. From Luke's perspective, Jesus is not done to death for what he did. It is *who he is* that is the heart of the matter, whatever the historical charge-sheet might have contained. And in this short exchange between the court and the prisoner, the whole gospel of God is placed before Luke's readers.

On our way with Luke to this place, we have learned what Messiah means. We know that, in the vocabulary of God, the word has no meaning unless it be preceded by another word:

Suffering. It is necessary that God's Messiah should come to this place because it is necessary, it is a divine decree that the depth of the riches and the wisdom and the knowledge of God should be shouted from a cross *(Letter to the Romans 11:33)*. But how difficult it is to fathom the wisdom of God! St Paul has but one slogan: *We preach Christ crucified! (First Letter to the Corinthians 1:23)*. He is realistic enough to point out, however, that this is an almost impossible leap for Jewish faith and, of course, for pagans it is just stupid. Thus the reply of Jesus is that there's none so blind as those who will not see: *If I talk with you, you will not believe; and if I ask you questions, you won't answer.*

From now on
the Son of man
will be seated at the right hand
of the power of God

So Jesus makes a voluntary statement to the court. The man from God, the one who knows the heart of God, the one who reveals the purposes of God, the very Son of Man *from now on* will be seated elsewhere. Not in this human court but in the heavenly court. *From now on:* that is to say, the exodus of Jesus, his going from this world, is not a defeat but a liberation for all whom God has placed in his hands. From this moment of defeat, God will open a new way to life. The journey does not end on the cross; there is a promised land. In the place of honour, invested with God's power, the Son of Man will dispense God's mercy on all who are lost:

> The Lord said to my Lord:
> 'Sit at my right hand,
> till I make your enemies
> a footstool under your feet.'
> *Psalm 110:1*

Of course, the most deadly enemy, and the last enemy, is death.

You are, then,
the Son of God?

It is not possible for those assembled in this court to ask such a question. If your quest is to seek out history here, then take your leave. For Luke means here the full Christian understanding of who this man is and that understanding is a matter of faith that cannot be scrutinised by the courts. Ironically, he puts his final word on who Jesus is in the mouths of his accusers (notice 'they all said', as if they were a chorus), all the more to emphasise that the true purpose being carried out here is God's. As we have learned many pages ago, no Jewish religious court could affirm what Christians affirm. That Jesus is Son of God in a unique sense, Son of God as no other may be so described, is beyond what mortals may truly know or understand. The Father knows his Son. Gabriel knows the Son of God. And Jesus knows who he is: *You say that I am.*

There can be only one verdict.

The end is not yet. There is more to come. We move to the foot of the cross and the same leaders of the people scoff at their victim, the people standing by, watching *(Gospel of Luke 23:35-38)*. The scoffing of the leaders and the mockery of the soldiers are orchestrated, not simply to heighten the drama and to plead for our sympathy (though those intentions are clearly there); the chief intent is to repeat and reinforce the portrait. Consider:

He saved others

If the scoffing rulers know that he saved others, why have they done him to death? We have witnessed the birth of the saviour who is Christ the Lord when we joined the shepherds around the manger. We have walked the way with him as he saved and made whole every kind of brokenness. And now he is to be condemned for it?

Let him save himself

There is really only one riposte to the scoffers:

… anyone who wishes to save his life will lose it, and anyone who loses his life for my sake will save it. What does it profit a man to gain the whole world but lose or forfeit his very self?

The Messiah of God

What irony! Here we have the leaders of the people echoing the very words of Peter, echoing the solemn declaration of Christian faith *(Gospel of Luke 9:20)*. The first readers and hearers of his Gospel will surely have marvelled at Luke's daring in putting such a Christian question in the mouths of those who have come to mock and not to pray. For the answer to the question is a resounding 'yes' for those who hear the story of the journey from Galilee to Jerusalem from our side of the resurrection. Jesus truly is anointed by God to save others by not saving himself.

God's Chosen One

This, the second of what is a startling litany of three profoundly Christian titles for Jesus, God's Chosen One, takes us back to the Transfiguration story which is our concern in this chapter. Peter's confession of faith that Jesus is the Messiah of God, God's affirmation of the true identity of the one born of Mary (*Gospel of Luke 9:35*), and Gabriel's declaration that the Lord God will give to that child the throne of his father David (*Gospel of Luke 1:32*), all of these affirmations are clustered around the cross. The manger, where the child lay wrapped in royal swaddling cloths (*Wisdom of Solomon 7:4-5*), was where great names were uttered: Saviour, Messiah, Lord. So now, at the cross.

King of the Jews

There are millions of books written about Jesus of Nazareth, from Gospels to Hollywood scripts. There is only piece of writing about Jesus written is his own lifetime. And it is this: *This is the King of the Jews*. The soldiers mock their victim, *If you are the King of the Jews, save yourself!* Again, the ungodly view that it is better to save one's life than to lose it in order to save it.

The mocking jibe is written up above the head bowing in death and it is shocking. The shock is that the King of the Jews, as every Jew in the crowd well knows, is God.

At the birth: Saviour, Messiah, Lord King. At the death: Saviour, Messiah, Lord King. *As it was in the beginning, is now, and ever shall be…*

The Middle

In the middle is the Transfiguration. The word 'transfiguration' is not used by St Luke, but that is what the story is called. It comes from an English attempt to translate a Latin phrase, itself trying to translate a Greek word used in St Mark's Gospel, on which Luke depended for much of his own work. The Latin phrase, *transfiguratus est,* comes from the Vulgate, the Latin Bible of St Jerome (c.347-420 AD) which, despite the opposition of St Augustine, became the Bible for Christianity in the West. An English priest, John Wyclif (1333-1384), initiated a translation of the Bible into English and it is to this that we owe the phrase *he was transfigured before them (Gospel of Mark 9:3).* We shall explore the matter further. For the moment, and to set our thoughts on the right road, here is a short story:

> When Moses came down from Mount Sinai with the two flat stone slabs of the commandments in his hands, he did not know that, as he came down the mountain, the skin of his face had become radiant because he had been talking with God. When Aaron and all the people of Israel saw Moses, behold, the skin of his face was radiant, and they were afraid to come near him. Only when Moses called to them did Aaron and all the leaders of the gathering of people come to him. Moses talked with them. And after that all the people of Israel came near, and he enjoined on them all that the Lord had said to him on Mount Sinai. And when he had finished speaking with them, he put a veil on his face. But when he went in before the Lord to speak with him, he took the veil off, until he came out again. When he came out, he told the people of Israel all that had been commanded. The people of Israel saw the face of Moses; they saw that the skin of his face was radiant. And Moses used to put the veil on his face, until he went into the presence of the Lord to speak with him.
>
> *Book of the Exodus 34:29-35*

The Transfiguration of Jesus comes in the middle, between the birth in Bethlehem and the resurrection in Jerusalem. It comes as a final answer to Herod's question and as conclusion to the lesson that true following involves taking up one's cross every day and the promise that faithful followers will be recognised when the day of glory comes. We will have to read carefully, for in a moment or two we will be asked to set our faces to go to Jerusalem and to be prepared for what will happen to us there *(Gospel of Luke 9:51).*

After These Words ...
After Herod's question,
after the actions of
    welcoming,
    talking,
    healing
    feeding,
after Peter's word: *The Messiah of God*,
after the warning of necessary suffering,
after the cost of discipleship is plainly stated,
after all these words –

transfiguration comes.

After about eight days

The first phrase of this Transfiguration story, *after about eight days*, hints at another story but the hint is rather obscure. As we shall see, there are three tents in this story and in the *Book of Leviticus* 23:37-44 the proper way to celebrate the Feast of Succoth (tents, huts, tabernacles, whatever) is laid down. It was a local harvest festival celebrated by farmers but by the time of Jesus it had become as big fun week out in Jerusalem for those who could make it there (though imperial oppression had politicised the feast from the days of the Maccabees to the rebellion of Bar Kokhba). People erected tents and camped out in them for seven days rejoicing before the Lord. A good time was had by one and all in memory of the years in the desert when God fed his people with manna and fat quails. But on the eighth day the festival ended in a solemn rest. After the week long celebration, on the eighth day, a Sabbath rest was observed to recall that, after the fireworks of the Exodus and the desert wanderings, God led his people to rest, to quiet, to gentle peace. Does Luke want us to see in the Transfiguration a taste of what it is like to come home, to be brought to glory, finally to come into the kingdom? Certainly, taking us up a mountain is taking us to where we are likely to meet God face to face.

Peter, John, and James

Following on the words about taking up one's cross everyday and about the Son of Man in glory recognising those who walk with him, there is a very strange saying:

In truth I say to you, there are some standing here who will
not taste death until they see the kingdom of God.
Gospel of Luke 9:27

Does this mean that the 'some' are Peter, John and James in the
next sentence? And does it mean that the experience of the
Transfiguration is the ultimate revelation of what it means to be
in the kingdom of God. I think so, and I shall proceed with that
conviction in mind.

When Jesus came to the house of Jairus, his twelve year old
daughter lay dead *(Gospel of Luke 8:40-56)*. A messenger had told
Jairus so but Jesus insisted on making his way to the house of
mourning with astonishing words. Instead of a kindly and
heartfelt 'I'm sorry for your troubles', which, with the best will
in the world, is the best that we can do, Jesus says two things.
First to Jairus,

'Do not be afraid!
Only believe, and she will be saved!'
Gospel of Luke 8:50

Then, to the mourners,
'Don't cry!
She's not dead, just asleep!'
Gospel of Luke 8:52

He allowed no one to enter the house except the distraught father and mother and, for some unexplained reason, Peter, John
and James. And before their very eyes, taking the dead child by
the hand, he says, 'Child, arise.' And she does. Early on in his
teaching days, Jesus called Simon Peter, and James and John (no
mention of Andrew), the first to be called, and they left everything and followed him to take up a new trade: *fishers of people*,
in our familiar hearing of the translated words. But the strange
thing is the exact words with which Jesus calls Simon Peter:

'Do not be afraid!
From now on you will be taking people alive.'
Gospel of Luke 5:10

Fishermen usually kill what they catch; I confess that the weight
in my bag for hitting fish on the head is called a priest. But Jesus
is calling the three fishermen to abandon fishing and take up life

saving. Their vocation henceforth is to save people, take them alive, preserve them for life, gather them safely into the net of God's kingdom. For the next time we meet the three they are with Jesus when he gives life to a little girl who has died. Literally, he takes her by the hand out of the jaws of death. And there to see and to learn what the job is about are Peter, John and James. Both the call of the three by the side of the lake and the raising of Jairus' daughter are resurrection stories – if you think about it.

And here they are, called to the mountain, to be with Jesus in his glory, not tasting death before they witness what the enterprise is all about and experiencing how good it is to be with Jesus where God is.

The mountain

Mountains are where you meet God. This is true for anyone who has ever climbed a half decent mountain. It is true in the Bible and Luke is well aware of the tradition that meetings with God tend to be on mountains. Angels, you may have noticed, are sent to where people are. God holds open house on the tops of mountains.

Mount Sinai is God's mountain. Others mountains come into many stories but Mount Sinai or, as it is also called, Mount Horeb, where Moses met with God face-to-face, is *the* mountain. To escape arrest for killing a man, Moses fled Egypt and, attaching himself to the family of a man called Jethro, a priest of Midian, he found himself looking after sheep. His shepherding brought him to *Horeb, the mountain of God (Book of the Exodus 3:1)*. The voice from the burning bush spoke, warning Moses to take off his sandals for he was standing on holy ground, and reveals that the time for liberation has come:

'I am the God of your father, the God of Abraham, the God of Isaac, and the God of Jacob … I have seen the affliction of my people who are in Egypt, and I have heard their cry because of their taskmasters; I know their sufferings, and I have come down to deliver them out of the hand of the Egyptians, and to bring them out of that land to a good and broad land, a land flowing with milk and honey …'

Book of the Exodus 3:5-8

When the battle with Pharaoh was won, Moses led the people back to Mount Sinai (Horeb), and again the Lord called to
him out of the mountain, saying:

> 'Thus you shall say to the house of Jacob, and tell the people
> of Israel: "You have seen what I have done to the Egyptians,
> and how I bore you on eagles' wings and brought you to my-
> self. Now therefore, if you will obey my voice and keep my
> covenant, you shall be my possession among all the peoples;
> for all the earth is mine, and you shall be to me a kingdom of
> priests and a holy nation." These are the words you shall
> speak to the children of Israel.'
> *Book of the Exodus 19:32-36*

Every detail surrounding Mount Sinai and its part in the Exodus
story, the rôle it came to play as a symbol in Israel's religious
imagination, ought to concern us as we climb up the mountain
of the Transfiguration. I will call to mind just two other incidents. First, clouds:

> On the morning of the third day there were thunders and
> lightnings, and a thick cloud upon the mountain, and a very
> loud trumpet blast, so that all the people who were in the
> camp trembled. Then Moses brought the people out of the
> camp to meet God; and they took their stand at the foot of the
> mountain. And Mount Sinai was wrapped in smoke, because
> the Lord descended upon it in fire; and the smoke of it went
> up like smoke out of a kiln, and the whole mountain quaked
> greatly. And as the sound of the trumpet grew louder and
> louder, Moses spoke, and God answered him in the thunder.
> And the Lord came down upon Mount Sinai, to the top of the
> mountain; and the Lord called Moses to the top of the moun-
> tain, and Moses went up.
> *Book of the Exodus 19:16-21*

What follows is the giving of The Words or what we call (but the
Bible does not) the Ten Commandments. When Moses *went up to
receive the two tables of stone, written by the finger of God (Book of the
Exodus 31:18),* we are told that 'the cloud covered the mountain'
and that 'the glory of the Lord settled on Mount Sinai' *(Book of
the Exodus 24:15-16).*

The fiery prophet Elijah, a companion of Moses in the

Transfiguration story, also has dealings with God on Mount Horeb (Sinai). Having routed the false prophets of Baal and in the process incurred the wrath of the equally fiery Queen Jezebel, Elijah made a run for safety and found himself at Horeb, the mountain of God *(First Book of the Kings 19:8)*. Then, in what is one of the most famous of passages in the Bible, Elijah was commanded to take his stand on God's mountain:

'Go forth, and stand upon the mountain before the Lord.'

And behold, the Lord passed by, and a great and strong wind rent the mountains, and broke in pieces the rocks before the Lord, but the Lord was not in the wind. And after the wind came an earthquake, but the Lord was not in the earthquake. And after the earthquake a fire, but the Lord was not in the fire. And after the fire a still small voice. And when Elijah heard it … *First Book of the Kings 19:11-13*

A mountain, God, clouds, Moses, Elijah, tents, voices, talking, listening – all imported into Luke's story to help us to understand what it is all about. What is beyond doubt is that Luke's mountain is Mount Sinai. I do not for a moment suggest that Mount Sinai is in Galilee. Luke's mountain is a theological mountain, a mountain built on memory, image and symbolism which transformed a mountain in the Sinai Peninsula into the mountain of God. We might say that traditional religious insight and Luke' theological daring have transfigured the mountain itself. And don't forget that Elijah did not find God in the wind nor in the earthquake. He was invited to listen to the still, small voice. To listen.

To Pray

That Jesus went up the mountain to pray will come as no surprise. What we need to notice is that it is in the praying that transformation comes: *while he was praying, the appearance of his face became different, and his clothing white and dazzling.* Everyone in Luke is transformed, changed, transfigured by prayer. All great moments in Luke's drama, as we have seen, are shot through with prayer. On another mountain, the Mount of Olives, Jesus prays. The disciples sleep.

Transfiguration

The scene is set. We have checked the props. Now we can attend to the play. And we notice first the make-up and the costume. The change of Jesus' countenance, the dazzling white which transformed his clothes signal what it is that the three disciples experience: the hidden glory of Jesus is revealed to them. As we are told,

> But Peter and those with him were overcome with sleep. Waking up, they saw his glory and the two men who stood beside him.

It is the context of this revelation which begins the process, not simply of transforming, transfiguring Peter, John and James, but of transforming and transfiguring you and me who read Luke's story.

First, we are directed to Moses and Elijah *who appeared in glory*. The man who brought torah down from the mountain of God, who opened the hearts of a stubborn people to the words of God, is again on God's mountain, again pointing to where glory is to be found. Moses represents the foundational documents of faith, for long thought by Jew and Christian to have written the five books *(Genesis, Exodus, Leviticus, Numbers, Deuteronomy)* which show us and lead to the glory of God. Secondly, we have Elijah, that firebrand of a prophet with a passion for justice. Elijah it was who discovered God in the still small voice on God's holy mountain, Elijah the man who did not die but was taken up to heaven in a chariot of fire, fanned by a whirlwind *(Second Book of the Kings 2:11-12)*. Because the biblical account of his mighty deeds did not record his death (and thus consign him to the nothingness of Sheol), tradition assigned to Elijah many rôles in God's future, most tellingly, as the prophet who would herald the days of the coming Messiah.

What Moses and Elijah stand for in the Transfiguration story is plainly explained by the stranger on the way to Emmaus and the one who came to quiet troubled and frightened hearts. On the way to Emmaus:

> And beginning with Moses and all the prophets, he interpreted to them in all the scriptures the things concerning himself.
> *Gospel of Luke 24:27*

And to the whole band of frightened followers on that same
Easter Day:

He said to them,

'These are my words which I talked to you about while I was
still with you, that it was necessary that everything written
concerning me in the torah of Moses and the prophets and
the psalms should be fulfilled.'

Gospel of Luke 24:44

A third piece must be put in place before this corner of the jig-
saw is complete. What were Moses and Elijah talking about?
They were speaking of his exodus which he was to fulfil in Jerusalem.
His *exodus*? The two great figures who stood on the mountain of
God, the one God's appointed leader of the great act of saving,
forever to be known as The Exodus, the other the doughty fight-
er who championed God's right to be God in Israel, these two
speak of a new journey, a new way out, a new exodus which will
take place in Jerusalem [in Greek: *ex* = out; *hodos* = way; *exhodos*
= way out].

What Luke is telling his readers, with the awesome authority
of Moses and Elijah, is that everything that will happen in
Jerusalem is a new exodus which leads to the glory where they
now are. If readers listen to what they tell, if readers and hearers
attend to the words of the torah and the prophets, they, too, will
come to the glory which awaits on the mountain of God. The
exodus of Jesus is all that will come to pass in Jerusalem: supper,
agony, trial, death, resurrection, ascension, glory.

When Jesus went to the Mount of Olives for the last time,
being in agony he prayed more earnestly and when he rose from
his prayer he found the disciples sleeping *(Gospel of Luke 22:44-
46)*. On the mountain of God, though heavy with sleep, Peter,
John, and James keep awake and they, too, see the glory of Jesus
and of the two men with him. In this theatre of prayer and scripture, glory comes.

The desire of Peter is to prolong the vision, to make three
tents or booths, to ensure permanently the joy of the Feast of
Booths, in the company of Jesus, Moses and Elijah in glory. But
Peter is wide of the mark. That is not the way to glory; the way to
glory is through the necessary fulfilment of the torah and the

prophets. To discover how glory comes, they will have to go into the cloud and be taught by God.

The cloud, as we have seen, is Bible-speak for God's presence. There is overshadowing and fear (as with Mary!), familiar indicators of divine nearness. And, as with Moses and Elijah on the mountain of God, there is the voice out of the cloud and the word of God comes to earth:

And a voice came out of the cloud,
'This is my Son,
my Chosen One.
Listen to him!'
Gospel of Luke 9:35

That is all we know, and all we need to know. Everything we have seen on our journey through Luke's pages about the Son is confirmed in God's naming of him as the Chosen One, chosen to be for us as no one else can be: *in the happening of the voice, only Jesus was to be found.* Ponder an exact translation: *in the happening of the voice.* In that moment of revelation, Jesus stands alone, the only way to glory. To take up the cross and lose one's life, is to find life and come to glory. The one who, as Moses, Elijah, and all the prophets reveal, must set his face toward Jerusalem, to the Place of the Skull, to the table laid out in Emmaus, is the One to whom we must listen.

We are transfigured by listening.

Jesus in our time
Jesus in our place

Here then is
the Jesus who was,
in the ancient pages of St Luke's Gospel:

JESUS WELCOMES PEOPLE

JESUS CHATS AND TALKS ABOUT THE KINGDOM OF GOD

JESUS HEALS THOSE IN NEED OF HEALING

JESUS FEEDS THE HUNGRY

JESUS PRAYS

JESUS IS THE MESSIAH OF GOD

JESUS CALLS ON PEOPLE TO FOLLOW HIM

JESUS SUFFERS AND DIES

JESUS IS RAISED FROM THE DEAD

JESUS WILL COME IN GLORY

JESUS IS GOD'S SON, THE CHOSEN ONE

JESUS IS THE ONE TO LISTEN TO

If the Jesus who was, the Jesus who walked the hills and byways of Galilee, and the Jesus who walks in the pages of St Luke's Gospel, is to be the Jesus who is, in our time and in our place, then we must see him in a portrait for our time and for our place:

MY CHURCH WELCOMES PEOPLE

MY CHURCH TALKS ABOUT THE KINGDOM OF GOD

MY CHURCH HEALS THOSE IN NEED OF HEALING

MY CHURCH FEEDS THE HUNGRY

MY CHURCH PRAYS

MY CHURCH IS THE MESSIAH OF GOD

MY CHURCH CALLS ON PEOPLE TO FOLLOW

MY CHURCH SUFFERS AND DIES

MY CHURCH WILL BE RAISED FROM THE DEAD

MY CHURCH WILL COME IN GLORY

MY CHURCH IS GOD'S FAMILY, A CHOSEN PEOPLE

MY CHURCH IS THE ONE TO LISTEN TO

but ...

DOES YOUR CHURCH WELCOME PEOPLE?
a. Who does your church welcome?
b. Who does your church turn away?
c. Is your church a haven for tax collectors and sinners?

DOES YOUR CHURCH CHAT/TALK
ABOUT THE KINGDOM OF GOD?
a. Does you church chat/talk with people?
Or speak at people? Or, speak down to people?
b. What is it that pre-occupies your church?
c. Does it ever listen?

DOES YOUR CHURCH HEAL PEOPLE
WHO NEED HEALING?
a. How is healing done in your church?
b. Is it open to all who need healing?
c. Or does it operate private health care only?

DOES YOU CHURCH FEED THE HUNGRY?
a. Who are fed?
b. Who are turned away from the Lord's Table?
c. Who decides?

IS YOUR CHURCH THE MESSIAH OF GOD?
a. Is your church a clear sign of God where you live?
b. Does your church hunger and thirst for justice?
c. Does your church fulfil anyone's hopes?

DOES YOUR CHURCH PRAY?
a. Or does it just say prayers?
b. Does it pray to hear the word?
c. And then to keep it?

DOES YOUR CHURCH CALL PEOPLE TO FOLLOW?
a. Into the pews?
b. Into the world?
c. Into the gospel of God?

DOES YOUR CHURCH SUFFER AND DIE?
    a. What's killing it?
    b. Is it losing its life to save it?
    c. Or saving its life – and losing?

WILL YOUR CHURCH BE RAISED FROM THE DEAD?
    a. Will it be worth the effort?
    b. Who will do it?
    c. What will it be like?

WILL YOUR CHURCH COME IN GLORY?
    a. Is your church big on hell?
    b. Is your church so looking forward to
    the Second Coming that it has missed the First?
    c. What does your church teach about glory?

IS YOUR CHURCH GOD'S FAMILY,
GOD'S CHOSEN PEOPLE?
    a. How can you tell?
    b. Does it much resemble its Father?
    c. Is it a happy family? Not dysfunctional?
    Sons and daughters treated equally?

IS YOUR CHURCH THE ONE TO LISTEN TO?
    a. Has it anything interesting to say?
    b. Is it deaf?
    c. When it talks, do people hear the voice of Jesus?

Does your parish, your religious community, your family, your school, your Sunday congregation, does each little cell of Christian people welcome, chat, heal, and feed and be all that it takes to be Jesus in our time and our place?

And then there's the really distressing realisation that *I* must paint the portrait of Jesus in *my* time and place.

I welcome people.

I talk about the kingdom.

I heal where healing is needed.

I feed the hungry …

… and I better stop here.